With Our Heads Bowed

Studies on Culture and Society

Volume 1. Gary H. Gossen, ed.
Symbol and Meaning Beyond the Closed Community: Essays in Mesoamerican Ideas

Volume 2. J. Jorge Klor de Alva, H. B. Nicholson, and Eloise Quiñones Keber, eds.
The Work of Bernardo de Sahagún: Pioneer Ethnographer of Sixteenth-Century Aztec Mexico

Volume 3. Victoria R. Bricker and Gary H. Gossen, eds.
Ethnographic Encounters in Southern Mesoamerica: Essays in Honor of Evon Zartman Vogt, Jr.

Volume 4. John Gledhill
Casi Nada: A Study of Agrarian Reform in the Homeland of Cardenismo

Volume 5. Brenda Rosenbaum
With Our Heads Bowed: The Dynamics of Gender in a Maya Community

Volume 6. Mary G. Hodge and Michael E. Smith, eds.
Economies and Polities in the Aztec Realm

With Our Heads Bowed

The Dynamics of Gender in a Maya Community

Brenda Rosenbaum

Studies on Culture and Society
Volume 5

Institute for Mesoamerican Studies
The University at Albany
State University of New York

Distributed by
University of Texas Press

For submission of manuscripts address the publisher:
   Institute for Mesoamerican Studies
   The University at Albany
   State University of New York
   Albany, New York 12222

For copies address the distributor:

   University of Texas Press
   Post Office Box 7819
   Austin, Texas 78713-7819

*HQ
1465
.C52
R6
1993*

Cover: Photograph of cloth dolls made by Chamula women to sell to tourists.

Library of Congress Cataloging in Publication Data

Rosenbaum, Brenda.
   With Our Heads Bowed: The Dynamics of Gender in a Maya Community.

Library of Congress Catalog Card Number: 92-76220
ISBN 0-942041-14-3

to Fredy

and to our parents

Dora and Rafael Picciotto
Rosita and Guillermo Rosenbaum

Truly now,
Double thanks, triple thanks
that we've been formed, we've been given
our mouths, our faces,
we speak, we listen,
we wonder, we move,
our knowledge is good, we've understood
what is far and near,
and we've seen what is great and small
under the sky, on the earth...

Popol Vuh
translation by Dennis Tedlock

Contents

List of Illustrations ix

Acknowledgements xi

Preface xv

1. Women and Gender in Chamula: *A General Framework* 1
   Researching the Dynamics of Gender
   Fieldwork in Chamula

2. San Juan Chamula: *Community, Historical Setting, and Ethnicity* 15
   Transformations of Gender in History
   Ethnicity and Gender

3. From Birth to Maturity: *Women and Men Through the Life Cycle* 39
   Children and Young People
   Wives and Husbands
   Gender Interaction Through the Life Cycle

4. In Our Ancestors' Words: *Women and Men in Chamula Oral Narratives* ... 65
   The *jtotik/jme'tik* Paradigm
   The First Man/First Woman Paradigm
   The Earth Paradigm
   Summary

5. The Other Eye, the Other Side of One's Face: *Courtship and Marriage* 89
   Jak'ol: The Marriage Petition
   Separation and Reconciliation
   Trato ta juera: the Deal Outside the House
   Acquiring a Second Wife
   The Monetization of the Marriage Transaction

6. The Struggle for Life 121
   Social Stratification in Chamula
   The Case of Tzajal Vitz
   Division of Labor by Gender in Tzajal Vitz
   Economy and Marital Relationships
   A Word on Ideology

7. The Quest for Prestige and Power 147
    Historical Context
    Assessing the Role of Women in Cargos
    Officials and their Duties in Chamula
    Helping the Deities Carry Their Burden
    Gender Symbols in Cargo Ritual
    Religious Cargos and the Marital Relationship
    Women and Civil Cargos
    Gender Ideology and Women in the Chamula Court

8. The Dynamics of Gender Interaction 179
    K'op riox: Religious Conversion and Gender
    Conclusions

Appendix 191
References Cited 227

Illustrations

FIGURES

1. Map of central Chiapas, Mexico 16

Following Page 120

2. A Chamula house

3. A woman weaves a woolen *jerkail* for her husband

4. A young woman shrinks and felts her father's *jerkail*

5. Children begin to work at a young age

6. A girl makes bracelets to sell to tourists

7. Brothers and sisters play together

8. A young woman sells woven belts to tourists

9. Chamula women sell fruit at the market

10. A family engages in conversation around the hearth

11. An older woman earns money carding wool

12. A woman teaches her son to use a hoe

13. A woman begins a cloth doll for sale in the tourist market

TABLES

1. Structure of events in two narratives 76

2. Economic activities of wives and husbands 129

Acknowledgements

With a candle, with a flower, one of a handful of Chamula women who are literate, and use this skill to earn a livelihood, frequently addresses the deities as follows:

> Please do not let me forget how to read.
> Please do not let me forget how to use your paper.
> Please do not let me forget how to use your pencil.
> Set it firmly in my head.
> Set your book firmly in my heart... (Linn 1976:235)

Having lived most of my life in a third world country where education is the privilege of only a few--rarely women and even less frequently married women with children--I feel tremendously privileged to have had the opportunity to pursue higher education and to publish the results of my research.

The origins of this book go back to 1983 when I went to Chamula, Chiapas to engage in research for my dissertation. Because of the multiple and often conflicting commitments that shape a woman's life, teamwork is sine-qua-non for reaching any substantive goal. The effort and support of family and friends sustained me through the almost ten-year process of research, writing a dissertation, and making numerous revisions before the manuscript of this book was ready for publication.

Above all, I am deeply indebted to the many Chamula women and men who allowed me into their homes and hearts. Not only did I learn from their culture, but also from their example as courageous and resourceful human beings. To protect their privacy, I do not name them here; throughout the text, I employ pseudonyms to refer both to them and to their hamlets. In 1993, we celebrate the success of their 500 year struggle against oppression and their remarkable survival as a people. May Chamulas continue to go from strength to strength.

I would like to thank my professors at SUNY-Albany. Their dedication to teaching and their high academic standards continue to inspire me. Gary Gossen shared his profound insights on Chamula society and showed me the importance of viewing individuals as agents of their own lives and history. Further, he generously gave me access to his fieldwork files from Chamula. Robert Carmack led me to examine the impact of global forces and trends on the local cultures that anthropologists study. Through her critical stance on social theories, June Nash taught me that a gendered perspective does more than add women to the human record: it revolutionizes one's view of society. I thank them, and also Gail Landsman, and Jan Gasco, Research Director of the Institute for Mesoamerican Studies, for their continued encouragement to publish this book.

The comments and insightful critique of Louise Burkhart, Helen Elam, Liliana Goldin, Robert Laughlin, June Nash and Mario Ruz were of great assistance during my many revisions of the manuscript.

Over the years, many people have helped me to understand Highland Chiapas. Jan and Diane Rus, Christine Eber, and Robert Laughlin, longtime students of the area, have offered their perspectives and knowledge to help me find answers to my questions. Their intellectual generosity and their long-term commitment to the indigenous population with whom they work set an example of what truly humanistic scholarship is all about.

While in the field, friends and colleagues enriched my experience and made it more enjoyable through their companionship, hospitality, and advice. I thank Martha Rivera, Conchita Thomae and Nacho García, Marcey Jacobson, Janet Marren, Nancy Modiano, Mimi and Robert Laughlin, Duncan Earle, Erika Verrillo, Olya Szyjka. I thank, especially, my friend Donna Engleman who shared with me the joys and tribulations involved in exploring the complexities of Tzotzil culture.

As a native Spanish speaker, I overcame my great frustration of writing in English, a language I will never master completely, only through the outpouring of support and the assistance of many friends. They revised version after version of this manuscript, translating "my" English into English. Faye Silton, Lyle Campbell, Jean Easton, Sonia Rosenbaum, Mary Patlen, and Shel Horowitz gave generously of their time and skills to this project. Cindy Heath-Smith spent many months working intensively on the consistency, clarity, and coherence of this final volume. I thank her for her hard work and her committment to represent my ideas faithfully. My friend Mike McCarthy eased the writing task a great deal by offering his computer expertise and by setting up everything for me so that I could just sit down and write. Hatsune Hatanaka was of great assistance in revising the bibliography. I thank the Museo Ixchel, Guatemala City, for permission to reprint some of my photographs that appeared in one of its publications. I am grateful also to Plumsock Mesoamerican Studies for its financial support in publishing this volume.

This book would never have seen the light had it not been for the unfailing support of my family. From the moment I began to plan my research, through my time in the field, and later the long months of transcription, analysis, writing, and endless rewriting, my family has rallied around me. My sister Elena and my brother-in-law Isaac took care of my children when I was in the field. My mother made innumerable trips between Guatemala, Mexico, and the United States to help me care for my family. Knowledgeable about the workings of academia and the writing of books, my sisters-in-law, Sonia and Lilian, guided and encouraged me. From little girls, my daughters Susie, Elena, and Dora Lisa have grown into young women while their mother was engrossed in this project. They always accepted the situation with good spirit, accompanied me in the ups and downs of the road, and with patience and humor brought me back many times from gloom.

Finally, I thank my husband Fredy. He has always encouraged me to do what I think is important, regardless of the difficulties involved for him. My Chamula friends never let me take him for granted. To begin with, they could not understand how he could agree with my dragging our children to a distant place with the purpose of learning another people's ways. Furthermore, they could not believe that he would willingly support me financially in this frivolous venture! According to them, he either "had a very kind heart" or had been bewitched! My husband has had a major input in this book. He took on a lot more than his share to liberate my time for writing; he read and discussed this manuscript with me at length, leading me to sharpen ideas and arguments. More than anything else, his absolute faith in me strengthened my resolve to see this work through to its completion.

Preface

Since the early 1980s, Mexico has suffered a dramatic economic crisis that has had a profound impact on its population. This crisis has hit especially hard the people who live at the margins of survival, such as the indigenous peoples of Highland Chiapas. At this critical juncture, men and women struggle to cope with the hard times that have worsened their already difficult situation, creatively seeking alternatives for survival. Expected behaviors are modified in order to subsist. Traditional discourse and division of labor clash with the hard surfaces of reality. Economic and political transformations affect the gender system—which permeates the fabric of social life—often sharpening ideological contradictions and conflictive interactions between men and women.

This book explores the dynamics of gender interaction in Chamula, a Maya community in Highland Chiapas. It examines the deep symbolic roots of gender ideology and the way in which this ideology is reinforced and contradicted by other cultural statements and behaviors. Although for more than a century Chamula has been an integral part of the national economy, like many other indigenous groups in the area, Chamulas resist total assimilation into a system in which they have a clear disadvantage. Expressing their commitment to their ancestors' traditions and values through ritual, oral narrative, socialization practices and so forth, Chamulas insist on their separation and survival as a distinct people. The gender system, thus, is shaped by a complex interplay between local beliefs and practices, on the one hand, and historical, political, and economic forces that impinge upon the community, on the other. Since the arrival of the Spanish, Chamula men have had more contact with the outside world than have Chamula women. Men have had no alternative but to learn Spanish, to negotiate with first colonial and later national administrators and landowners, and to transform the structure of native governments to fit the demands of the dominant society. Through the centuries Chamula women generally have remained monolingual and have continued to weave garments and to prepare foods with the same basic techniques employed by their ancestors. They have become, vis-à-vis the men, bearers of the most traditional aspects of Chamula culture.

Feminist research in Mesoamerica and other regions has demonstrated the negative effects of the integration of peasant communities into the larger capitalist economy. Relatively egalitarian gender systems tend to develop into hierarchical systems in which men control the production process and have access to political positions, and women become subservient to them. The male bias of the larger society usually decreases women's economic and political options. The position of Chamula men on the lower rungs of the national economic ladder, however, modifies this general statement on the effects of capitalism on the gender system. In the last decade, with the deepening of the economic crisis, Chamula women have resorted to a series of activities in order to obtain a cash income. Many have turned to artisan production that is geared toward the tourist market—a lucrative sector of the economy. The new opportunities opened to women furnish a badly needed income for their families and grant women a measure of economic independence from their husbands. Not only do women make a modest cash contribution to the household, but they do so without threatening their own cultural integrity. Men, on the other hand, spend weeks or months away from their highland homes, working for a wage or in the informal economy and assimilating Ladino (non-Indian, "western") ways in the process. Given that Chamulas place such emphasis on their cultural autonomy from the dominant society, men's immersion in the nonindigenous world causes them anxiety and affects their interaction with women. There is still, however, the potential for a huge economic gap to develop between men and women. The North American Free Trade Agreement (NAFTA), for example, could become a major catalyst in fostering this gap. It could force communities such as Chamula into a rapid modernization process in which women—largely monolingual, tied to traditional technologies and ways, with few contacts outside their community—are likely to be the losers.

Recent feminist scholarship suggests the need to move away from causal explanations of gender hierarchies based on one or a few determining variables. Gender pervades all aspects of social life and ideology and varies in the ways it is manifested in each; therefore, it is important to study gender representations in several different areas. This book begins with a general theoretical orientation, which lays the foundation for the analysis of gender as a complex interaction between behavior and symbol, practice and ideology. Each chapter that follows presents an analysis of gender practices and ideology in a specific area of social life. I begin with an investigation of the historical context, both to incorporate women into the historical record of Highland Chiapas and to trace the transformations of gender conceptualizations and practices through time (chap. 2). I move on to an analysis of gender interaction through the life cycle (chap. 3) and the representations of men and women and their relationship in oral tradition (chap. 4) and in the ritual and practices of marriage (chap. 5). Next I delve into the roles of women of various income levels in the economic system (chap. 6) and their participation in the prestige and power hierarchies of their community (chap. 7). Finally, I present some preliminary information on the effects of religious conversion on gender interaction among Chamulas (chap. 8). Because conversion to the "new religions" (Protestantism and Catholic Action) leads to expulsion from the community (and usually settlement in crowded squatter colonies around San Cristóbal de las Casas), conversion radically transforms the Chamula way of life.

In each chapter, I examine gender ideology and practices as analytical constructs of an indivisible social whole. In most chapters I attempt to deal as much with ideology as with practice. Because of the nature of specific subjects, however, chapter 4 (on oral tradition) stresses the symbolic aspects of the gender system, while chapter 6 (on the economy) stresses its behavioral aspects. The overall picture of gender in Chamula displays an intricate dynamic in which symbol and practice restate, complement, contradict, subvert, or conceal one another. Women appear simultaneously as powerful and vulnerable, dangerous and easily victimized, independent and subjected, complementing men and submitting to them, building up men and destroying them. The particular behaviors of women and men, and the various definitions applied to them, depend on institutional and situational contexts. The effects of policies, economic changes and ideological influences that stem from the larger society further complicate this picture, obliterating or exacerbating local gender ideas and behaviors.

In the examination of social life, from the distant past up to the present, Chamula women emerge as central actors. Adjusting to dramatic changes and struggling to survive; serving religious cargos with their husbands to secure divine blessings on behalf of their families and community; making economic decisions and manipulating social networks in order to improve their options and to exercise power—the roles of women are essential to an understanding of this society. Furthermore, most Chamula men and women recognize that only within their own society are they able to lead meaningful, dignified lives. In many respects, Chamula women have borne the responsibility of carrying on their ancestors' traditions and dreams into the twenty-first century.

1

Women and Gender in Chamula
A General Framework

In January 1984, Miguel de la Madrid, president of Mexico, and Absalón Castellanos, governor of the state of Chiapas, arrived in Chamula. They had come to present a new plan to develop the indigenous communities of Highland Chiapas. On a typically chilly, highland morning, seven enormous helicopters swept into the Chamula ceremonial center.

Antel, a middle-aged Chamula friend, stood with me as we watched the helicopters appear on the horizon and asked, "Isn't it true that the president is the second one in line after God?" As the helicopters clattered over our heads, she commented, "The president must be looking at us from up there and saying: 'Oh, how many children I have already!'"

Antel had prepared herself for the event. She, along with the thousands of other natives who were converging on the plaza, had heard the repeated radio announcement for everyone in the area to congregate at Chamula Center that morning. The announcement had gone on to say that free transportation and a payment of 300 pesos ($2.30)[1] would be provided to those in attendance; at that time 200 pesos was the normal, daily wage.

Unlike most of the audience, Antel was not a passive spectator. She had meticulously embroidered a blouse, of the type she sells to tourists, to present to the president. After asking me to write the names of her hamlet and township, Chamula, on the left-hand, front corner of the blouse, she had proceeded to embroider them onto the garment. As we waited for the officials to speak, she asked me to follow her to a quiet street. Away from the growing crowd, she dictated a letter in Tzotzil to the president and asked me to translate it into Spanish. In the letter she informed the president that she represented her hamlet in the cooperative of weavers, Sna Jolobil, and that she had taught more than twenty women, her "workers," how to embroider and sew pretty garments. She asked for help to obtain fabric so that she could continue this work. She added that she was appealing to him for assistance because she and her husband had just finished their service in the *cargo* (office) of *kominarol* for which they had incurred a great debt.

The president and other officials, including the presidents of all of the indigenous highland townships, sat on a stage erected in the central plaza. The stage was encircled by men. At the periphery women cared for their children but remained attentive to the activities on the stage. Antel waited, frequently asking which individual was the president and which was his wife. When the president's departure was announced, she rushed into the crowd to assail him but was unable to reach him. He was so heavily protected by armed bodyguards that, even on stage, he was totally obscured. Furthermore, he never addressed the people.

Antel was slightly disappointed, but she is not one to give up easily. In his speech the governor of Chiapas had mentioned that the government would invest many millions of pesos to assist the indigenous population of Chiapas. A few days later Manvel, Antel's husband, asked me for help to write a letter to the governor of Chiapas requesting jobs for himself and his sons. A week after the president's visit, I went to the hamlet for the last time, intending to work on the letter. Manvel, who had been drinking, stood on the path threatening to hit anyone who approached him. Antel signaled me to follow her into the house. Once inside she stated that, given Manvel's condition, she would dictate the letter. Antel addressed her own agenda, however: she requested an audience with the governor's wife in order to ask for help to buy yarn at a low price.

This anecdote portrays many aspects of the study that follows and introduces the dynamics of Chamula social life and male-female interaction. For example, in social gatherings women and men form segregated groups—men usually at the fore, in the most visible position, and women behind them. This spatial distribution reflects the attitude that men have a status superior to that of women, especially with regard to political contacts with the outside world. The segregation of men and women also reveals a division of activities, of social worlds; men's and women's concerns and activities are thought to belong to different spheres. The underlying reality, however, is that cooperation between husband and wife is fundamental for survival and for the acquisition of power and prestige in this community.

Antel identified the highest authority in the country, the president, with the figure of the Sun/Christ—a central male deity in the Chamula pantheon. The Sun/Christ always has a female counterpart by his side, as do Chamula religious officials. In prayer Chamulas always address male and female deities consecutively, underscoring the importance of the complementary whole. This male/female complementarity explains Antel's assumption that the Mexican president would be accompanied by his wife at any official function.

Women often take over household business when their husbands drink too much, as demonstrated in the incident of the letter. Because of alcohol related problems, women frequently are forced to engage in activities that are considered exclusively male. Antel's mention of the couple's service in a cargo is interesting because officially only men hold cargos (especially civil cargos such as *kominarol*).

Antel endeavored to address directly the foremost authority of the country, intending to initiate the relationship with the presentation of a gift. This anecdote dramatically illustrates the contrast between one of the prevailing ideological images of women—vulnerable, devoted to traditional household activities, with limited mobility and outside contacts—and real life interactions that show Chamula women to be strong and independent. The precarious economic situation compels women to look persistently for ways to increase their family income. Monolingual in Tzotzil and illiterate, Chamula women are at a disadvantage in dealing with the outside world when compared with men. Nevertheless, they still strive to create links with the dominant society in order to increase their resources.

To be sure, Antel is an extraordinary Chamula woman. Through many years of hard work, she and her husband have carved out a position of prestige and wealth in the community. They have served many religious and civil cargos. They also have established ties with Ladinos (nonindigenous Mexicans) and Americans in San Cristóbal de las Casas (the closest metropolitan center), who provide Antel with work. At the time of this study, Antel worked with 15 other women in the hamlet, to whom she taught sewing skills and provided material. She sold the garments produced by this group at considerable profit by Chamula standards.

Not all Chamula women are as successful as Antel, but most work extremely hard to bring in some cash or food to augment their husbands' contributions. Antel was not always as independent and powerful as she is today. When she was a still a girl, Antel's parents accepted a gift of liquor from a suitor, which committed her to marry the boy. The marriage transaction is a powerful, symbolic expression of male control; formally, it is a transaction between men. A boy selects a girl for marriage and, following a series of petitions, pays a brideprice and takes the girl to his home. The girl is a commodity, literally "bought" and "sold" (*man* and *chon* in Tzotzil), transferred from one household to another. Through a detailed examination of the marriage process (chap. 5), however, I show that complex interactions and symbolic meanings challenge the notion that men dominate the process. Several years after she married, Antel endured a temporary and very conflictive situation of polygyny involving her younger sister.

A strong interdependence and an equality of responsibilities characterize the relationship between husband and wife. As in all societies with a subsistence economy, husband and wife provide goods and services for one another that cannot be attained otherwise. In the ideal division of labor, men and women support one another (*malk'in sbaik*). The husband contributes the corn and beans he has sown as well as money to buy other necessary foodstuffs. The wife prepares the food to nourish the family, weaves the family's clothes and blankets, performs household chores, and cares for the children. The difficult economic situation of most Chamula families mars this ideal. Since the middle of the nineteenth century, thousands of men have been forced to leave their highland homes for several months of the year to work as wage laborers or, less commonly, as sharecroppers in the lowlands. Feeding the family has turned into a difficult and frustrating task. Women have become the pillars of stability, continuity, and ethnicity. Because they remain in their homes, women take responsibility for socializing the children into a Chamula way of life and for caring for the family's sheep, home, and any highland crops.

Chamula ideology expresses contrasting views of gender relations that encode complementary dualism, male superiority, and female power. Although the three paradigms coexist, the identification of men with the supreme deity (Our Father the Sun/Christ) seems to prevail at the most explicit level, underscoring men's superior power. The Sun/Christ's heat, gifts, and beneficial influence over his children outshine those of Our Mother the Moon/Virgin, with whom women identify. While superior heat connotes men's strength and courage, the opposite traits define women. Mythology related to the Earth, however, challenges the definition of women as weak and vulnerable.

Strong contradictions exist among different ideological pronouncements as well as between the ideological assertion of male supremacy and the reality that women's input is as indispensable as that of men and, in many cases, more essential to the survival of the family. Although cultural values encourage a complementary division of labor, they also give men the right to rule over women, to have more than one wife, and to move about freely. Such inconsistencies generate tensions in male-female relations, especially between husband and wife. These contradictions lead to a deep-seated ambivalence towards women. According to Gary Gossen (1974:44), this ambivalence is quintessentially embodied in the idea that the female principle preceded the male principle; men are always born of women. *Jtotik*, the Sun/Christ, came from the womb of the radiant and powerful *jme'tik*, the Moon/Virgin. As a child, however, he tricked his mother by throwing boiling water at her face and burning one of her eyes in order to make her less powerful.

This pattern of men usurping the originally superior position of women recurs in many myths and historical events (Gossen 1986c, 1989a). For example, women were the instigating force in the two major revitalization movements that took place in Chamula, in 1712 and in 1867. In both cases, the movements attempted to create cults to provide the people with a native deity that they could worship legitimately. Women initiated the cults through mystic communication with female supernaturals, but men took over the organization and leadership of them (Bricker 1981).

To this day women continue to symbolize the origins and continuity of the Chamula culture and people. The power of women, however, must be kept under male control to prevent the system from falling into the hands of more powerful male factions or demons. The following myth illustrates this pattern:

> Long ago there lived only crazy women, pure crazy women. This is what they did. They wanted to find husbands. *Me'tik* Lorisia (Our Mother Lorisia) lived then, a tall white woman with a long black skirt and a long black shawl. She held a knife in front of her two folded hands. She was a haughty woman and a saint. This was the time before Christ died on the cross. The crazy soldierly woman hung him on the cross.
> The women prayed to *me'tik* Lorisia and she abetted their love affairs. She killed the jealous husbands. The women then did not want husbands. They did not want a holy good saint. But the men rose up in arms and pushed *me'tik* Lorisia into the fire. She died and a new female saint came and taught the women to be good and submissive. She taught them to wait at home with bowed heads and be married by formal petition. (Lacy 1976:63)

Many Chamula origin narratives present the view that once men overpower women, the latter are defeated permanently. Lingering ambivalence towards women asserts itself in mythic projections of powerful women overcome by submissive and compliant exemplars of femininity.

RESEARCHING THE DYNAMICS OF GENDER

This study is an ethnography of Chamula from a feminist perspective.[2] Impoverished, overpopulated, dispersed, and incorporated into the dominant economic system for over a century, Chamula has been, nonetheless, extraordinarily successful in retaining its cultural vitality and separate identity. In order to understand the dynamics of such a situation, it is crucial to examine the roles that women play in Chamula society; to view women and men as actors at the confluence of conflicting internal and external forces; and to consider the gender system as a variable that affects the impact of these forces on Chamula and, in turn, is transformed by them.

I am mainly concerned with the *dynamics* of gender relations in Chamula— the interaction between ideology and practice in the negotiation of power and status between men and women. This interactive approach does not assume a priori the privileged position of either social practices or ideas, but instead analyzes the relative salience of both and their interrelationship. It enables the ethnographer to construct a picture of the complex fabric of social relations and corresponding institutional and symbolic structures. While stressing the importance of the economic system, the social relations that derive from it, and the idea that ideology may rationalize a state of affairs, this approach extends the analysis in other directions. It grants ideas a place of their own, thereby precluding sociological reductionism. Ideas and social behavior are considered as interdependent, but nonhomologous, analytical systems; that is, they are treated aspects of a single process, and their interaction must be viewed within a historical context in order to understand their operation in the present (Yanagisako and Collier 1987).

The idea of two different analytical instances in the study of society and the dialectical relations between them was introduced into modern social sciences by Karl Marx, inspired by G.W.F. Hegel. Because he was countering the overwhelmingly idealistic, intellectual climate of his time, Marx's analysis became entangled with the issue of the predominance of material life over ideas and the "determination of the economy in the last instance" (Engels 1978:765). This entanglement has caused unending controversies about the roles of ideas and culture in society. Marxists often see ideas as distorted views of the productive process and culture—the social relations that ensue from this process—as epiphenomenon. Raymond Williams (1977) argues that this position leads to a dead end because the reduction of the symbolic realm to a dependent, superstructural role replicates the separation of ideas and material life in idealist social thought that has been so severely attacked by Marxists. Marx's monumental contributions to the study of society remain his emphasis on the importance of material life in society and his conclusion that a one to one correspondence between social life and the way it is expressed in ideology does not exist.[3]

My approach derives primarily from the conceptual frameworks espoused by Robert Murphy and Clifford Geertz. These scholars view social life as a constant interplay—a conflict, more or less critical at different times, between those symbols that define reality and guide behavior and what Geertz (1973:142) calls the "hard surfaces of reality" (i.e., the political, economic, historic, and biological systems). The hard surfaces of reality exert strong pressure on social practice, and the symbols expressed through social practice may represent open contradictions of the official definitions of reality that a culture offers. These symbols may represent compromises, consciously justified in terms of more urgent demands of survival, among the cultural ideals and constraints that individuals confront as members of a group. Ideas, therefore, are more than a reflection or a symbolic restatement of action; they may deny, contradict, reinterpret, simplify, and/or distort behavioral reality (Murphy 1971:158). On the other hand, social structures are not to be defined a priori as timeless configurations but as structures expressed by individuals through their actions and experienced by them as possibilities and limitations. Although structures shape individual experiences, people enact struc tures, and there is always the potential of modifying or transforming them (Yanagisako and Collier 1987:43; Comaroff 1987:65).

Yanagisako and Collier (1987) recommend a theoretical approach that focuses on the interaction between behavior and symbol in social life. They see this approach as a central strategy to transcend dichotomies such as domestic/public, nature/culture and reproduction/production, which obscure our understanding of gender systems.[4] By positing these structural oppositions as universals able to explain women's inferior position in all societies, ethnographers impose their own culture's folk categories and evaluations on the groups they study (Rapp 1987); thus, they take for granted phenomena they ought to explain. The dialectical view that Yanagisako and Collier (1987:18) propose seeks to overcome the static sameness these structural opposites entail and the dichotomized vision of ideas and actions that they evoke. Furthermore, this view counteracts the extreme idealism of other approaches in anthropology in which symbolic analysis is concerned exclusively with interrelationships between symbols. One symbol is shown to represent another, more elementary symbol, and culture becomes an hermetic system of ideas with an elegant internal logic, but no connection to practice.

An analytical distinction between discourse and practice also makes possible the identification of the loci of contradictions and weaknesses in existing structures by investigating the material and ideological bases of power and the meanings that stem from different social sources. The identification of these points is a prerequisite for the revelation of areas of potential critical transformations in social practices and ideas that is necessary to change the situation (Weedon 1987:124).

In Chamula female ownership of property and other economic resources gives women leverage in the marital relationship. Despite the importance of independent female behavior as a survival strategy, such behavior is defined as socially dangerous and is strongly discouraged. An autonomous Chamula woman threatens the "naturalness" of gender hierarchies (Weedon 1987:113). Common sense, jokes, myths, and various social practices of everyday life accentuate women's vulnerability and men's superior strength and dominance.

Many ideas and behaviors contest the "official" view of gender in Chamula. Their meanings, consequences, and relative prominence are investigated in the chapters that follow. My data do not reveal a separate model of reality for men and women; rather, contradictions in the prevailing view are integrated in the basic culture shared by men and women and highlighted by the intense ambivalence that characterizes gender ideology and behavior. In other societies researchers have uncovered female models of reality that contradict the dominant male models.[5] The former often remain muted because of their "subversive" nature and because of women's subject status.

Several ethnographers have noted that women implement diverse strategies to counteract their lack of formal power. These strategies include the creation and manipulation of social networks, the exercise of control over female resources, and indirect means of influencing decision making.[6] Chamula women also employ such strategies. Specific historical and social factors lay the basis for women's power in Chamula, namely, the extended absences of men from their homes and the ineffectiveness of men who drink to carry out their social obligations. In addition women's new economic possibilities enhance their position and give more flexibility both to married women (who no longer depend solely on their husbands' cash earnings for support) and to single, young women (who argue that they would rather support themselves than live with an undependable man).

Yanagisako and Collier (1987:38-48) propose a three-faceted, research program that leads to a complex, dynamic view of social life. This program includes (1) an examination of cultural meanings in everyday life, (2) an attempt to understand the specific structures of inequality in a given society, and (3) an evaluation of the historical processes through which practices and meanings have developed. Within this dialectical model, meanings and practices not only reinforce and reproduce each other but also undermine and destabilize each other. I have found the three facets of this program useful in my analysis of Chamula's gender system. My study of oral narratives (chaps. 2 and 4) and ritual (chaps. 5 and 7)—privileged symbolic domains in Chamula—uncovers a system of contrasting meanings that are expressed in everyday life and have diverse relationships to practice.[7] I analyze social interactions, the allocation of economic resources, and political and prestige structures (which are shaped by powerful external constraints and internal dynamics and ideological principles) to show how each of these aspects of Chamula society contour the experiences of men and women (chaps. 3, 6, and 7). The broad outline of the historical evolution of ideas and practices (chap. 2) provides the backdrop necessary to understand the contemporary situation.[8]

I close this section with a narrative that illustrates the fundamental importance of gender differences for Chamula.[9] A primary item in the agenda of feminist anthropologists calls for deconstructing the categories of "male" and "female" and questioning the universality of gender distinction (Yanagisako and Collier 1987:15).[10] Ethnographers should not presume that gender distinction is "natural," nor should gender categories be explained or justified strictly in terms of biological differences. In the study of a specific system, the researcher must investigate whether male and female exist as categories and whether their relations are structured by their differences.

This narrative, by a Chamula man, concerns the Lacandon, a Maya group inhabiting the tropical jungles of Chiapas. According to the narrator, the Lacandon people are as uncivilized as wild animals because the women and men look the same. Both sexes wear long hair and similar clothing, and Chamulas allege that it is impossible to distinguish between them. Even a Lacandon man, the story goes, is unable to tell if the person he approaches when seeking a wife is a man or a woman; to find out, Lacandon shamelessly touch one another's genitals. For Chamulas this travesty—the absence of radical differentiation between men and women—becomes a metaphor to define Lacandon society and behavior as generally immoral when compared with the righteous Chamulas. The Lacandon have no church, nor do they establish ritual relations with their children's godparents at baptism—a fundamental value in the lives of Chamulas. Instead, they baptize their children by themselves with a big stick. As if these differences were not enough, Chamulas claim that Lacandon starve unwanted children and toss the corpses into a ditch with the garbage to be devoured by vultures. This story reveals that, for Chamulas, the act of distinguishing male from female stands for the differences between human and animal, cultural and wild, moral and immoral. The difference between men and women appears to be the very essence of being human and a fundamental principle for ordering behavior in this community.

FIELDWORK IN CHAMULA

The research that forms the basis for this study was carried out from July 1983 through January 1984. I returned to the field for a few weeks in March 1986 to visit and finalize the translation process. During the first weeks of my initial stay, I lived in a relatively isolated Chamula hamlet that I refer to here as Tzajal Vitz. Later I moved with my family to the city of San Cristóbal, but I continued to visit the hamlet almost daily. My Chamula friends often invited me to attend private or public festivities with them; on those occasions I would spend two or three days in the hamlet.

Most of my data come from Tzajal Vitz, but I also spent many days in a hamlet near the city of San Cristóbal de las Casas (which I call Nichimtik), making observations and conversing with women. I had constructed a picture of women and the gender system based on information from Tzajal Vitz. The information that I gathered in Nichimtik allowed me to extend my generalizations to the whole township. Although these two hamlets have distinct economic profiles, their gendered division of labor and the interactions between men and women show no major differences. As I describe in more detail in chapter 6, Tzajal Vitz and Nichimtik differ in many respects. The close proximity of Nichimtik to the city determines its labor structure and the nature of its commercial enterprises. People from this hamlet often walk into the city. Tzajal Vitz is more distant from San Cristóbal, about an hour by bus, so residents cannot sell their products in the city as easily and inexpensively as the people of Nichimtik. The general economic profiles of the two hamlets also vary. Tzajal Vitz is one of the largest and poorest hamlets in Chamula township. The people of Tzajal Vitz own fewer lands than the inhabitants of most of the other hamlets. In Nichimtik, the proximity of the city encourages the development of horticulture as a supplementary activity and the employment of men as day laborers.

My first months were spent in intensive participant observation during which I learned Tzotzil, acquired basic background knowledge, and established the relationships that are indispensable to more formal stages of research. I attended several festivals, met many Chamula men and women, held innumerable conversations with people, and spent time with the women learning to do their work (e.g., tortilla making, the use of a tumpline to carry water and firewood, weaving, and embroidery). I accompanied Chamula girls and women to San Cristóbal, where they sell their products (vegetables, fruits, woven and embroidered goods) in the market, on the city streets, and to Ladino-owned stores.

During the last three months of fieldwork, I conducted formal interviews at my house in San Cristóbal, but I also continued to visit the hamlets. I elicited a general survey of Tzajal Vitz from one of the hamlet's most respected elders. The survey includes 97 families and covers about two-thirds of the hamlet's population. Together we drew a map of Tzajal Vitz with the locations of the households that constitute the sample. My informant described the composition of each family, the main economic activities of husband and wife, and some of the characteristics of the different members of the family (e.g., drinking behavior, participation in religious or civil cargos, cases of polygyny or domestic violence, and attitudes of individuals towards children and parents). This information proved to be an invaluable source for the different economic and religious activities in which specific women engaged; it also helped me to identify the positions of individual women in the economic strata of the hamlet. I used this information to select for formal interview women who represented diverse sectors and experiences. Nevertheless, the sample is limited since it is based on material provided by a single individual. Much of the data, however, were cross-checked in individual interviews.

I interviewed in Tzotzil more than twenty Chamula women and recorded many hours of conversation. Most of the women were from Tzajal Vitz, but a few were from Nichimtik. I transcribed the recordings in Tzotzil and translated them into Spanish. In addition to sampling for different economic strata and activities, I also selected women of different ages. Four broad age groups appear in the sample: girls of marriageable age, married women with young children, mature women with older children, and old women. The women spoke about general issues and narrated their life histories. They focused on family relationships, activities, sex, concerns and fears, specific problems (e.g., polygyny, court cases, divorce), and so forth. Women who had served religious or civil cargos, curers and midwifes, and women who had acted as petitioners for boys during courtship also talked about the details of their work. Additionally, every woman narrated dreams and myths. Because their culture places so much importance on speaking well, most Chamula women have a singular mastery of language. After I explained the kind of information I was seeking, my informants would often speak nonstop for a long time, moving easily and skillfully from one subject to the next and sometimes switching to the poetic, parallel structure that characterizes formal Tzotzil. I also interviewed a few men, including an agent of the municipal government in a distant hamlet who offered valuable information on court cases involving women and the way in which these cases are usually handled. I interviewed other men to elicit a male perspective on the issues brought up by the women.

Their history of tense relations with the exploitative outside world leads Chamulas to suspect the motives of all non-Indians and makes fieldwork in Chamula a challenge. As I discuss in chapter 2, ambivalent feelings toward the outside world are clearly expressed in Chamula narratives about the Earth Lord. On the one hand, all outsiders represent Ladinos, whose relations with indigenous peoples over the centuries have been exploitative and abusive. In the eyes of Chamulas, Ladinos are egregiously incarnated in the form of the Earth Lord. On the other hand, outsiders are seen as the source of all wealth, also an attribute of the Earth Lord. Chamulas say that wealthy people in the community obtain their riches by striking a deal with the Earth Lord; in fact, most fortunes in Chamula are made through contacts with outsiders. Chamulas dislike and fear Ladinos, but they also are attracted to them; by obtaining the favor of Ladinos, Chamulas may improve their own difficult situation.

The Pérez Tz'i' family of Tzajal Vitz agreed to board me. This family had developed close relationships with some American anthropologists who worked in the area a few years before. These anthropologists had helped the family to forge contacts with Ladinos and Americans in San Cristóbal. The Americans had found jobs for some of the men in the family and provided outlets for the women's artisan products. Perhaps the family accepted me in the hope that I would provide them further access to influential people in San Cristóbal. The rest of the people of Tzajal Vitz saw my presence and my potential to add to the Pérez Tz'i' family fortune as a threat to the fragile balance of power maintained in the hamlet. This situation posed a difficult dilemma for my hosts: If they encouraged me to meet and become friendly with other families in the hamlet, they could lose their exclusive claim over me and the benefits I might bring. If they restricted my contacts, they risked increasing their neighbors' suspicions that I intended to help them at the expense of other people in the hamlet. In Earth Lord accounts the souls of neighbors are sold by individuals seeking personal gain (see chapter 2). These suspicions would generate envy towards the Pérez Tz'i' family, who feared that witchcraft would be used against them.

Unaware of the concerns surrounding my presence, I decided to make an effort to meet more people. I began to venture out by myself, visiting other houses and conversing with the people. In those conversations I explained my reasons for living in the hamlet and my intention to learn the work of women and to find out about women's lives. On my return to the Pérez Tz'i' household, however, I met with angry and disapproving looks. I realized I would have to walk a fine line between trying to expand my network of acquaintances and keeping my hosts reasonably at ease. There were some problems, and I heard rumors that some people wanted to expel me from the hamlet, but my strategy of appearing ignorant of these problems proved successful in the end. In time I became well known to many people, most of whom grew more comfortable with my presence and ceased to fear me or suspect my motives. Some people, however, continued to watch me with distrust from a distance. Eventually the Pérez Tz'i' family realized that I would be a good friend to them but had nothing more to offer.

Once I had passed the awkwardness of first meetings and dispelled the initial doubts about my motives, Chamula women began to ask questions about my family and my work. In broken Tzotzil I described my research interests, my husband and children, and my home country. In one of our first exchanges, the women inquired about birthing practices in my country. With little Tzotzil and much gesturing, I informed them that women had to push, push, push the baby out! They laughed heartily and expressed surprise at the fact that we did it just as they did. They had believed that city women simply went to a hospital, took some kind of pill, and the baby was swiftly born. Sharing our experiences as women, wives, and mothers created a common ground on which to build initial acquaintance into warm friendships.[11]

After several weeks in the hamlet, I moved to San Cristóbal so that my children could attend school. I continued to visit Tzajal Vitz, and I received people from the hamlet at my city home. At my house I was able to reciprocate the hospitality I had received in the hamlet. My guests ate and slept at my home on several occasions, and our relationships grew stronger. Away from the scrutinizing eye of worried neighbors, the women felt freer to engage in longer, more involved conversations. Chamula women are extremely open and discuss intimate details of their lives without prodding. After one long interview, Maruch went out to meet her husband, who had waited in the patio. She turned to him and cheerfully said, "I told her everything!"

A few days before I returned to the United States, Veruch, one of the women I felt closest to, narrated her encounter with the Earth Lord. She recounted how this fearsome character tried to persuade her soul to remain in his realm (a situation by which Chamulas explain a slow, debilitating illness leading to death). Veruch explained that the Earth Lord gave her good food and good coffee in order to gain her confidence and added half-jokingly, "just like you."

Five hundred years of painful experiences in their dealings with non-Indians have made Chamulas wary of any ulterior motives outsiderers bring to their interactions with them. One cannot be surprised that our presence among them—disrupting a given state of affairs in their villages, invading their privacy to fulfill our professional requirements, establishing friendly relationships, and, then, as unexpectedly as we arrive, disappearing from their lives—should be construed with a metaphor like that of the Earth Lord.

NOTES

1.   Throughout this book I give monetary amounts in pesos, followed by the approximate U.S. dollar equivalent based on the exchange rate at the time of my research in 1983-84. This rate was roughly 125 pesos to the dollar. Where the work of other scholars is cited, I follow the particular author's system of noting monetary amounts in either pesos and dollars, or dollars alone. I indicate the exchange rate used in the study under discussion.

2.   Although the Chiapas highlands have been intensively studied by anthropologists for more than 25 years, none of the major investigations in this region have focused on women. Most published works refer to the activities of women only as a part of the general social background. Others, however, contain more detailed information on women and gender, enabling comparison. This study of the female perspective in Chamula, together with Eber's (1991) recent ethnography of San Pedro Chenalhó, represents a first step toward balancing our understanding of native communities in this region. These ethnographies are part of the larger quest to incorporate women into the human record and transform our theories of society to account for new issues and questions. This quest, prompted by the feminist critique of anthropology, began in earnest about two decades ago. At present, an increasing number of anthropologists, historians and sociologists are devoting their efforts to document and analyze the situation of women in Mesoamerica, including the Chiapas area. Their studies add an indispensable dimension to the knowledge of this complex region—a region beset by turmoil and undergoing rapid changes due to the massive penetration of the international economy, acute economic crises and politico-military conflicts. For a review of the burgeoning literature on women in Mesoamerica, see Bossen (1983) and Rosenbaum and Eber (in press).

3.   Some Marxist anthropologists incorporate the view of ideology as an active process of interpretation, rooted in and in continuous interaction with social life. They consider meaning as part of people's lives and actions, inherent in the general pattern of social relationships (for example, Dolgin et al. (1977)). Godelier (1977) extends Marx's ideas on ideology and finds that both history and the structure of thought are indispensable to understand the ideology of precapitalist societies. Most Marxist anthropologists, however, still give privilege to material life and relations of production in their analysis of gender (for example, Leacock 1981; O'Laughlin 1975; Sacks 1979).

4.   In their review article on anthropological studies of women, Mukhopadhyay and Higgins (1988:486) note that recent feminist theory pursues the construction of a theory of the relationship between action and symbol that allows for the integration of action and cultural meanings.

5.   For example, E. Ardener (1975); S. Ardener (1975); Gilligan (1982); Murphy and Murphy (1974); and Okely (1975). See Shapiro (1988) for a critique of the concept of "women's culture," and Strathern's (1981:169) related comment on the difficulties of anthropological methods to compensate for the symbolic male bias which characterizes many cultures.

6.   For example, see Bossen (1984); Chiñas (1983); Collier (1974); Harding (1975); Lamphere (1974); Rosaldo (1974); and Stephen (1991).

7.   I chose to focus on the study of ritual and oral narratives to penetrate into Chamula symbolism since they occupy a central position in this society. Ritual is almost an every-

day affair that takes place at the time of major and minor crises in the family (e.g., pregnancy and birth, marriage, death and sickness; building a new house, taking a trip, planting, and so forth also involve the performance of rituals). It is no exaggeration to say that people's lives revolve around public festivals. These celebrations represent times of heightened social interaction, cultural awareness, and religious fervor, as hundreds, sometimes thousands, flock into town to participate in them. Neither is the domain of oral narrative esoteric; on the contrary, it is also a part of everyday life. Through the narration of myths and stories, Chamulas explain and illustrate many aspects of nature and social interaction and try to induce specific behaviors. These domains, ritual and oral narrative, are not isomorphic or consistent, but share a symbolic core.

8.   Several ethnographic studies of women also employ a multifaceted perspective, showing the complex articulation of gender with economic, political, kinship, prestige and ideological structures in specific societies. Gender systems vary according to the way they connect with other structures in the social system. See, for example, Bell (1983); Bloch (1987); Bourque and Warren (1981); Collier and Rosaldo (1981); Comaroff (1987); Goodale (1971); Maher (1987); Murphy and Murphy (1984); Nadelson (1981); Ortner (1981; Ortner and Whitehead (1981); Strathern (1981); and Weiner (1976); see also Zaretzky's (1976) important study of the evolution of the family.

9.   This story comes from Gary Gossen's corpus of narratives.

10.   For a radical critique of the use of these categories in anthropology, see Strathern (1988).

11.   I describe the details of my interaction and friendship with Maruch, an older Chamula woman, in Rosenbaum (1990).

2

San Juan Chamula
Community, Historical Setting, and Ethnicity

San Juan Chamula is an indigenous *municipio* (township) located in the highlands of Chiapas, Mexico (fig. 1). With an area of 364 km² and a population of approximately 100,000, Chamula is the largest and most densely populated of more than thirty Maya-speaking communities in the area. The majority of Chamulas live in one of more than one hundred *parajes* or hamlets scattered throughout the basins, hills, and cliffs of this mountainous terrain. The civic-ceremonial center, the seat of government and location of Chamula's only church, has a small permanent population. Roughly fifty thousand Chamulas live in the municipio itself; the other fifty thousand have emigrated to found new colonies and communities both within and outside of the highlands, a process that began more than a hundred years ago. This migration continues today as economic pressures and political and religious conflicts force some Chamulas to leave. These new Chamula colonies retain some of the basic traits of Chamula culture such as the Tzotzil language, social organization, cosmological categories, and ritual observances, thus demonstrating the vitality and strength of the native culture (Gossen 1986b:228).

Because of their large numbers and ubiquity, Chamulas have become the symbol of "Indianness" in the area (Gossen 1986b:228). Ladinos condescendingly refer to all native peoples in the area as "Chamulitas" (little Chamulas). Moreover, when the president of Mexico and the governor of Chiapas announced a new program to incorporate the highland indigenous groups into the more progressive economic sectors, they chose Chamula Center as the most appropriate place to make their appearance.

Like most native populations of the Americas, Chamulas survive largely on corn, beans, and squash. This triad is supplemented by cabbage, potatoes, and

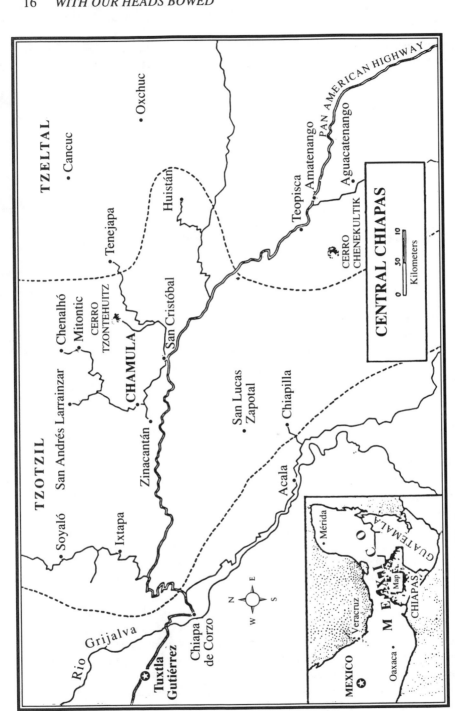

Figure 1. Map of central Chiapas, Mexico

turnip greens and flavored with salt, chile, and herbs. Chamulas eat chicken, eggs, and dried fish as ritual dishes. Corn is ground for tortillas, the staple food. *Matz'*, corn dough mixed with water, is the most frequent drink. *Ul*, a corn gruel, is a ritual beverage, and *pox*, cane liquor, is used prevalently in ritual life. *Pox* is used both in formal public ceremonies and in private, more secular ceremonial interaction. A request for a loan, a petition for a wife, a plea for forgiveness are among the many interactions that require both gifts of liquor and communal drinking. In recent decades soft drinks have been incorporated into ritual and social interaction, but cane liquor continues to be the ritual offering par excellence.

Most Chamulas live in one-room, thatch-roofed, wattle and daub houses. Recently tile has become a common roofing material. Wealthier Chamulas build relatively larger houses of brick and cement with tile or sheet metal roofs (fig. 2). A house usually shelters a patrilocal domestic unit, which most often includes a couple with their unmarried children, perhaps a married son with his wife and children, and sometimes one of the couple's parents. All members of the domestic unit share the food supply and the household shrine, and they cooperate with one another in economic and ritual activities.

In Chamula and surrounding indigenous communities, patrilineages have lost strength because fathers lack sufficient land to bequeath to their children (Collier 1976:98; Favre 1984:212). Young men begin to work for wages at age 14 or 15 and become economically independent. This independence encourages marriage at an early age and has resulted in increased birth rates. Chamula women marry at a younger age than the inhabitants of adjacent municipios (Collier 1976:153). Even though residence after marriage still tends toward patrilocality, husband and wife try to build their own house on or close to the husband's father's land, as soon as possible. If, however, the wife's family owns more land than the husband's family, the couple may move to her family's lands or hamlet, instead.

The domestic unit, or nuclear family, is the functional economic unit. Husband and wife depend heavily on each other for the economic survival of the family. The ideal division of labor in Chamula demands that a man plant his highland milpa, an act that symbolically reproduces the flesh of the Sun/Christ (corn) and brings heat and life (sustenance) to the family. The woman is expected to complement her husband's work by helping with certain agricultural tasks, especially during the harvest, and by preparing the products of the milpa for consumption. A woman's responsibilities also include weaving the family's clothing and blankets and caring for the children.

Unfortunately, only the richest men in Chamula can enjoy the privilege of making a living from highland milpas. The majority of families own tiny plots in the highlands that they plant almost as a token. On average these crops supply only 20 percent of a family's yearly requirements (Wasserstrom 1983a:202). Most Chamula men must work for wages outside the community. Some men also work as sharecroppers in the Grijalva River Valley, where they rent land for milpa from

Ladino cattle farmers. Even so, men cannot always harvest or purchase enough corn to satisfy the requirements of their families. Their wives must sell woven or embroidered garments or engage in other income-producing activities in order to purchase corn.

Several factors compound the difficulties of farming in the highlands. The yield of these lands is generally poor because of the altitude, which averages 2300 m. The soils are exhausted in many sections, probably because of intensive use over hundreds of years. The introduction of sheep in the early colonial period accelerated soil erosion tremendously (Collier 1976:148). Gradually pine and oak forests have been cleared for fields or cut down for industrial use or for firewood. As a consequence of land erosion, water holes tend to dry up before the rainy season. When the water shortage becomes extreme, Chamulas abandon their hamlets and seek other places to live. Chamula landholdings have been divided into minute parcels because of rapid population growth, land inheritance by both sons and daughters, and lack of economic alternatives. Chamula, therefore, has become a center for the provision of workers to the region's commercial economy (Collier 1976:153; Wasserstrom 1983a:201). Unable to depend on agriculture, many Chamula men and women choose to make a livelihood through the production of various craft items and other goods (e.g., pottery, pine furniture, firewood, charcoal, musical instruments, woven garments, and cane liquor). Unlike wage labor, however, craft specialization depends on local resources and therefore contributes to the destruction of the environment.

Women use the backstrap loom, a prehispanic invention, to make clothes that set Chamula men and women apart from both Ladinos and the other indigenous peoples in the region. Chamula women usually keep flocks of four to ten sheep to supply wool. Women employ simple, ancient technology for the long process of producing a garment: shearing the sheep; washing, drying, fluffing, and carding the wool; drop-spinning the wool into thread; measuring the yarn; setting up the loom; weaving the piece; dyeing, shrinking, and felting the fabric.[1] Women weave their own long, black skirts and the red belts that secure the skirts at the waist. Traditionally, women also wore brown, beige, or white woolen shirts with red tassels that they wove themselves; but today most women substitute white or blue cotton shirts that they buy in San Cristóbal or from local tailors in the hamlets. The *mochib* is a black woolen shawl (sometimes replaced by a long, usually blue shawl bought in San Cristóbal) that is used for modesty as much as for warmth (Linn 1976:9). Chamula women, especially young marriageable ones, cover their mouths, and sometimes most of their faces, so they will not be accused of enticing young men with a smile.

Women weave white woolen tunics (*jerkail*) and black woolen tunics with long sleeves (*chuj*) for their husbands (figs. 3 and 4). Men wear the *jerkail* daily over a simple cotton shirt and trousers and the *chuj* when it is very cold or on more formal occasions. Children wear clothes similar to those of their parents.

Before the onset of puberty, a girl's skirt is brown or gray and is woven with a simpler, less time-consuming technique than that used for the black skirts of adult women. Girls are easily identified as Chamula from a very young age. A boy, on the other hand, may not receive his first *jerkail* until he is eight years old and the black *chuj* even later. Until he is toilet trained at about age two, he wears the same type of skirt that a girl wears. Once he is trained, a Chamula boy wears clothes that are practically indistinguishable from those worn by Ladino boys. From birth girls have no alternative to Chamula dress; boys, on the other hand, do not don traditional clothing until they are older. This difference in dress between the sexes is not coincidental. Chamula men have absorbed many Ladino traits, but Chamula women have been less influenced by the outer world.

TRANSFORMATIONS OF GENDER IN HISTORY

In this section I attempt to incorporate women and gender into the historical picture of Highland Chiapas. This discussion is only an outline of a feminist view of the history of this region. In order to reconstruct fully women's roles in the history of Chamula and Highland Chiapas, a meticulous study of primary sources is required. Given that most historical accounts in Mesoamerica were written by nonindigenous men, such a reconstruction is especially challenging. As Burkhart (in press) points out, "gender became a contested domain now to be negotiated not simply between women and men but also between indigenous people and Europeans."[2]

The following account is derived primarily from secondary sources that were not written with any particular interest in the female perspective or female contributions. Despite these limitations, however, I believe the role of gender within a dynamic historical context is an important consideration. The main goals of such a task are as follows: (1) to present women as active agents of history—whether openly challenging the changes that demean their lives, developing mechanisms to minimize the effect of threatening forces, attempting to salvage the ways of life they treasure, or otherwise participating in the historical process; (2) to study gender relations and gender symbolism through time and evaluate how they functioned in terms of the larger society; (3) to determine how social changes affected gender relations and how men and women in this specific society came to have separate historical experiences (Kelly-Gadol 1987; Silverblatt 1988).

Although historical research on women and gender in Mesoamerica is in its infancy as a field of study, it promises to illuminate not only our understanding of gender in the region but also our discussion of central, theoretical gender issues.[3] Some of these issues include the nature of gender systems at different levels of sociocultural integration; the effects of statehood, the militarization of society, and colonialism on the role of women and gender interaction; and the development of ideologies through which elites manipulate gender.

Precolumbian Society

Little information is available from the prehispanic or colonial periods in Highland Chiapas to permit a detailed analysis of gender. Compared with the Guatemalan Highlands or Central Mexico, this area appears to have been only marginally involved in the social and cultural developmental trends of the great civilizations of Mesoamerica upon which the region depended. Chiapas maintained a lower level of sociocultural organization (Calnek 1988:59) than did these other areas. It is precisely this marginality that accounts for the general scarcity of information about this region.[4]

Rulership was inherited through the male line. Women were sometimes called *cacicas* (female of cacique or ruler). This term, however, seems to indicate that a woman was the daughter of a cacique, not that she herself was a ruler (Calnek 1988:41). Caciques married high-ranking women from other communities, and it was the children of these women—rather than those born to lesser wives—who acquiered the highest positions in the community. The elite practiced polygyny, but it was not their prerogative exclusively. Commoners who could afford to do so also acquired several wives (Miles 1965:281). The unit of social life was the extended household, comprising a patriarch, his unmarried daughters and sons, and his married sons with their children. Complementarity characterized the division of labor within an economy based on subsistence. The extended group constituted a self-sufficient unit. With maturation, heads of lineages were able to rise in a prestige hierarchy.

Upon marriage into patrilineal households, women's lives probably were not very different from the lives of women in contemporary indigenous communities that maintain a strong patrilineal orientation. Living among a closely knit group of men who were linked through kinship, women's influence in the affairs of the extended group would probably have been limited. But a woman's authority could be expected to increase as she aged, became an established member of the group, and was able to command the labor of daughters and daughters-in-law. Also, as Miles (1965:280) argues, marriage was a man's first step toward building his own patrilineage, and consequently it must have been highly valued by men. In subsistence societies, generally, women are esteemed and considered indispensable; their labor complements that of men and cannot be obtained except through marriage (e.g., Bossen 1984; Leacock 1981; Wiener 1976). The work of women must have been as essential to the survival of the household as it is today. The woven goods a woman produced for trade improved the economic standing of her family, a pattern found among other Mesoamerican groups (Burkhart in press).[5]

With regard to gender ideology in the prehispanic period, our only information derives from the Popol Vuh and concerns the Quiché of Highland Guatemala. This document reflects the perspective of the elite. It was written down during early colonial times and shows some Spanish influence. Unlike Highland Chiapas, Quiché society was heavily militarized before the arrival of the Spanish (Carmack 1981).[6] In this remarkable book women appear as originators or fertility symbols for both children and crops (for correspondences with Chamula, see chapter 4). For example, Xquiq (Blood Woman) salvaged the seed of Hun-Hunahpú and bore his children. She also displayed the ability to magically increase corn by filling a large net from only two ears found on a single plant.[7] Xmucané (Grandmother) and Xpiyacoc (Grandfather) made the first human beings of corn dough, but it was Xmucané who actually formed the humans from the same corn with which she prepared her tortillas.

Men, however, appear at the center of the cosmogony. The heroes of the story are the male twins Hunahpú and Xbalanqué, who ascend into the sky as the Sun and the Moon. The gender ambiguity of Xbalanqué, however, should be noted: since Classic times Maya mythology has depicted the moon as female. The prefix *x* at the beginning of the name Xbalanqué is a common indicator of female names or occupations in Maya languages. Other associations with this hero twin also suggest gender ambiguity (Carmack 1983:36, 196, 201). In the more historical section of the Popol Vuh, women appear primarily as wives and are only mentioned as the bearers of the children of the Quiché forefathers. Perhaps this reference illustrates that women from the nobility often played a conservative role, insuring the succession of legitimate offspring to the throne (Gossen and Leventhal 1993).

Colonial Period

After a century of Spanish occupation, the native population of Mesoamerica was reduced by 90 percent. Epidemics continued to ravage the population during the following century, and the remaining indigenous peoples experienced tremendous pressure to fulfill the onerous tribute and work obligations imposed by the Spanish (Wasserstrom 1983b; MacLeod 1973). In the lower elevations, many communities lost their lands to encroaching haciendas. Chamula and other highland communities (e.g., Tenejapa, Oxchuc, and Huistán) were able to retain their lands, and the land tenure of these communities was legitimized by the Spanish crown (Favre 1984:46). Although the highland communities continued to practice small-scale, subsistence agriculture and peddling (Wasserstrom 1983a:105), they were not spared from exploitation.

Throughout the colonial period, native communities were accosted from every angle by greedy colonial administrators, priests, and Spanish entrepreneurs. These ambitious men competed among themselves for control over the indigenous labor force and its economic productivity. The Spanish used various means to impose tribute and forced labor obligations on indigenous communities; in Highland Chiapas, however, a system of *repartimientos* was employed as well. In exchange for goods such as dried beef and knives, the natives were forced to transform cotton into cloth (Wasserstrom 1983a:47) or to procure cacao or cotton for colonial administrators. Often they had to trade their own corn crop to acquire the demanded goods. *Repartimientos* affected both men and women. Women worked extremely hard to produce the yarn and woven goods demanded by the Spanish. Men transported the requisite goods to distant places, where the Spaniards sold the items at great profit. Exhausted and sick from constant traveling, men often died young, and their wives outlived them.

During those centuries of harsh exploitation, indigenous peoples did not accept their lot passively; whenever possible, they rebelled. In many cases this resistance took the form of religious insurgence instigated by women. Faced with an apparently hopeless situation and closely supervised by priests, who sought to obliterate all traces of "paganism," native peoples struggled to create a religious ceremonial of their own. They hoped to construct a spiritual and communal refuge from the painful realities of exploitation, death, and constant migration. Among the most important attempts to create an independent religious life were the Virgin cults of Santa Marta and Cancuc (Bricker 1981:68). These cults represent only two in a series of apparitions, miracles, and prophets that emerged in several highland communities at the beginning of the eighteenth century.[8]

According to legend the Virgin appeared in Santa Marta, a town of the Chamula parish, in the fall of 1711. A Chamula woman, Dominica López, saw the Virgin first, in a cornfield. The Virgin requested that the people build a chapel in her honor in the town. The people brought the Virgin into town, where she turned into a wooden image. The chapel was built, and Dominica and her husband were appointed *mayordomos* (stewards) of the Virgin. The Virgin communicated her messages to the people only through Dominica, who always stood by the side of the image. In her messages, the Virgin offered to reward the people with "much maize, beans, and many children" (Bricker 1981:57). When the Spanish discovered this cult, which was attracting a great number of people from the surrounding communities, they supposedly removed the image to San Cristóbal. After a few days the image was banished, and the ecclesiastical authorities brought Dominica López and her husband to trial.

At the time of the trial in June, 1712, the Virgin appeared again, this time in the nearby Tzeltal town of Cancuc. She appeared to María de la Candelaria, a native girl of 13 or 14, who was married to Sebastián Sánchez. The Virgin demanded that a chapel be built in Cancuc on the spot where she appeared. Once the chapel was finished, the organizers tried to get ecclesiastical approval for the cult by petitioning the Spanish priest to perform a mass. The petition was denied, and the entire delegation was imprisoned (Bricker 1981:60).

At this point Sebastián Gómez, a Maya from Chenalhó, claimed to have spoken with the Virgin. In this conversation, said Gómez, the Virgin demanded that an indigenous priesthood replace the Spanish one. As Bricker (1981:60) notes, this assertion was an explicit declaration of war against the Spanish colonial system. Thirty-two towns participated in the revolt. A group of *fiscales* (indigenous assistants of Spanish priests) were ordained as priests and took over the functions of the ousted Spanish priesthood (Bricker 1981:61). Although these indigenous priests were all male, María de la Candelaria was the *mayordoma mayor* (main steward). The other Stewards of the Virgin were elderly men organized in *cofradías* (religious sodalities). The Virgin statues were clothed in traditional blouses, and María de la Candelaria was seated nearest the altar, flanked by two native priests who served as her scribes. In the same manner as Dominica López, María de la Candelaria communicated with the Virgin.

Under the leadership of Sebastián Gómez, this cult developed into a confederation of towns and an army, "the soldiers of the Virgin." In August 1712, the indigenous army massacred the Spanish population of several highland towns and, for a while, successfully held its ground. Finally, after fierce fighting and many casualties on both sides, Cancuc was captured by the Spaniards in November. When the people realized they would be overwhelmed militarily, they tried to engage supernatural forces to help them:

> Four Indian women who were reputed to be witches were hastily carried to the river in chairs completely covered by mats to protect them from the sun, to invoke magical weapons against the enemy. Each woman represented a natural force: earthquake, lightning, flood and wind... (Bricker 1981:64)

The exploitation and control of the native population intensified after the rebellion of 1712. Native life deteriorated to such an extreme that many people abandoned their communities permanently (Wasserstrom 1983a:89-90). By this time, many more haciendas had been created in the Grijalva Valley, and the native people were incorporated into the hacienda work forces.

In the mid-eighteenth century, haciendas expanded and encroached on lower, more productive terrain. Although Chamula and other communities in the higher elevations continued to control their own lands, the severe impact of diseases and exploitation had drastically transformed even these communities. Immediately following the initial struggle between the Spanish and the indigenous people, Chamula Center had about 400 houses, and there were an additional 100 to 200 houses in two of the hamlets, for a total population on the order of 3,000 to 4,000 people (Calnek 1988:32). By 1611 the number of heads of households had been reduced to 219, and 150 years later the population had still not reached its precontact levels.

Under conditions of severe demographic decline that threatened the survival of the group, women's role as mother appears to have dominated. Emphasis on the importance of women for the continuation of the group is dramatically portrayed by the Virgin cults. The deities around which these two movements centered were female, and twice they appeared to very young women. In both cases the deities were probably *jme'tik* (Our Mother), who in modern Chamula cosmology represents the Moon and Mother Earth and is identified with the Virgin (for other associations of *jme'tik*, see chapter 4). As the Earth, Our Mother symbolizes fertility, that is, life and the renewal of population and of crops. In the Virgin Cult, she appears at a time of hunger and hopelessness and offers to bless the Indians with abundant food and children. Young and recently married, the two main figures who initiated the cult, Dominica López and María de la Candelaria, also could be interpreted as symbols of fertility and hope. The association of this cult with the Earth is further confirmed by the recruitment of female witches who enlist the forces of nature—wind, earthquake, flood, and lightning—to destroy the Spaniards. These forces are still believed to reside in the Earth and as discussed in chapter 4, represent the dark, ominous aspect of the female Earth.

Women assumed the role of mayordoma in the cults. In the case of Cancuc, María de la Candelaria was more important than the elderly male mayordomos, which suggests that women were active in the religious organizations of their communities in colonial times. As Bricker notes (1981:68), other aspects of the organization of the cults followed the basic lines of the *cofradía* system; therefore, the appointment of women to religious positions probably was accepted practice.

Post-Independence Period

The economic conditions of indigenous communities worsened after independence from Spain in 1821. The number of haciendas in the lowlands increased enormously, especially after the government simplified the system for granting titles. Beginning in 1826, landowners were able to acquire title to native communal lands. After 1850, with the tremendous investment of French, American, German, and Spanish capital, hacienda owners diversified their crops (Wasserstrom 1983a:113). These new developments affected native communities in different ways. At the highest altitudes, previously ignored by the hacienda owners, the communal lands of the municipios were seized, and the people were forced to migrate to the lowlands as sharecroppers or laborers. The alternative for native people was to remain in their communities and work as laborers on lands that once belonged to them but had been appropriated by the very outsiders who now employed them. Only by serving as laborers for Ladinos were the native people allowed to plant their own milpas on a portion of the land, undoubtedly a humiliating option (Wasserstrom 1983a:119).

During the mid-nineteenth century, the indigenous population of Highland Chiapas was trapped in the midst of an ideological struggle between Conservatives and Liberals and the ensuing administrative and religious transformations that took place when power changed hands (Rus 1989).[9] Both Conservatives and Liberals exploited the native peoples. The Conservatives appropriated native lands close to San Cristóbal and proceeded to extract rent from the former indigenous owners who continued to plant their cornfields there. In the Grijalva Valley, Liberals had a hard time finding enough field hands for the haciendas since the Conservatives monopolized them. Furthermore, Creole priests were pressuring indigenous communities to change "...their extravagance, their propensities and strange customs..." (Wasserstrom 1983a:131). Chamula officials responded with a formal protest against priestly intervention in their local Catholic practices.

The stage for a confrontation was set. The worst incident took place in Chamula from 1867 to 1870. Cuscat's rebellion, called the "War of St. Rose" by local people, started as a religious revitalization movement. This religious movement turned into a political confrontation aimed at the extermination of the Ladino population only after Ladino authorities dismissed the religious aspects of the movement as "idolatrous" and stressed its potential for ethnic conflict by calling it a "caste war" (Bricker 1981:125). In the manner of the Virgin cults of 1712, the revitalization movement began with a young girl, Agustina Gómez Checheb. The girl claimed to see three stones fall from the sky while she looked after her sheep in the hamlet of Tzajaljemel. Later, the *fiscal* of Chamula, Pedro Díaz Cuscat, took over the organization of the new cult. Through Gómez Checheb, the stones talked to the people who came to worship them. Cuscat declared that Gómez Checheb had given birth to the stones and that therefore she was "the mother of God" (Bricker 1981:120). The new indigenous saint was identified with Saint Rose, an important figure in the Chamula pantheon.

The cult grew dramatically when Díaz Cuscat incorporated it into the traditional festival cycle and *cofradía* system. He also established a market that attracted large numbers of people for recruitment into the cult (Bricker 1981:121; Rus 1989). The movement ended in open confrontation. The Ladino authorities in San Cristóbal, reinforced by state troops, attacked an indigenous army about 600 strong, which had marched to the city to demand the release of one of its leaders. Approximately 300 Indians and many Ladinos were killed (Bricker 1981:124). In the following weeks, the natives continued sporadic attacks on defenseless Ladino settlements. Nine Tzotzil towns participated in the rebellion. By 1870, however, the Indian attacks on Ladinos subsided. According to Bricker (1981:125), the War of Saint Rose won a degree of religious freedom for the native population of Highland Chiapas similar to that achieved in Yucatan following the Caste War. The Catholic priests were never able to regain control over Chamula religious life.

Cuscat's rebellion, like the cults of 1712, took place at a time when despair and exploitation were peaking. Again, people strove to establish a cult that would unite them in the worship of a distinct, native deity. The stones that ignited the spark for the rebellion were another expression of the female Earth and its wealth, defined in terms of crops, animals, or money. Agustina Gómez Checheb, as "mother of God," was identified with Saint Rose. In contemporary Chamula, Saint Rose is linked to women's interests. In contrast with the Virgin Mary, Saint Rose demands to be dressed by women during festivals because "men have dirty, impure hands" (Linn 1976:255). Saint Rose has an influence over women's earthly concerns and is the patroness of weaving. It may not be possible to determine if the associations between Saint Rose and women's concerns existed during the Cuscat rebellion, but if they did exist, Saint Rose may have symbolized not only women's fertility and wealth but also female productivity at a time when men were being forced out of the local communities. Female participation in the movement was so central that wives fought beside their husbands in the battles. According to the folklore of Chamula and other highland communities, women decided to participate in the struggle with the hope that their "cold" female genitals would "cool" the guns (a "hot," male item) of the Ladinos (Bricker 1981:150). This account substantiates the contemporary view found in many indigenous communities that female genitals are "cold" in nature, no doubt associated with the coldness of the Earth's womb. The account also reveals the solidarity of husband and wife and the decision of men and women to fight their oppressors in a final attempt to rescue their society from seemingly inevitable destruction.

Following Cuscat's rebellion, the situation of indigenous peoples continued to deteriorate. Export business vastly increased, and entrepreneurs established new and larger haciendas dependent on native labor from the highlands. Chamulas and indigenous men from other communities were forcibly recruited through an infamous system of *habilitación* or *enganche*. Under this system, representatives of the landowners gave native men an advance payment in exchange for a commitment to work several months on a specific hacienda. The money was usually distributed during a celebration at which the men were deliberately encouraged to spend it. Once the money was spent, the men could repay their debt only by working on the hacienda. Those individuals who did not honor their obligation to the hacienda were jailed by the Ladino authorities.

The unfortunate laborers usually had to walk long distances to their destination. On the hacienda, the men became further indebted to the landowner because they were required to purchase their necessities on credit at the hacienda store. Their earnings were small, and often they were unable to repay their debts and became virtual slaves on the hacienda. Those men who were able to return home were frequently overworked and succumbed easily to diseases like malaria. Many never returned to their communities (Favre 1984:79). By 1910 thousands of men had sold themselves into debt peonage (Wasserstrom 1983a:152).

The migration of Chamula men to lowland farms and plantations, where they work for weeks or months at a time, continues today. The Mexican Revolution abolished debt peonage and *habilitación* in 1914, but migration in search of work continued. Additionally, the Chamula population grew so rapidly after the agrarian reforms of the late 1930s that the benefits of the reforms were quickly undone. In 1970, Wasserstrom argues (1983a:203), most Chamulas planted only minuscule cornfields, and about 76 percent of all married Chamula men migrated in search of wage labor. For 150 years, Chamula men have performed seasonal labor away from home, usually under oppressive conditions. In general, women have not migrated to engage in wage labor but have remained at home in the highlands.

The intrusion of the national Mexican government in the governance of native communities in the late 1930s had an important and continuing effect on gender in Chamula. The Cárdenas government required indigenous communities to establish *Ayuntamientos Constitucionales* (Constitutional Town Councils)— governing bodies that would represent their communities before state and national authorities. Through these bodies, the national government could control and manipulate indigenous communities in order to gain support for its programs. By law, the officials elected to these councils had to be bilingual and experienced in dealing with Ladino governmental bureaucracies. In this way, the government bypassed traditional indigenous rulers, who were primarily monolingual and held isolationist preferences, and became firmly entrenched inside native communities.

Women, who had been actively engaged in religious cargos for centuries and who had religious obligations complementary to their husbands' civil cargos, had no role to play in the newly created civil positions. First, Mexican officials themselves were overwhelmingly, if not totally, male.[10] These officials were accustomed to dealing exclusively with male leaders in indigenous communities.[11] Second, most Chamula women were and continue to be monolingual and have little or no contact with Ladinos in San Cristóbal. Women had no opportunity to establish a presence on the council. Over the years, the members of the Chamula council have become tremendously powerful. Politically, these men have established strong links with Ladino public institutions and officials. Economically, they have manipulated their positions to obtain handsome economic benefits. The council has come to stand for a new kind of power in the community—a power that is totally male, strongly secularized, and displays vast economic superiority to the majority of the population. The complementary presence of women, customary in native cargo systems, is lost within the Constitutional Town Council.

Summary: Gender in Historical Perspective

What little we know about gender in precolumbian Highland Chiapas indicates a relatively egalitarian gender system. As the heads of extended patrilocal households, men probably had more authority than women over decisions affecting the group. Gender symbolism, however, reveals that women were important for their role as the creators of human beings and for their control over the Earth's fertility—a fundamental value in a society which depends on agriculture for survival. The male position of primacy in the Popol Vuh represents a view of men as central in shaping and establishing world order so that human life would be possible (perhaps similar to contemporary myths that narrate the struggles of the Sun/Christ over the forces of evil, chap. 4). Might the presence of the more "feminine" Xbalanqué indicate that this role of arranging the world could be performed by a man/woman pair, analogous to the contemporary religious cargo system in which husband and wife together help the deities to carry their burden?

Having retained their lands during the colonial period, Chamula's extended patrilineal groups probably continued to function albeit compelled to work for Spanish masters. In practice, the authority of the patrilineal head must have decreased substantially once he was no longer able to command the work of the extended family to accomplish his own goals. One cannot be sure, however, what effect this loss of authority had on gender interaction. If one compares the colonial situation with that of today, in which Chamula men have seen their authority suffer dramatic erosion within Ladino society, one observes that feelings of powerlessness may drive men to exert their authority within the family in despotic ways.

As early as colonial times, indigenous men were forced to leave their communities to work on haciendas or to serve as bearers or mule drivers in the transportation of *repartimiento* goods. This situation was the beginning of a specific, gendered division of labor in which native men were forced to leave their communities temporarily and women remained at home. This division was increasingly strengthened to the point where, after the mid-nineteenth century, it became a defining aspect of the Chamula way of life. With forced recruitment and, in the twentieth century, demographic pressures, Chamula men have had no choice but to emigrate each year for several weeks or months. In this manner, Chamula men have been incorporated into the national socioeconomic system on the lowest rungs of the economic ladder. Meanwhile, from the colonial period to the present, women have remained in their hamlets where they care for the children, the highland crops, and the ritual obligations and weave to earn extra cash to support their families.

Perhaps Chamulas and other native peoples from Highland Chiapas consciously devised this gendered division of labor as a way to protect women and children at a time when sickness, hunger, and death prevailed. There is no question that this strategy sheltered women and children from the worst abuses of the system and, in the midst of drastic transformations, allowed the reproduction and continuation of at least some elements of Chamula society and culture. In the long run, however, this strategy had a profound effect on the way Chamulas character-ize gender. It shaped an ideology in which men are depicted as courageous, will-ing to face risks; but women appear as vulnerable, easily scared, and therefore they must remain close to home. As I note below, this depiction, predominant in contemporary Chamula ideology, is often flaunted as male superiority and em-ployed to justify limitations on female mobility.

Although both men and women suffered and continue to suffer the impact of exploitation, men have been affected in more direct ways. Apart from constant emigration under strenuous conditions, male authority within the extended family group has diminished considerably. Long absences lessen men's influence over family and group decisions, and their loss of lands (whether by appropriation or by division of the land among heirs into parcels too small to meet basic subsis-tence needs) decreases their control over the economic future of their children. Furthermore, when the men left, women became more involved in productive activities and took on many jobs previously carried out by men. Survival would have been impossible, otherwise.

In an interesting study of ritual dramas from Zinacantán, Wasserstrom (1983a:217ff) analyzes how women were put back in their place after having per-formed for many decades roles previously defined as male. When the agrarian reform laws returned the lands that the Zinacantecos had lost to the haciendas, Zinacanteco men were able to return to their community. Once home, the men redefined women's roles in order to regain their own position of control in the community. They created new rituals from which they excluded women shamans. In the ritual dramas that Wasserstrom interprets, women are publicly scolded and shamed for attempting to do men's work and thereby risking damage to their reproductive organs. By taking on male responsibilities, women jeopardized their most important role—child bearing.

In terms of the symbolic representation of gender, I have shown how in colo-nial times, when the survival of native societies was severely imperiled, women's roles as mothers and symbols of the fertile Earth became paramount. The instru-mental role of women in the religious movements of 1712 and 1867 reveals their active involvement in the social life of their communities. Indeed, in both in-stances, perceiving the hopelessness and devastation of their communities, women initiated contact with a divine being who had the power to transform the painful reality of indigenous life. In both cases, however, a male took control of the orga-nization of the cult. He placed the female leader under his patronage and imposed a military structure upon the movement.

These revitalization movements, according to Gossen (1989a), illustrate a paradigmatic configuration underlying Chamula sacred narratives that manifests itself in critical historical events involving this community. From an original phase of social malaise, a female mystical force or creative power emerges. As soon as this female force manifests itself to a native woman, a male personage attempts to snatch away the woman's power. Once he has subdued her, the male personage enters into conflict with other males for control of the flow of events (Gossen and Leventhal 1993). According to this interpretation, paradigmatic historical events begin as a conflict between the sexes and become a struggle between male adversaries for political, economic, and religious power. Chamula women's active role in their community's history and social life is indisputable and clearly recognized by Chamulas themselves.

ETHNICITY AND GENDER

The violent Spanish invasion, the subsequent demographic devastation of the native population, the systematic despoiling of indigenous resources and labor, and the intensive program of evangelization by the Catholic Church fractured the social life and culture of native communities in Highland Chiapas. Old meanings and social forms vanished. From fragments of their ancestors' way of life and new elements often adopted under pressure, each indigenous group struggled to construct a new synthesis—a meaningful universe to shelter it and enable it to retain its integrity as a group.[12] Through the centuries indigenous peoples have succeeded in creating distinctive cultures in spite of or, perhaps, because of outside control over their economic and political life.

The tasks of building and maintaining relatively distinctive worlds generate ongoing strain. New situations, threats, and challenges continuously compel people to rethink boundaries and reestablish their sense of group; sometimes they resist, and sometimes they yield to powerful outsiders. Chamulas redefine themselves not only vis-à-vis Ladinos and indigenous peoples from other communities but also with respect to other Chamulas who disagree with traditionally accepted views. Recently, under the direction of community leaders, thousands of neighbors and friends who have rejected Chamula religious traditions in favor of either Protestantism or "New Catholicism" have been expelled from the community (see chapter 8). Unwilling to abide by tradition and celebrate in the accepted way the central corporate symbols of Chamula (i.e., the Sun/Christ and the saints), these converts are no longer considered members of the group.

In this discussion, I analyze Chamula ethnicity as a subjective construct through which men and women express their understanding of their positions in the wider social system and delineate a space for themselves.[13] In contrast to Friedlander (1975), who finds that the label of Indian denotes exclusively a low socioeconomic status in the national stratification system, I argue that in Chamula the opposite is true. The decision by Chamulas to retain a separate identity demonstrates a keen awareness that only within their own society can they become respected people, accrue power, help the deities to carry out critical responsibilities, and follow in the footsteps of their forbears. In other words, only within their own society can Chamulas live a meaningful, dignified life. Were they to be incorporated entirely into Ladino society, Chamulas would become no more than poor peasants.

Stephen (1991:20) notes that the Zapotecs of Teotitlán del Valle project a monolithic ethnic identity to the outside world with the purpose of attracting consumers of indigenous culture.[14] This projected identity fails to reflect the complexities and contradictions of the internal representations of Zapotec identity in their own society. This image of humble weavers, working at simple looms to reproduce designs from a glorious, ancient past, conceals increasingly crystallized class divisions that permit some individuals to buy labor and extract surplus value from others. Even though large income differences exist among Chamulas, the appropriation of surplus value is generally indirect. For example, wealthy Chamulas monopolize sales of liquor and soft drinks and are able to afford trucks, with which they transport other people's goods for a fee. They sell their products and services at high prices to other, usually impoverished Chamulas. Like their counterparts in Teotitlán, these wealthy Chamulas hold the highest positions of authority; however, they are able to extract the labor of civil and religious cargoholders to support the operation of the social machine and at the same time enhance group solidarity. For the most part, surplus labor is not obtained directly through the sale and purchase of labor within the community.

Chamula ethnicity does not project a facade of romantic homogeneity rather it stresses its opposition to one adversary, Ladino society, which ceaselessly threatens its survival. There is no mystification about internal stratification; it is clearly identified and explained in the idiom of ethnicity: wealthy Chamulas are ladinoized, greedy and exploitative; worse, they enter into deals with Ladinos to obtain riches at the expense of others. As Scott (1976) observes, reciprocity and redistribution are essential characteristics of village life. Because subsistence is a fundamental social right, the poor have a legitimate claim to the resources of wealthier neighbors. Reciprocity and redistribution break down with increasing internal differentiation, and exploitation emerges within the community (Goldin and Rosenbaum in press). Chamulas seem to have an acute understanding of this situation; although they recognize Ladinos as their strongest adversaries, they also use the social weapons available to them against those Chamulas who ally themselves with the Ladino culture. Wealthy individuals live under tremendous fear of envy and witchcraft. The latter is a powerful deterrent against accumulation and conspicuous consumption.

Of all the indigenous communities in Chiapas, Chamula is perhaps the most self-conscious. It is among the few communities in Chiapas that forbid non-Indians or foreigners to reside or own land within their territories. Unlike the Zapotecs Stephen describes, Chamulas do not present an amiable face to attract tourists to their community. Although they sell their products to tourists, there have been many instances of attacks against visitors in Chamula Center. Usually the visitors have not respected rules that forbid taking pictures inside the church or during religious festivals.

In 1974 the Chamula elders expelled a Catholic priest who lived in the ceremonial center. Following years of Church criticism of indigenous religious practices, Chamula officially broke with the Catholic Church in 1985 when the community found a bishop from the Mexican Orthodox Church who was willing to abide by Chamula traditions. Based on recent and past experiences of explosive interactions with Ladinos, Chamulas have a reputation for conservatism, separatism, and rejection of Mexican national culture (Gossen 1984:256, 1986b:228). How have they been able to endure close contact with the Ladino system for so long without succumbing to it?

In practice the Chamula community's strong sense of identity reflects their powerfully centralized political system. The few families that comprise the oligarchy do not allow the existence of dissident groups, whether political, religious, or economic. Dissidents are killed or banished from the community. The religious system is also centralized. Unlike neighboring communities, such as Zinacantán, where churches have been built in several hamlets, Chamula has only one church, which is located in the Ceremonial Center and is the site of the most important ritual festivals. Several times a year, men and women from near and distant hamlets assemble to collectively worship their deities.

Since colonial times, indigenous communities have strengthened their internal solidarity through public rituals (Wasserstrom 1983b:109). These rituals kept alive a spirit of resistance against the oppressive dominant society. In times of chaos and despair, native peoples envisioned the revitalization of their communities with new, autochthonous cults. The cults led to armed confrontations that rallied a collection of indigenous groups in the fight against non-Indians.[15] Public rituals continue to reinforce the basic principles of Chamula society.

Gossen's (1986b:249) analysis of *k'in tajimoltik* (the Festival of Games, or Carnival), an extremely complicated five-day festival, shows how the different ritual sequences bring life to history and social reality before an enthralled audience. The audience vicariously participates in the strife as the destruction of Chamula society is ritually overcome in a battle similar to people's daily struggles with aggressive outside forces. Chamulas manifest awareness of their centuries-long disadvantaged position in the larger society and justify their internal conformity and defensive posture against the outside world. The festival also offers a lucid, economic commentary. Acknowledging economic dependence on the larger society, Chamulas contend that Ladino goods have value in their society only as they are used in the service of the deities. Chamulas ambivalence toward the intrusive Ladino system finds expression in the double role of the Passion character in the festival. This character represents both the Sun/Christ and the destructive forces of antagonistic ethnic groups. Gossen (1986b:254) argues that the Passion character articulates a deep-seated ambivalence; each Chamula is "an amalgam of ethnic patriot and potential Mexican mestizo."

Through centuries of contact with the larger world, Chamulas adopted a dual strategy that enabled the persistence of many cultural and social forms. Spanish androcentrism, with its insistence on the proper place of women, led to the separation of the public and the private spheres (Kellogg 1991); indigenous men, with a tradition of male patrilineage leadership, became the brokers. As the representatives of non-Indian rulers, these men collected taxes, organized labor, and so forth. They had no choice but to modify the structure of public systems and to enforce foreign domination in their communities. The most visible aspects of the native system (e.g., government, judicial procedures, and public rituals) underwent radical transformations; in the peripheral hamlets where most people lived, however, many practices and beliefs were either hidden or considered nonthreatening by priests and colonial and modern authorities. Domestic production and social reproduction, which occur in the domestic arena, were relatively protected from forced intervention (Gossen and Leventhal in press).

In time men, as symbols of the center (i.e., public life), came to stand for the unavoidable compromise with outsiders. Although not completely absent from public life (chap. 7), women became symbols of life in the periphery, where the more conservative aspects of their tradition endured. The assimilation of Chamula into the dominant economic system is all but complete today; however, household production, usually performed by women employing traditional cultural arts, has become a tool of resistance. Artisans struggle against complete absorption by the invasive capitalist system and its consequent commoditization and alienation (Nash in press). Both cosmology and history express and validate these basic features of Chamula life, namely, women's cultural conservatism and men's compromise with the Ladino world. I have shown that when Chamulas and their culture are threatened from the outside, a female deity or oracle appears and spells hope for the renewal and continued life of her children. Society goes back to its origins, always symbolized by women. Within this paradigm, men wrest control away from women and appear therefore as opportunistic actors who trick women in order to gain control.

Men's compromise with Ladino culture is poignantly expressed in the ideology of the Earth Lord. This supernatural Ladino has blond hair and fair skin; he dwells within the earth with his wife and children. He owns large expanses of land; herds of cattle; a large, elegant house; a car; and a great deal of money. He seeks workers to plant his crops and to care for his animals; his wife searches for servants to care for her children and perform housework. The Earth Lord and his wife try to capture the souls of Chamulas. They abduct Chamulas and make them work in exchange for food. The Earth Lord snatches souls in a variety of ways. For instance, if a person is startled by a sudden fall, by a serpent, or by an unexpected loud sound, his or her soul immediately leaves the body. The Earth Lord emerges from a water hole, cave, or some other opening in the Earth, and leads the soul to his underground abode. That large numbers of men and women narrate personal stories of encounters with the Earth Lord reveals the threat Chamulas believe Ladinos pose to them as individuals and to their culture as a whole.

Chamulas who envy their neighbors are believed to strike a deal with the Earth Lord. Since the Earth Lord controls all riches, Chamulas say that a person only becomes wealthy by promising the Earth Lord many souls of his or her people in exchange for money, good animals, or singularly good crops. Eventually, the Earth Lord demands payment from the person upon whom he has bestowed wealth; these individuals become his permanent servants and are condemned to work endlessly inside the Earth. The myth of the Earth Lord shows that Chamulas perceive the threat of individual and cultural destruction as coming from both within and without their society. In the final decades of the nineteenth century and the beginning of the twentieth, Ladino administrators and landowners compelled Chamula officials to register the names of men to be sent to work on lowland haciendas and farms. For a commission, some Chamulas helped *habilitadores* recruit needed field hands. Since many indigenous workers died or returned home sick and debilitated, it may have appeared to the Chamulas that someone had "sold" the men's souls and become rich in the process. Today, forced recruitment no longer exists; their disadvantaged position in the economic system, however, continues to force Chamula men to work for wages on other's farms. Those who labor for the Earth Lord are still said to have been sold to him, and their work is equated with wage labor. Earth Lord accounts, therefore, continue to reinforce the view that working for rich Ladinos is undesirable and, sooner or later, leads to death.

As part of his strategy to snare laborers, this supernatural Ladino may tempt people with money, good food, or a car ride. For example, a young Chamula woman told me that she dreamt of a Ladino woman who was desperately looking for a maid. The Ladino woman approached the Chamula woman's wandering soul and handed her several thousand pesos. The Chamula woman acknowledged with relief that her soul shrewdly refused to receive the money or to follow the woman. Another Chamula woman, Veruch, narrated her experience at the Earth Lord's house. She said that after work she was given "good food" such as chicken, meat, and bread—foods that Chamulas consider luxury items because they rarely have the opportunity to enjoy them.

> Every night I saw in my dreams the Earth Lord's place. It was a
> very nice, big house, like the houses in San Cristóbal. The house
> was huge. It had a good table and good chairs, and they always
> offered me good food. They gave me all kinds of food. That is

why my soul liked it there; it was deceived into thinking there
was nothing wrong with being there because the food was so
tasty. Delicious tortillas, good coffee... When I finished eating,
I would take care of the Earth Lord's child. I was a servant,
nothing but a maid. I washed the clothes of the father and mother.
I washed the clothes of the children. I was their servant, their
peon. But during the time I lived there, approximately one month,
I was dying. My soul was deceived because in reality I was
dying.[16] (Veruch C61-44)

In the Earth Lord's domain, Chamula men and women work as peons or
servants. They marry one another and have children inside the Earth. In addition
to working for the Earth Lord, men plant their own corn, and women prepare
meals, just as they would in the real world. The longer a soul remains inside the
Earth, the more difficult it is to retrieve it, to convince it to return to the body.
Meanwhile, on the brink of death, the unfortunate soulless body weakens day by
day.

What a powerful description of ethnic interaction and Indian ambivalence
toward the Ladino world! Ladinos own all riches, and indigenous people who
want to partake of them must betray their own kind; but eventually, Ladinos will
destroy the natives, anyway. The message is clear—those who adopt Ladino values and strategies to become rich at the expense of their fellow Chamulas will
suffer eternal damnation. By surrendering to the powerful attractions Ladinos offer, Chamulas renounce their autonomy. In the long run, those Chamulas who
leave to earn wages from Ladinos become dependent on their wealthy masters
and increasingly accustomed to Ladino commodities. Time is a critical factor,
once Chamulas "get used to the good things" with which Ladinos lure them, they
are permanently lost to Chamula society. If curers are unable to retrieve the captured souls of men or women and if these people die while their souls are under
the Earth Lord's control, they will never again be free.

In spite of this compelling commitment to their own lifestyle and values, a
symbolic choice of life over death, Chamula men must spend much of their lives
outside of their community in the employment of and in constant interaction with
Ladinos. A woman, however, views her experiences inside the Earth as a result of
her soul's mindless wanderings or a neighbor's betrayal. In actuality Chamula
women rarely compromise their loyalty. It is unusual for a Chamula woman to
work as a servant or peon for Ladinos. Unable to speak Spanish, women interact
with Ladinos in San Cristóbal solely in terms of short commercial transactions.

At the present time, women represent the most traditional expression of
Chamula culture,[17] but men must compromise in a situation perceived as dangerous for both themselves and their culture. Men daily experience the temptations
of the outer world and the pain of Ladino condescension and outright contempt.

They confront, on the one hand, a language and culture they never fully master and, on the other hand, the guilt of their compromise. Women's advantage in this regard may be resented by men, even more so because women have been able to make cash contributions to the family economy through traditional activities.

As symbols of the preservation of tradition, Chamula women are greatly valued in their society.[18] Chamula men appreciate the efforts of their wives to reproduce the lifestyle of their ancestors. On the other hand, men also brandish their own worldly experience as evidence of their greater sophistication and courage. Since this worldliness is accompanied by guilt and anxiety, men who invoke it to enhance their status only add to their already intense, conflictive feelings. Their ethnic identity and Ladino enticements pull men in different directions.

NOTES

1.   Except for wool and the hand-card used to comb it (both of Spanish origin), most of the process of producing a garment is done with very old, native techniques. The backstrap loom and the tradition of spinning with a spindle shaft and whorl come from prehispanic times. Moreover, in contrast with most Mesoamerican groups where commercial dyes have displaced natural ones, Chamula women still use the latter to dye their garments. The principal dye is made from dark mud obtained from marshes and leaves of *bik'it chate'* (*Eupatorium chiapense*) or *muk'ta chaté* (*Eupatorium ligustrinum*) (Gómez Quiles ms). Weavers purchase, however, both white and red cotton thread to combine with the wool of the men's white tunic and the women's red belts. For a detailed description of the weaving process in the words of a Chamula weaver, see *Ta jlok'ta chobtik ta k'u'il* (*Bordando Milpas*) by Maruch Komes Peres (1990).

2.   Burkhart (in press) addresses the difficulties in sifting through the information written by Spanish priests and officials, who imposed their own perspective and value judgments on the strange reality they confronted.

3.   See, for example, Nash (1980), Burkhart (in press), Brumfiel (1991), Kellogg (1991), and Rodríguez (1988), for Central Mexico. Inspired by the pioneering work of Proskouriakoff (1961) on Classic Maya hieroglyphs, new studies that allow a deeper understanding of the roles of women in Classic Maya culture will soon be available.

4.   See Calnek (1988) for details of the sources available to reconstruct the prehispanic and colonial periods in this region, the information they offer and their limitations and problems.

5.   Burkhart's (in press) piece on Mexica women illustrates splendidly the complementarity between men and women, even within a radically militarized society. The Mexica, she finds, invested the household with the symbolism of the battlefield, and a woman's activities at home had a definite impact on her husband's fate in war. Aside from the military elements of Aztec society and culture, there are astonishing similarities between some of the characteristics of Aztec women's activities and symbolic configurations,

as described by Burkhart, and those of Chamula women today. For example, the Aztec midwife presented the newborn girl with the tools of weaving just as her counterpart does in Chamula. A baby boy received weapons; in modern Chamula he receives a tiny hoe and digging stick. Weaving continues to be an essential element in the definition of womanhood in Chamula, as it was for the Mexica (Rosenbaum 1992). The Mexica symbolic associations of women with the west, the position of the setting sun, and with darkness and coldness also prevail in Chamula today (chap. 4). The similarities between the ancient Mexica and modern Chamula relate to the continuities of some basic aspects of Mesoamerican material life and their corresponding cosmology.

6.   See Carmack (1981, 1983) for details on syncretistic elements in the Popol Vuh.

7.   The link between women and the fertility of the Earth has ancient roots in Mesoamerica, as evident from the remains of small, hand modeled figurines of pregnant women that archaeologists interpret to have been fertility symbols (Adams 1977:126).

8.   Bricker (1981:55-59) describes two other miraculous apparitions that took place at around the same time. In one instance a Ladino hermit preached in Zinacantán that the Virgin had descended from heaven to help the Indians. His image of the Virgin, he contended, gave off rays of light. The other event took place in Chenalhó, where the image of St. Sebastian reportedly sweated twice and that of St. Peter emitted rays of light. There was no official spokesperson for the miracles of Chenalhó.

9.   The Conservatives and Liberals were engaged in a civil war as a result of French imperialism. Within Chiapas, highland Conservatives sided with the French, and lowland Liberals supported Juárez (Rus 1989:1035).

10.   In most Mexican states women did not win the right to vote until 1944 (Stephen 1991).

11.   The practice of administrators dealing only with male indigenous leaders probably had been in effect from early colonial times, as reported by Burkhart (in press) for the Mexica.

12.   Chamulas do not predicate their ethnicity on continuities from a prehispanic past that somehow legitimize the authenticity of their culture. A group of Maya professionals in Guatemala are leading such a project, attempting to define what is truly Maya as a basis to construct a pan-Maya identity (Warren in press). It is probably next to impossible to designate "uncontaminated" cultural features. Anthropologists should instead examine the exceptionally creative syntheses, which, in the midst of devastating experiences, made survival possible. In Chamula continuities from ancient times include symbolic and material elements related to corn production and the transformation of corn into daily and ritual foods, and weaving (see, for example, Morris (1988); Rosenbaum (1992); and Otzoy (in press)). Even these fundamental elements of their culture, however, show outside influence. For example, Chamula women weave *batz'i k'u'iletik* ("true clothes," as they call their own clothes in contrast to those of Ladinos) with ancient techniques; however, where their prehispanic ancestors used cotton, today Chamula use wool from sheep, which were introduced by the Spanish. Conversely, Spanish or Mexican items and beliefs suffered dramatic transformations as they were fitted into native configurations. For example, the Virgin of the Dominican missionaries had to undergo significant transmutation to reach the point where she was identified with the "three stones falling from the sky" seen by Agustina Gómez Checheb.

13. For current theoretical issues in ethnicity and their application to Mesoamerica, see Stephen (1991) and Warren (in press).

14. Stephen (1991) uses the term "consumers of indigenous culture" to refer both to tourists and to entrepreneurs who broker native culture in the world markets.

15. At present, indigenous peoples in Highland Chiapas identify themselves primarily in terms of their community affiliation. Even though they are in close contact with and sometimes marry people from other indigenous communities, there is not, to my knowledge, a strong sense of identity transcending the local level (such as a pan-Tzotzil or pan-Maya feeling). Although the economic and political relationships between the other communities and the Ladino population are not identical to those of Chamula (Rus ms, in press), these groups also shape their identity vis-à-vis the dominant society. It is possible, therefore, that in a direct confrontation with Ladinos, such as occurred in 1712 and 1867, indigenous communities might again come together to fight a common adversary.

16. Throughout this book, quotes are literal translations of the statements of Chamula women (and occasionally men). The literal translation attempts to retain the "flavor" of the speakers' diction and stresses what is important to them. The letters and numbers following these passages identify the fieldwork documents from which the quotes were taken.

17. Difficult economic conditions are persuading Chamula parents to send their daughters to school, not just their sons as used to be the case. As women become bilingual, we can expect more openness of the Tzotzil household to the outer world. Women will probably face dilemmas similar to those men have encountered for over a century.

18. There is not enough specific data on the subject of ethnicity in other Highland Chiapas indigenous communities to generalize about the importance of women as symbols of ethnicity in the region (for general information, see Bricker (1973:146, 1981:127ff.); Wali (1974:43)). Everywhere in the highlands, indigenous men have been in contact with Ladino society more than women and have assimilated several of its traits; they speak Spanish, wear western style clothing and shoes, buy calculators and tape recorders, and so forth. As in Chamula, the all male civil institutions of these communities have had to yield to the influences of the Mexican government. Women remain more tied to traditional activities, clothing, and consumption patterns. Relatively speaking, they are more conservative than men.

3

From Birth to Maturity
Women and Men Through the Life Cycle

During the first decade of life, boys and girls go out to the fields together to pasture sheep. They share many other chores such as drawing water from distant water holes, helping their parents in the milpa, and preparing wool for their mothers to weave. Boys grow up in households in which they are surrounded mostly by women; they experience a dramatic break at the onset of puberty when they leave their homes and communities to begin what will probably be lifelong careers as wage workers. At puberty a strict separation between the sexes also takes place. Young men suffer an identity vacuum since they are required to abandon the security of family to face work responsibilities in a strange, hostile environment. They also are forced to reject many of the tasks they once enjoyed, but now find off limits because these activities are considered "female" in nature. A young man's new group of reference, the peer group, socializes him into behaviors considered appropriate for men, such as drinking and conquering women. Marriage signals a return to family, but sometimes men continue to drink and pursue women, which makes for a turbulent relationship between husband and wife.

Machismo, the glorification of virility, is bred mainly within the peer group and is reinforced by men's unstable and fragile economic situation.[1] Unquestionably machismo affects interaction between men and women in Chamula. Men's failure to provide for their families becomes a metaphor for their feelings of sexual inadequacy; these feelings in turn lead men to doubt their wives' fidelity and to assert their own virility in terms of the pursuit of and control over women. Interdependence between husband and wife in the struggle for survival and in the quest for power and prestige partially counteracts the negative effects of machismo.

In her study of Chenalhó, Eber (1991:341) arrives at similar conclusions: traditional Maya values and activities—complementarity between the sexes and a view of spiritual strength based on collective rather than individual achievement—foster respect for women. Increasing pluralism and the prevailing ideology of female subordination among Ladinos, however, affect traditions in Chenalhó and lead men to abuse power, especially during bouts of heavy drinking.

The ideology of *marianismo* (Ehlers 1991:2-8), posited by several authors as a counterpart to machismo, argues that women tolerate male abuse and irresponsibility to support a view of themselves as eminently spiritual, closer to God, and morally superior to men. Their quiet suffering, resembling that of the Virgin Mary, ennobles women and elevates them to a superior status as semidivine beings. Ehlers (1991:4) contends that this argument, which glorifies women's restriction to the domestic arena, might hold true for middle-class Latin American women but breaks down completely when applied to poor women who must work to feed their families.[2] Furthermore, I argue that the ideology of marianismo is completely alien to Maya thinking as illustrated in the context of Chamula. First, in contrast to the Hispanic emphasis on the suffering Virgin Mary, Chamulas underscore the Virgin's dialectical nature (chap. 4). Chamulas stress the Virgin's power as the Earth goddess and her vulnerability (which they do not idealize) as the Moon/Virgin; they do not, however, stress her martyrdom. According to local wisdom, a woman should not tolerate indefinitely an abusive, irresponsible husband. Second, Chamulas lack a cult of domesticity to sanction marianismo. Third, both women and men view sex as an enjoyable activity. Chamulas do not attempt to link women to sexual innocence or purity, in contrast to middle-class Latin American women, who follow a model of sanctity by emulating the Virgin.

Women do not put up with male domination because they are compelled by the mystifying force of marianismo (Ehlers 1991). Rather, in a patrifocal system—where economic development limits women's access to resources—women become more economically dependent on men. Without the means to lead an independent life and support her children, a woman has no alternative but to stay with an oppressive, unfaithful husband. The majority of Chamula men, unlike their counterparts in the Maya townships Ehlers studied, do not have access to well-paid jobs, nor do they have capital to establish their own commercial ventures. The interdependence between husband and wife remains strong and indispensable in Chamula.

CHILDREN AND YOUNG PEOPLE

Babies are everyone's darlings in the household. Siblings delight in the newest arrival; except for the youngest, who has been displaced by the baby and no longer receives constant attention from the mother. Both parents strongly desire children for the companionship they provide.[3] Also, parents say that children make them feel powerful; they have someone to obey them and run errands for them. Children do household tasks and contribute to the family economy from about age 10 and therefore are not regarded as burdens (figs. 5 and 6).

Some men and women expressed a desire to have fewer children because they find it difficult to raise them. One woman mentioned that her husband resented her new pregnancy, but by and large, children are given a warm welcome. Infant mortality is very high, about 25 percent during the first two years of life (Rus 1990:12). Since only a few children survive, it is necessary to have many. Neither information about birth control nor contraceptive materials are available to Chamula women because birth control clinics in San Cristóbal do not have personnel who speak the native languages of the area. Women commented that they would be utterly embarrassed to undergo a medical exam, especially one administered by a male doctor. Should large families one day become a problem in Chamula, the power of women, which is ideologically linked to fertility, would be affected.

Mothers and fathers often prefer children of their own gender. Pozas (1959:156) and Lacy (1976:19) mention the disappointment and anger of some Chamula men who had only daughters; in one case, a father wanted to sell his daughter. Nonetheless, daughters are not considered more burdensome than sons; they, too, make an important contribution to the household. Fathers desire sons for their companionship. A father wants a son to work with him, to accompany him to the farms and to the hot country. For the same reasons that men want sons, women desire daughters. A mother wants a daughter to assist her with tasks and to talk with her. Both parents are affectionate with their young children, but because fathers are frequently away from home, they play a less important role than mothers in the socialization of children too young to work.

Chamulas act in a solicitous way toward their babies. Women cart them around on their backs; at an infant's least whimper, the mother offers her breast. Chamulas tenderly caress, kiss, and play with their young children. Babies may be given soft drinks—or almost anything else they demand—in order to appease them. The baby is like an extension of the mother; the two are always together. Although women sometimes mention that small children curtail their productive activities, they go about their daily routines—carrying firewood and water, weaving, working in the fields, and so forth—seemingly unhampered by the babies on their backs. Having babies and taking care of them are such common occurrences in the life of a Chamula woman that a mother adjusts her baby to her activities and obligations (in contrast to the pattern in Western society in which the mother alters her schedule to accommodate the baby).

Antel's baby, for example, was born in Chamula's ceremonial center on the day Antel hosted the celebration of her religious cargo. Antel was dancing and praying when labor began. The house the couple had borrowed to host the fiesta was crowded because all of the cargo helpers were sleeping there for a week. Antel had to ask people to leave the small kitchen where she went to give birth. Some of the women who were taking part in the celebrations assisted at the delivery. They also prepared Antel's meals during the first days following the birth. Two days later, with her baby on her back, Antel went to church to continue her ritual obligations.

Children are weaned at about two years of age. At that age they may go out on the family patio or venture out of the household with their brothers and sisters, especially those close to them in age. When a child is still quite young, one of the older children cares for it for short periods while the mother works. Both girls and boys take care of the family's baby, carrying it on their backs in a shawl, cleaning it, and taking it outside to the fields to relieve itself.

Mothers seem to be more casual and less attentive with their older children. Children three years and older wander away from their mothers, sometimes under the supervision of an older sibling, sometimes by themselves. During my fieldwork an epidemic of whooping cough swept the highlands, and many children caught the disease, some very seriously. In one instance, I observed a three-year-old girl cough so badly that she almost choked. She had accompanied her mother to another house, where her mother went to get fabric and to embroider garments to sell to tourists. Several women had come for the same purpose, and they chatted loudly while they worked. Despite her severe coughing spells, the little girl's mother paid little attention to her. Only her eight-year-old brother tried to help her by patting her back and holding her each time she coughed. Children are expected to become independent and fend for themselves at a very young age.

In general, older children trek about with their mothers and help carry burdens. They are sent on errands—for example, to buy cane liquor or eggs, or to return empty bottles to beverage vendors. When they accompany their mother on a visit or an errand, they wait quietly until she is ready to leave. If she lingers a long while, they begin to play without interfering with the adults. Only if their play becomes disruptive do the adults intervene. From seven to twelve years of age, children behave in a noticeably quiet manner, especially during family meals. They become very self-conscious as they internalize their culture and are expected to behave in the appropriate Chamula way at all times. Shame is a basic tool of socialization, and children are afraid to say or do anything that might cause their older siblings, parents, or other people to embarrass them.

There are no major differences between activities of boys and girls during the first 10 years of childhood. They play together in the fields as they watch the sheep. Although occasionally they play with other children, most of their time is spent with cousins and close neighbors. They climb trees, catch frogs, play tag, build little houses of sticks and burn them, grind soil to make small pots or tortillas, or play in a stream. Both Chamula women and men talk of childhood with nostalgic delight. Although they already had some responsibilities, adults remember childhood as the most carefree period of their lives.

During these early years, strong camaraderie and cooperation develop among siblings who are relatively close in age. Occasional friction occurs among siblings because some assigned tasks may be regarded as easier or more pleasant than others. Also, as Favre (1984:247) indicates, there may be conflicts between older and younger brothers (*bankilal* and *itz'inal*) because the older child is supposed to have authority over the younger one according to the principle of seniority. Many stories and myths refer to older brothers who abuse their authority over younger siblings only to be punished or destroyed later. There may also be difficulties between an older sister and her younger brothers because the principle of authority based on seniority comes into conflict with the principle of authority based on gender. Such conflicts, however, normally do not erupt until later in life. As children, brothers and sisters play together and share in adventures and games; they enjoy the freedom they experience away from their parents' supervision (fig. 7).

Every Chamula boy, up to age 10 or 11, cares for sheep. Chamula girls, on the other hand, continue to look after sheep until their own children can take over the flock. At around 10, children are supposed to start helping significantly at home, and tasks begin to be gender-typed. Both boys and girls carry out jobs such as hauling water from the water holes, grinding corn, and helping with the younger children, but by 12 or 13, boys stop performing these chores. Although all activities related to weaving (including fluffing, carding, and spinning) are considered exclusively feminine chores, both boys and girls fluff and card wool, and one woman mentioned that her son had learned to spin. Once boys have been integrated into the masculine world, however, they join adult men in the rejection of activities related to sheep. The association of sheep and women is so profound that when men get angry with their wives, they often threaten to kill and eat the sheep.[4]

A comic book, written and illustrated by a Chamula man, narrates the true story of a Chamula boy who eventually became municipal president. The boy looked after the sheep and wore girl's clothing so that Ladino authorities would not force him to attend school. Many informants affirmed that some decades ago when government officials tried to enforce the law requiring male attendance at school, boys wore skirts in public places such as the market or the church in order to avoid compliance. Chamula boys were tremendously mortified at donning their sisters' clothes because they associate womanhood with weakness and vulnerability—qualities diametrically opposed to those that every boy must strive toward. In the comic book, the little boy is obsessed with the thought that his penis is being overheated by the skirt while he makes tortillas near the fire. He agonizes not only over wearing women's clothing but also over caring for the sheep. When he goes into the field with the flock, he pretends the sheep are bulls, animals usually cared for by men.

Sheep and women are literally and symbolically very close. Day in and day out, women of all ages spend time in the fields with the sheep. They walk long distances to find pastures during the dry season. Much of women's economic role within the household revolves around the production of woolen goods. But the relationship between women and sheep goes beyond mere economic dependence. In general, girls and women become very attached to their sheep. They describe them as beautiful cotton balls; they give them human names, as if they were part of the family. When a woman is sad, her sheep are said to sense her misery; they, too, grow sad and die. Like women, sheep are associated with wealth and fertility. A milpa planted in a place fertilized by sheep grows well. Sheep represent a major part of a family's nonmonetary income.

Boys often go to school for part of the day, but girls stay home to work.[5] Parents try to keep several of their children home to help with household activities. The children's economic contribution is indispensable to the family's survival. Out of four or five children, only one or two, usually boys, may be selected to go to school; the rest will never attend. Upon returning from school at noon, the children work at home. Parents say boys need more schooling than girls because as adults they will have to deal with Ladinos in San Cristóbal and on the farms (see also Siskel 1972:87ff.). Many adult women, however, regret not having gone to school. Today's Chamula woman needs to speak Spanish to communicate with the owners of businesses and to sell her goods. Young women commented that their parents would not send them to school out of fear that if they learned to read and write, they might leave the community, abandon their parents, marry Ladinos, and lose their Chamula heritage. Chamulas voice similar concerns about men, but because women constitute the backbone of Chamula culture and identity, ladinoization of women may be perceived as more threatening to the community's survival. Furthermore, people say that men have no alternative but to deal with Ladino society and that they have already incorporated Ladino material and behavioral traits, anyway.

By age 10, girls start to make tortillas. They are usually initiated into the womanly arts of spinning and weaving at 12 or 13, although they may wait a few years if they are the primary caretakers of the sheep. Many girls are also taught to use a hoe and to plant, weed, and harvest the milpa. They find this work strenuous but argue that it is much easier to learn than weaving. The long process of refining textile skills begins with shearing the sheep and culminates in spinning and weaving. Learning these techniques demands patient training over a long period of time. Dyeing, shrinking, and sewing are demanding as well, but not as difficult as weaving.

Until the age of nine or ten, a boy spends most of his time in a household comprised mainly of women. His father may be far away, working for wages. If the father plants a milpa, his son begins to accompany him to the fields at about age eight; otherwise, the boy is initiated into wage labor on the farms or in the hot country at 12 or 13. By the time they turn 18, most young men have tried their hand at several types of work—farm work, wage labor under Chamula or Zinacanteco men in the hot country, menial jobs in San Cristóbal, and popsicle vending in one of the region's larger cities. During this phase of early adulthood, young men become "worldly." They have traveled to distant places, learned some Spanish, and learned to deal with Ladinos on the farms. This knowledge, they feel, gives them an edge over women.

Girls are fully trained by the time they are 16, yet they remain a great deal more provincial when compared with boys of the same age. Usually, a girl's travel has been limited to a few trips to San Cristóbal or to nearby Indian towns like Zinacantán and Tenejapa. A few girls accompany their fathers to the hot country to prepare meals. Girls speak little or no Spanish and have little contact with people outside their families and hamlet. In recent years young Chamula women have begun to travel in small groups of relatives or friends to San Cristóbal, where they sell their woven or embroidered goods. Their business activities require them to deal with Ladino buyers, and they must rely on their own scanty Spanish or the broken Tzotzil of the Ladino storekeepers to conduct their transactions. To be sure, the language barrier causes difficulties and misunderstandings; nevertheless, garments do get bought and sold. Women also sell vegetables, woven bracelets and belts, and cloth dolls on the streets or in the marketplace of San Cristóbal (figs. 8 and 9). The interaction between buyers and sellers is limited, but these young women do become city-wise. They are no longer afraid of cars or of losing their way. They negotiate the streets of San Cristóbal to sell their goods, to purchase raw materials for their work, and to buy food.

A girl may have friends, but her life revolves around the household, where she keeps busy all day. A boy's life, in contrast, changes a great deal when he begins to work at 13 or 14. He leaves the hamlet for several weeks at a time. He usually joins a peer group and starts to drink and to talk about women. Strong notions of manliness emerge as his sexuality develops. Perhaps out of rebellion against the predominantly female environment of his childhood, he rejects anything associated with women and identifies himself in opposition to them. The discontinuity experienced by a boy as he leaves his familiar surroundings for a hostile world causes the critical leap to consciousness of his identity as a male.[6]

Young men who have not yet made an explicit, participatory commitment to Chamula values and traditions experience powerful tensions as they are confronted with the Ladino world. On the one hand, their rudimentary knowledge of Spanish and of Ladino culture gives them a sense of insecurity and awkwardness. On the other hand, they feel attracted to Ladino material comforts, products, and ways, and they may question the value of their Chamula identity.[7] This conflict may be one cause of heavy drinking among young men. Young women do not experience these frustrations and temptations (Siskel 1974:9). Their Chamula identity remains strong and relatively unchallenged.[8]

The strength of the male peer group is related to boys' early independence from the household, which has both an economic and an ideological basis. Single young men spend a great deal of time with their peers, and this pattern does not always change when they marry. Instead of devoting time and money to their familial obligations, some married men spend most of their money with friends and challenge one another to look for other women.

Young women are expected to remain under the control of their parents until they marry, even if they are economically independent. The opportunities to sell goods in San Cristóbal have created the possibility of young women's peer groups. These groups operate mostly during travel to San Cristóbal and during business activities in the city. Back in the hamlet, family control and household obligations keep young women tied to home.

Boys and girls have minimal contact with each other from the age of 12 until they marry. The exceptions to this pattern are brothers and sisters, and cousins who live next door to each other. A girl learns to avoid eye contact with males. She must not smile or talk to a boy. If she gives him any sign that she is interested in him, the boy may proposition her, which could cause her a great deal of trouble. A young woman knows that she is not an independent being and may not decide on her own to initiate a relationship.

From a young age girls learn to fear men. They are taught that men seek to steal them from their parents without due compensation. Girls feel constantly persecuted. Most women I spoke with reported at least one incident in which a man unexpectedly talked to them, grabbed them, or waited for them along the paths to the water holes or while they were washing clothes. Feelings of persecution come out transparently in the dreams of Chamula women; in many of these dreams, the woman is chased by animals and men. In dreams, as in real life, women are not always victimized; often they respond aggressively, sometimes killing the animals and injuring the men. In many instances they may climb a tree or, as happens in real life, run away to escape the attack. Maruch was still a child when the following happened to her:

> I was about 11 years old when I went with my father to the hot country. I walked to fetch water, and a man was waiting for me on the path. He appeared suddenly and grabbed me.
>
> "I want to marry you, I want to marry you" he said.
> "No," I replied startled. And I began to scream until the other workers who were there came to help me. I got very scared. I lost my spirit. The man was older. He already had a wife and children. I told my father what happened.

"Why," he asked the man, "do you come to bother my daughter? Why do you come to bother my girl? Is it perhaps that she smiled at you? Or did you think that she likes to be talked to? Tell me the truth, did she accept your propositions?"
"No, I don't know what came over me," the man responded.
Then my father and the other men beat him up.(C29-10)

Thus, from about age 10, girls are frightened of meeting boys or men when they go out by themselves. They realize that their sexuality makes them vulnerable. They deeply fear rape, and no matter the time of day, they prefer to go out with a companion, especially when they have to walk long distances.[9] Girls and young women contend that men are physically stronger than women and are able to overpower them easily and rape them. This kind of behavior is usually attributed to drunken men, for rape is viewed as a serious offense that leads to a long sentence in the San Cristóbal prison.

Young women also fear that men may try to initiate conversations with them along the road. Boys and adult men are forbidden to talk to girls who are not relatives. There is a specific Tzotzil noun for men who engage in this proscribed behavior; they are called *jk'oponvanej*, literally "man who talks to woman" (Laughlin 1975), a word with strong negative connotations. To engage in conversation with a *jk'oponvanej* carries dangerous implications for a woman. Although she may be paralyzed with fear, the woman must respond in an aggressively angry manner to the man's attempts to converse with her. If the *jk'oponvanej* is angered by the woman's response, he may hurt her.

In most cases the *jk'oponvanej* is testing the young woman to see if he can get away with talking to her or perhaps secure a promise for a future conversation. Despite interdictions, boys and men frequently attempt to talk with young women on the roads. On the other hand, young men also fear the woman's reaction; she is expected to tell her father, who may tell the young man's parents about their son's transgression. If the boy attempts to engage the girl in conversation more than once, her father will probably summon him to court and present the case to the president of Chamula. The young man could end up in jail or be fined.

For the girl, however, the attentions of a boy or man spell trouble because he may spread gossip that she has responded to his advances. She could become the subject of angry gossip that accuses her of challenging the traditional rules for getting a spouse. Men spread gossip quite frequently, especially when they are obsessed with a specific young woman and want to take her as a second wife. A man may become infuriated when the woman rejects him and may go so far as to tell her parents that she has accepted him (implying a sexual relationship) so that they will force her to marry him.

Young Chamula women spoke about the shame and frustration they experience when the whole hamlet gossips about them.[10] They feel like killing themselves, like running away, but there is no place to hide. It is not unusual for a young woman to be the subject of gossip; on the contrary, it is almost inevitable. A woman's parents and siblings may not always support her against her accusers; they may also doubt her story. Moreover, parents feel deeply ashamed and disappointed in their daughter because they are ultimately responsible for her behavior. Young women usually face the situation quietly, praying and fasting until the gossip abates or a new event in the hamlet captures people's attention. Women claim that gossip of this nature ruins their reputations and dissuades decent young men from courting them. A stained reputation, however, does not seem to be permanent. Once people have "satisfied their hearts" through malicious gossip, the young woman is left alone.

Young women must avoid speaking to or looking at men, but young men are encouraged by peers to prove their manliness by propositioning the young women they meet on the road. Often they tell the women that they will marry them. Later, a young man may lie, falsely bragging that a woman accepted him. Sometimes a woman appears to be a pawn in a struggle between her suitors, who are young and low in status, and her father. Society bestows respect and prestige upon older men on the bases of age and of service in religious or civil cargos. Individual attractiveness, youth, and manliness struggle against prestige and status; tradition is at stake. If a man secures a wife in the traditional way, he reinforces the status quo, bowing to authority and acknowledging the father's rights over his daughter. In contrast, the *jk'oponvanej*, who tries to convince a young woman to accept him without her father's consent, directly attacks the father's position. By stealing the man's daughter, the *jk'oponvanej* makes the father appear powerless. Not all older Chamula men have participated in the cargo system, and not all of them are relatively better off or more prestigious than younger men. Nevertheless, the seniority principle requires younger men to show respect for the superior status of older men. Ideally, a suitor acquires rights to a girl with humility, respect, and a series of gifts that express his intention to create a lasting relationship with the young woman's parents.

Tradition notwithstanding, a young man may feel even more powerful if he successfully conquers the daughter of a high status man. The more important the father's position in the community, the more people will gossip over the event. If the father is well known, the gossip will spread as far as Chamula Center. Prestigious, well-known individuals are more likely to be envied and to find their misfortunes the subject of gossip than are ordinary men. Despite the threat of punishment by the president, a young man may still brag to his friends, and his reputation among them will grow. Respect for the woman's father temporarily dwindles because of his failure to control the behavior of his daughter; her mother is also shamed.

A recent problem in Tzajal Vitz illustrates this battle. Young men started a fad of playing marbles along the hamlet's paths. Every afternoon groups of marble players congregated in various parts of the hamlet. The older men protested that their daughters were afraid to go out on errands because the marble players would whistle at the young women or try to talk to them. It is not difficult to visualize how young men started to challenge one another to approach passing young women. The fathers took the case to the president of Chamula and were able to stop the marble playing on the paths. The president ruled that young men should limit their games to the enclosed school grounds where the women need not pass by. Later, when one of the marble players went to ask for a woman's hand in marriage, he was rejected on the grounds that "he would not be able to support her, for he could do nothing but play marbles."

WIVES AND HUSBANDS

As in the past, newly married couples establish residence close to the home of the young man's father and sometimes in the same lot. This pattern continues even though the young couple may be financially independent. Although relations vary with the relative distances the couple lives from each set of parents, stronger bonds usually exist among patrilineal relatives—probably because they grow up next door to one another. Children usually feel closer to their father's parents and brothers than to those of their mother. Landless older men travel with their grown sons to work on farms or to sharecrop in the lowlands. In these cases, the father's authority over his children seems to hinge on the traditional respect that children owe their parents. Also, the difficult struggle for money and prestige in Chamula makes cooperation between parents and their married sons and families mutually beneficial.

Localized patrilineage groups have not disappeared completely although their functions and bases have been radically altered. As long as her parents are living, a woman usually maintains close relations with her family of origin, especially when the family lives in the same hamlet. Nevertheless, through marriage, a woman becomes incorporated into her husband's family. Most of her daily interactions are with her husband's relatives, and eventually her ties with his family may become stronger than those she has with her own brothers and sisters. For example, when Xunka' lost her brother, she did not seem much affected. "It had been such a long time since she 'ate with him'...," explained her daughter-in-law. Eating together under the same roof is a symbol of continued interaction, affection, and economic cooperation; only the members of a domestic unit eat together. Because Xunka' had become an integral part of a new domestic unit decades before, her meaningful relationships were no longer with her family of origin.

Inheritance is bilateral in Chamula; women may own plots of land, house lots, houses, or other property. In this respect, Chamula women are more independent and less submissive than women in neighboring communities such as Zinacantán and Oxchuc, where only men inherit and patrilineages tend to be stronger.[11] One result of bilateral inheritance is the predominance of relatively autonomous, nuclear households. Today most plots bequeathed to descendants of either sex are tiny; nevertheless, Chamula women are aware of being not only sexually but also economically desirable (Favre 1984:213).

The relationship between husband and wife appears cordial and communicative. Although open demonstrations of affection are rare, one senses a feeling of companionship and care. Moreover, the husband/wife dyad functions as a true economic and status partnership. The contributions of both are indispensable to the family's precarious economic life as well as to accrue prestige in the community. In contrast with Ladino women, for whom sex is ultimately viewed as sinful and only justifiable in terms of the idealized relationship between mother and child, Chamula women desire and enjoy sex; in fact they frequently demand it.[12]

In addition to being an attractive sexual partner, a good wife works hard and tries to please her husband. She should have his food ready when he returns home, participate actively in the household economy, take care of the children, and generally submit to him (Favre 1984:238). A good husband works consistently and arduously, brings in food and money to satisfy his family's needs, treats his wife and children with consideration, and always shows concern for his family's welfare.

Manvel and Antel illustrate this type of relationship. An older couple, they have been married for over 30 years. During the day they both engage in separate activities, and even though the family is relatively wealthy by Chamula standards, Manvel leaves to work on the coffee farms every few months. When both are home, they speak together all the time. They converse about the events of the day, their activities, the people they meet, and local gossip. Money is an incessant topic of discussion: How much have they earned from sales of liquor and soft drinks and will they need to buy more soon? How much has she received for her woven goods? They exchange information about the various important people in Chamula, the activities of particular religious or civil officials, and the approach of upcoming festivals and the family's plans to participate in them. During the time I stayed with them, they would talk until very late at night, only to wake up at four in the morning and begin again. Manvel gets involved in Antel's business, commenting on the women in her group and the quality of their embroidery. He explains to Antel the details of work on the farms and the prices of products and transportation. As everywhere in Chamula, a large part of the conversation revolves around the latest gossip. In this sense, Chamula is a very exciting place. Something is always going on, and everyone makes sure that the information reaches every corner of the community.

Frequently husband and wife joke, talk, interact with their children, and eat together by the hearth (fig. 10). They enjoy this time together. Husbands ask for their wives' opinions about purchases and talk to their wives about the different customs and foods of the Ladinos in San Cristóbal. Husbands often translate from Spanish for their wives and read to them.

The first years of marriage, however, are usually difficult and unstable. Husband and wife do not know one another well, and the adjustment may be stressful, especially for the young wife. She must learn to follow the ways of her husband's family. Her mother-in-law supervises her closely during the time the young couple live in his parents' home. Friction is not uncommon in in-law relationships (chap. 5). The husband's parents complain about his wife, and his wife complains about them. If the young man does not handle the situation well, his wife may decide to return to her parent's house. Often, after reconciliation, a young woman will talk her husband into building a separate house, which he usually builds near his parent's home. In her own house the wife has more freedom to do things her way (cook, wash clothes, and so forth) without constant supervision and criticism.

As part of the marriage contract, the husband sometimes moves into the home of his wife's parents for a year or two. This allows her parents to observe their son-in-law's work habits and his behavior towards their daughter as well as to continue training their daughter in her role as wife. After a year or two of living with his in-laws, a man sometimes finds it difficult to take his wife out of her parent's home, but in most cases, a woman follows her husband and stays with her in-laws until her husband builds a new house. Occasionally, if the man comes from another hamlet and the girl's parents will not allow their daughter to go to a distant place or if the man is very poor or has no parents, he may come to live with his in-laws permanently. After the first years of marriage, the situation usually stabilizes. The young wife devotes most of her energies to raising the children, fulfilling household duties, and weaving the family's clothes, but even at this busy stage of life, she also exerts herself to bring some cash income to the family.

As the children grow up and gradually take over household tasks, their mother becomes more independent and engages more actively in income-producing activities. Daughters and daughters-in-law relieve the mature woman (about age 45 and older) of most of the daily chores. Older women move about more freely because they are less fearful of men's advances. They are able to go out alone. Thus, a woman's power and economic activity increase as her children grow older, and she becomes more independent of the demands of children and household.[13]

The spousal relationship of an older couple may be conflictive if the husband continues to try to control his wife's actions. Many husband/wife relationships in Chamula are, unfortunately, tinged with conflict. In some marriages, wife beating occurs only a few times in the woman's life; in other marriages, it happens frequently. Women often excuse mistreatment by a drunken spouse when it occurs on the husband's return from wage labor on the plantations. They interpret it as a backlash from the abuse men suffer when working away from home.[14] A man's excessive drinking, however, can impoverish the household and terrorize his wife and children.[15] The strategies employed by women to face this problem vary and depend on the length of the marriage, the number of children in the family, the frequency of the problem, and whether the husband supports the family well. Drinking is a problem in Chamula, and there are many cases of both young and mature men who drink a great deal and cannot provide adequately for their families.[16]

Drinking is sine qua non in Chamula social interaction and ritual life. People say that *pox*, the local liquor distilled from sugar cane, heats and strengthens the body, thus furnishing the most desired characteristics of *jtotik*, the Sun/Christ. Chamulas use *pox* to create, maintain, and patch up relationships both among themselves and between them and their deities. Liquor serves important functions in ritual and in specific social contexts, and people must drink in these situations. If, however, a man seems to be wasting his life away drinking, he and his wife may decide to take up a cargo, or civil officials in Chamula may try to convince him to do so. People believe that serving a cargo moderates excessive drinking. This may seem paradoxical since cargos require celebrations every 20 days as well as attendance at several major festivals, and a great deal of drinking goes on at these events. The cargo, however, places drinking in a religious context and circumscribes it. Practically speaking, commitment to a religious cargo forces a man to stop drinking and to start working hard in order to save for the many expenses this responsibility entails. A man who petitions for a cargo and later fails to assume the responsibility is jailed and can expect to suffer punishment from the deities.

Chamulas do not condemn excesssive drinking when it occurs in a ritual context; indeed, they expect it to happen every so often, and they accept it. What they reject is incessant drinking for its own sake, especially when it imperils the survival of the family. A man is not considerd to have a drinking problem if he drinks occasionally on his return to the hamlet after several exhausting and demoralizing weeks of work on lowland farms or if he occasionally shares a social drink with friends (although his wife may angrily accuse him of wasting precious money). Nor are there serious consequences if a man gets drunk and passes out as long as he is able to work normally the next day. It is not uncommon, however, for men just back from the farms to drink until they have spent all the money they have earned. After a week or two, these men must return to the farms, leaving their wives behind with no money and no corn. In such emergencies, women scramble to sell firewood or woven goods, or to borrow money to buy corn for their children. Many men leave their wives in this predicament. Drinking causes much suffering for women.

> When my husband got drunk he yelled at me. When he didn't everything was all right. He kicked me out of the house at noon. He kicked me out of the house at dusk. Sometimes he kicked me out of the house at dawn, I still had not prayed to Our Fa-

ther. But I put up with it. I tolerated it. I talked a lot to Our Father.

"How can it be?" I said. "But why?" I asked. "Why does he scold me so much? Why does he hit me so much?" But he went on getting more and more drunk. Then I prayed to Our Father, to Our Mother:

"Please make him bow his head, make him kneel," I told them. "Give him your blessings, confer your kindness upon him, treat him like your child, treat him like your offspring," I begged. "Look at my poor body." My eyes were blackened by his blows. (Maruch C29-50)

My brother is very mean, he gets drunk, and scolds, and beats his wife and children. It's a problem when they get drunk, for they torment us a great deal.

"Go with your lover," they say. "I know you have another man. Go look for him." That's what they say.

My poor sister-in-law has to flee. She has to go elsewhere to sleep. If she stays, he might hurt her with a knife, a machete, or whatever else he finds.

"You don't respect me," he tells her. "There are all your lovers waiting for you."

I don't know why she puts up with it. She doesn't think of taking him to court so that they punish him. (Vel C58-17)

What alternatives does a woman have? If she is young and has few or no children, she may return to her parent's house. Usually they welcome her back. If a couple has been married only a short time, it is easier to end the marriage than if they have been together a long time.

A woman who has been married many years, and who has probably born many children, must find other ways to confront the problem. She may flee with her children while her husband is drunk, or she may punish him by denying him food or sex. If the situation becomes intolerable, she takes her husband to court; there he is publicly shamed and sent to jail. But women realize that jail will not change a husband's behavior permanently. A mother of many children has difficulty separating from her spouse because she is unable to feed her children alone.

The most she can expect legally from her husband is a one-time payment for each of the children. These payments do not cover the children's needs for even a year.

Chamula men and women believe that a good, hard-working woman can help her husband to stop drinking. A wife is supposed to scold her husband and to threaten him with court; she cannot stand by as her husband wastes away. At court, the president gives the man an ultimatum: if he does not reform, his wife will leave him. If she is forced to leave him, he is jailed and must pay the one-time child support fee to his wife. If he has no money, policemen escort him around the hamlet as he tries to obtain loans from family or friends. He may be set free to work on the farms, but he knows that he must come up with the money, or he will not be able to return to Chamula. He works for several weeks, returns with his savings, and tries to reconcile with his wife. When a man realizes he is about to lose his wife and children, he may drink more moderately or stop drinking altogether. Some wives are resigned to their husbands' drinking and have given up any effort to stop it. Instead they seek ways to ensure that they can still hold their family together, however precariously, as an economically viable unit. The following account illustrates this point:

> "Stop drinking, don't drink anymore," I told my son-in-law.
> "But I can't stop, I feel so much like drinking!" he said.
> But when he drinks, he drinks so much! So I told my daughter:

> "Just take care of your chickens. Since he brings corn, you can feed your children. You can live off the chickens. You can sell some chickens, sell some eggs, since their prices keep going up. Don't take it too much to heart the fact that he gets drunk so frequently, girl. Because if you do, you will get sick," I told her.

> He works in the milpa and harvests his corn. When he looks for a job, whatever he makes is to pay his debt—the debt he has on account of liquor. Even if he has money, he doesn't give her a penny.

> "Don't let him take away the hen or the eggs," I said.

> With regard to his children's clothes, he doesn't buy any. Only their godfather and godmother buy them clothes. They buy their pants. They buy their shirts. (Xmal C38-75)

A wife influences her husband's success and may bring him "good luck." Akuxtin used to drink constantly. He lived in abject poverty and had been married twice before. People say things did not work out for him until he found his third wife. She tolerated his drunkenness and worked hand in hand with him in the production of liquor. Eventually, they saved enough to purchase horses to deliver cane liquor to their customers. Then, they began to take cargos. Little by little Akuxtin stopped drinking. Over time, he and his wife managed to forge a stable economic situation for themselves, and now they lead a peaceful, happy life together.

Chamula women are expected to be patient with their husbands and help them to change. Yet, Chamulas do not support the idea that women should be martyrs. When abuse is extreme, and the man makes no effort to change, his wife is not expected to tolerate him forever. She should take some action. Indeed, people think that a woman who puts up indefinitely with a husband who drinks constantly, mistreats her harshly, and fails to support her economically must be under a spell of witchcraft; no one would endure such treatment, otherwise. A woman who "has a good heart" does not scold her husband or refuse to feed him, but he must demonstrate an effort to change his behavior. When a man does not stop his excessive drinking, his wife may decide to leave him, especially if their children are older and able to help her support the family.

Women generally do not drink in excess; rather they care for their drunk husbands or fathers. Women feel they are not really free to drink themselves into a stupor because they cannot leave their young children unattended. Mature women with no small children may get drunk. For example, a young widow, who was left with five children and never remarried, earned her livelihood planting milpa and peddling charcoal from house to house. She began to drink when her children became independent. When her children tried to stop her, she told them to leave her alone, that she had the right to drink now because they were already grown up, and that her drinking would harm no one even were she to die from it. Older, single or widowed women who have held cargos, or women whose husbands drink a great deal, may also drink too much.[17] There are a few couples in Tzajal Vitz in which both husband and wife drink continuously. They are pitiful, extremely poor, and appear somewhat deranged. People make fun of them but also feel sorry for them, offering food or drink when they see them. These couples are usually older.

Another source of tension between husband and wife is the man's search for other women. Drinking and acquiring a second wife account for most divorces in Chamula.[18] Many men and women have been married two or three times in their lives; divorce is not a very complex procedure (chap. 5). During their 20s or early 30s, many Chamula men engage in affairs with other women. To have a second wife, a man must be a hard worker. He must plant a great deal of corn or earn a large amount of money to buy enough corn for two families. Most men barely make enough to support one family. A second wife may decide to leave if her husband fails to provide her consistently with corn. Or she may wait for a while and leave only when she realizes she will not succeed in ousting the first wife.

Temporary liaisons are explosive, and lead to bitterness. The first wife, without exception, goes into a rage when her husband brings home the new woman. Both wives complain angrily to the husband about each other, and sooner or later, the women's verbal conflicts deteriorate into physical fights. A man tends to side with his new wife because he is infatuated with her and wants the relationship to succeed. His first wife appears as the obstacle. When the first wife creates problems and announces her departure, the exasperated husband beats her before sending her away.

Many men dream of having two (or more) wives who live in the same compound, perhaps in different rooms. They would both care for him, prepare his food, wash his clothes, and bear his children. One could go with him to the fields or the hot country; the other would stay at home to care for the sheep or a store. The husband could parade both wives at the fiesta celebrations in Chamula; at night, he would have a choice of sexual partners. This is the ideal situation, according to many Chamula men. If only the wives would "have a good heart" and accept the situation, it would be possible. As long as a husband did not favor one wife over the other, either economically or sexually, the situation would be stable. This ideal, of course, is rarely met. Most women fight until the man throws one of them out, or if he is rich enough, builds separate houses for them in different places where he visits them in turn. Paxku' explained what happened when her husband brought home a another woman:

> Well, we used to have our money together. We bought what we needed with our money until he looked for another woman. I got very angry... He has had that woman for 12 or 13 years. She came to my house at the beginning, but I did not want her there. I got angry at her and beat her.

> "What are you looking for here? You are coming of your own free will to take away my husband. How is it? Are we both going to tend to him? Is that the idea? Look, he doesn't have a great deal of corn. He doesn't have much of anything. And you, what do you do? What kind of work?" I asked her.
> "Well, I will learn how you work," she replied.
> She wanted to learn my work. So I got even angrier.
> "Well, then go fix your husband's bed since that is what you came here for. Go! Go sleep with him!" I said.

> Then she started crying. There she was bending, fixing her husband's bed. My head exploded in fury. I took her by the hair and hit her with all my strength... She did not stay in my house for long, maybe three or four days. I left for my parents' house,

but I returned afterwards. The woman left. Since then he visits
the woman and takes her to San Cristóbal. He lives at my house
and sleeps there as well. (Paxku' C51d-24)

Favre (1984:239) notes, and Chamula men admit, that polygyny is not only
very unstable but also erodes the husband's authority; he has no power to reconcile the conflict. This paradoxical effect of depriving the powerful man of his
authority over women is clearly understood and manipulated by women. To make
matters even worse, men frequently choose relationships with their wives' sisters.
Men are forbidden to approach other young women, but they are allowed to talk
with their sisters-in-law. For a Chamula woman, insult tops injury when her husband selects her own sister as a second wife. Such betrayal from an intimate wounds
women deeply (chap. 5; Lacy 1976:31). All the women I spoke with reject polygyny ardently. They say that it brings sadness to their hearts, a rage that makes
them sick and eventually kills them. Their children suffer watching the constant
fighting that ensues when both women try to get rid of each other. Even the few
women who learn to live in a polygynous arrangement remain bitter and critical
of their husbands, and the interaction between husband and wife deteriorates.

The community, in general, condemns men who look for additional wives.
Women comment angrily against young women who knowingly get involved with
married men. Such "morally loose" women are deemed responsible for the suffering and hunger that the original wife and her children experience when her husband abandons them. The ideological justification of men's behavior so permeates
society that in the eyes of both men and women, the young, unmarried woman
bears the onerous responsibility of discouraging men's advances. Chamulas argue that men will always chase women, but if young women reject them, they will
not accomplish their goal. Women especially disseminate gossip about young
women who give in to men, and everyone condemns such actions. Gossip, then,
acts as a strong mechanism to dissuade women from entering into relationships
with married men.

The double standard is clearly illustrated in Lolen's story. Lolen, one of
Andres's three wives, told him she might look for another husband because he did
not contribute in any way to the support of her children:

"Well, if you find another husband, if you find another man,
you will not live for a long time with him. Maybe for a year,
maybe for half a year, but I will kill you. If I cannot kill you, I
will call the witches from San Bartolo. You will die. You will
get so thin, you and your husband," he told me, "because they
will throw a disease upon you."
"But I did not throw a disease upon you when you looked for
another wife," I argued.

"Oh, but I am a man, and men can do it, you know," he said. "That is a custom of men."

"But so can women, they can look at other men. Isn't it true that men and women work the same way, eat the same way? So women can do it too," I said.

"But can't you see that you are women. If you women do that, you will be killed. You will be killed. We may do it because we are men. There are many men who look for two or three wives, but women don't." (Lolen C44-37)

As a whole, the community makes things more difficult for a man who takes a second wife or otherwise mistreats his wife. For example, if the community believes a man has sent back a first wife without cause and then wants to get another one, they make it very hard for him. When he goes to petition for a new wife, the community reproaches him, saying that he has a wife, she is suffering, he sent her away without justification, and so forth. Female public opinion, in particular, expresses sympathy for the first wife since any woman could find herself in the same predicament. By condemning all women who become involved with married men, the married women try to uphold the ideal of monogamy.

One may wonder why men criticize polygyny since they themselves may have lived polygynously at some time or have played with the idea. I suggest three main factors: first, men feel envious of the man who accomplishes what they have not been able to do; second, they resent the economic achievement of a man who supports two wives; third, having two wives underscores a man's virility, so a man with only one wife may feel comparatively less manly. To be sure, the idea of monogamy as the decent, responsible way to live is still strong in Chamula. Cargoholders and respected members of the community feel pressure to uphold monogamy. A few older men told me that they would like to have a second wife, but it would be embarrassing since they have served cargos, and people look up to them. Yet, because they are in a better economic position than most Chamula men, several of these older *pasados* (men who have held religious or civil positions) have two wives.

To illustrate how the community sides with the first wife, consider a case in which the man could not find assistants for his cargo because he wanted to hold the position with his second wife:

Well, when he went to solicit the help of the cargo assistants they would ask him:

"With which of your wives will you serve the cargo? With the second one? Well, if you are serving the cargo with the second one, we really don't want to help you," people told him.

"I am sorry, Standard Bearer, we don't want to serve with you
if your second wife will take up the cargo. Maybe in some other
opportunity," they told him.
"No, we can't," replied others. "Think about it, send her back to
her parents," they advised him. (Tumin C31-52)

They pressured him to such an extent that his second wife finally left. The reaction of the community was one of the decisive factors in their separation.

Polygynous households have to divide their economic resources. Indeed, the
presense of a second wife means that the first wife must renounce the possibility
of a better house, better food and clothing, more land, or some of the other things
she may desire. She must share her husband's income with another woman and,
eventually, with the new wife's children as well. Chamula women say that the
second wife steals the husband's money:

When he went to visit his other wife, he would always take 2000
pesos or so with him. He went out drinking, and then he would
go to sleep with the woman. When he came back to my house
next morning, he didn't even have five pesos left. His other wife
had taken the money. He lost everything. He did not have any
money left. He did not have any corn. Nothing. I told him,

"Think about it, see if you feel happy about not having any
money."

It was not until he left her that he started doing better. He had
his money, his corn. He bought clothes for his children. He felt
happy. (Tumin C31-65)

The first wife also must share her husband sexually. Many Chamula women
say sex is an activity that husband and wife indulge in frequently, every night
when the men are home. But when there is more than one wife, the husband must
give them equal attention. This situation is very disadvantageous for the woman
who once had her husband all to herself.

Married women get involved with other men much more rarely. Such an affair has serious consequences.[19] The woman's husband, who has likely been working far from home, will probably beat her, reject her, and ask for the return of his
brideprice either from the woman's parents or from her lover. Usually the woman's
lover ends up jailed and fined; in some cases, this situation leads to murder or
mutual accusations of witchcraft. Women who take on a lover are severely criticized by the community; such behavior is considered an outrage. Men point to the
occasional instances of female adultery as justification for their widespread fears

of wifely infidelity; they often voice this concern when they are drunk.[20] As Favre (1984:239) mentions, men's profound anxiety may originate in the perceived sexual aggressiveness of Chamula women. Men express anxiety about satisfying their wives sexually by claiming that their wives have betrayed them.

As mentioned above, women contribute significantly to their husbands' successes and failures; but women are also believed to be capable of destroying their husbands by stupefying them and robbing them of their superior strength and virility. Indeed, when a married woman has a lover, she is metaphorically stripping her husband's virility. Her need to take a lover implies that her husband is sexually inadequate and has lost his authority over her—a central component of his masculinity. Chamulas talk about special potions women supposedly prepare to destroy men. One potion includes dirt removed with water from the woman's heels, armpits, and sexual organs. This water is mixed with corn gruel, which symbolizes male sexuality and is destroyed by fluids from women's intimate parts. The dirt from the heels represents the cold, female Earth on which women walk barefoot. In fact, one of Earth's aspects is a powerful and sexually aggressive woman, the *pak'inte'* (Favre 1984:240). Women prepare this potion when they want to get rid of a husband in order to marry a clandestine lover. If the husband drinks the potion, he will become mentally incompetent, lose his strength, and finally die.

The sexual insecurity men constantly verbalize when they drink also expresses a deep-seated sense of inadequacy as the family breadwinner. This anxiety stems from a lack of landownership and poverty. Moreover, men's long absences from their communities require them to leave their wives in charge of the household and to depend on their wives' assistance to make ends meet. Perhaps this insecurity provokes men to respond to their wives' reprimands when the children have no food as follows:

> But these are your children, they are not my children. Who knows
> who their father is. So *you* support them now. (Lolen C44-38)

The husband thus acknowledges both his incapacity to satisfy his wife sexually and his failure as a provider.

In the difficult economic situation which men and women face, a man's despair and insecurity may be expressed in heavy drinking, and mistreatment and domination of his wife and children:

> My father drank a great deal. He got very angry and tormented
> my mother. He beat her many times. When he was drunk, he
> pushed her. Once he threw a stone at her. He almost killed her.
> When we were little, he used to push us too.

"Get out of here. Go!" he said. "Go and see where you can get
your food." How could we know where to go when we were so
little? I was only around 10 years old. (Matal C50-2)

Both sexually and economically, manhood resides in providing for both a wife
and children. To an insecure man, his children as well as his wife may appear
responsible for his frustration and represent an appropriate vent for its release.

GENDER INTERACTION THROUGH THE LIFE CYCLE

A pattern of complicated, conflictive interactions surfaces in the examination of
the particularities of male/female relationships through the life cycle. Companionship and sharing pervade early interaction, but puberty brings separation and
polarization between the genders. Young men experience a drastic discontinuity
and loss; within the peer group, young men learn to oppose young women. While
the young men challenge tradition, the young women live in dread of men's attempts to engage them in illicit conversations or affairs. Machismo emerges with
strength in young adulthood, urging men to prove their boldness and worth, often
at the expense of women. Marriage is supposed to bring the young man back in
line with communal traditions, establishing an interdependent relationship between
husband and wife in which both strive to "mother and father their children" (i.e.,
love and care for the children in a responsible way). This ideal, however, is frequently marred. After marriage men and women may continue to interact in a
conflictive pattern. Men doubt their wives, beat them, and search for other women.
They simultaneously control women and endow them with power. Women respond in various ways, appeasing or antagonizing their husbands, searching for
the best way to prevent the complete breakdown of the family. A man's failure to
fulfill his expected role of main provider causes him to sink deeper into despair
and leads to more conflict. Chamula traditions, however, furnish paths leading to
respectful relationships between men and women, particularly through cargo service. Returning to the fold of tradition, by bowing to the wisdom of the elders and
by forsaking the authority of the male peer group, enables many Chamula couples
to enjoy a rewarding interaction.

NOTES

1.   My findings concur with Ehlers's (1990:156) analysis of machismo: tensions arise when idealized sex roles clash with economic realities that compel women to participate actively in the support of their households. These tensions strain the relationship between husband and wife and lead to the imposition of stronger controls over women. Consequently, machismo grows when expectations for the submissive and dependent roles of women contradict reality.

2.   The influence of feminism and the effect of the debt crisis in Latin America have, however, altered this ideology even for middle-class women. Nash (1989) examines the increasing incorporation of Latin American women at different levels of the work force.

3.   Generally, in indigenous communities in Highland Chiapas, children are viewed as the wealth and happiness of a family. In Chenalhó, a rich family is one with many children; a household with only a few children is deemed poor (Guiteras-Holmes 1961:112). Because of children's social importance, the relationship between parents and their offspring serves as a model for public leadership roles. In Amatenango, for example, the term for leader is *statal*, from *tat* (father). People who guard the community's traditions and mores (judges, curers, civil officials) are called *me'iltatil* (mothers-fathers) (Nash 1985:101ff.).

4.   As Pozas (1959:257) notes, sheep are never eaten in Chamula since they are considered to be part of the family; therefore, Chamulas, especially the women, are revolted by the smell of mutton.

5.   Today, parents are more aware of their daughters' need to learn Spanish in school (chap. 2, n.17).

6.   See Chodorow (1974, 1978) for a discussion of this perspective.

7.   Jacinto Arias, a Maya anthropologist from San Pedro Chenalhó, comments about the problems of young Pedranos who leave their community to study in San Cristóbal and become teachers. His comments echo the feelings of young Chamula men who work for Ladinos in low-paying jobs:

> Drinking for many of them has become the main escape from their "self," which inevitably asks the universal question "Who am I?" This question causes constant pain to such transitional people, so that most prefer avoiding to answer it. Loneliness is a common existential experience for these people who have abandoned the at least partially meaningful things which they used to fill their "self" some time in the past...They have not found something else that could feed their beings..." (Eber 1991:335)

8.   Eber (1991:323ff.) discusses the transformations in women's lives in Chenalhó when they undergo strong acculturative forces and become relatively ladinoized. These women live in a "no man's land;" Pedranos criticize them harshly, and Ladino or ladinoized lovers, husbands, and employers abuse and mistreat them.

9.   The threat of rape justifies the restriction of mobility imposed on girls and young married women in other highland communities, as well. Blaffer (1972:132) reports that in

Zinacantán young women who flirt openly are vulnerable to gang rape because they have robbed men of the right to "conquer" them on the paths.

10. Ehlers (1990:140) notes that in San Pedro Sacatepéquez, a rapidly changing Maya township in Guatemala, gossip functions as a vehicle of social control whereby men keep women in their place. Gossip usually tarnishes the reputations of women only; men's reputations are enhanced by it.

11. Inheritance is also bilateral in Amatenango, and women own lands. Landownership fosters women's independence in this community, where plots are larger than in Chamula, and women can hire men to plant them (Nash 1985:271). A Zinacanteco woman has a more difficult situation because she does not inherit, except in special circumstances. If her parents are dead and lands have already been distributed among her brothers, she will have nowhere to go should she decide to leave her husband. If she divorces before her parents die, they may bequeath her some land.

12. Chamula women's attitudes toward sex present a sharp contrast to the situation described by Ehlers (1990:150ff.) for San Pedro Sacatepéquez, Guatemala. In that community, women marry or engage in liasons with men mainly to produce children; for women, the relationship between mother and child is the only stable one in economic as well as emotional terms. Women find little enjoyment in sex but tolerate their husbands' needs for sexual relief. Men do nothing to please their wives sexually and would become suspicious if their wives took pleasure in sex. It is possible that people in this township have absorbed Ladino sexual attitudes and behaviors as they have become increasingly integrated into the national economic and cultural systems.

13. In all indigenous communities in the highlands, the status of women seems to increase with age and experience. Nash (1985:271) stresses that women in Amatenango become freer only after they have passed their childbearing years; they can drink and dance at fiestas and do not have to appear as modest in public. It is only after menopause that a woman takes her first role in ceremonials as "woman speaker."

14. Diane and Jan Rus, personal communication to Eber (1991:569).

15. Wife beating also is not uncommon in Amatenango, Zinacantán and Chenalhó. In these communities, as in Chamula, it underscores men's superior strength and authority and, at the same time, their insecurity. In Amatenango, wife beating is tolerated, especially if the man is drunk; it is even thought to be his privilege. But, a woman has the legal right to beat in front of the judges any man (other than her husband) who hits her (Nash 1985:281). Wali (1974:55) reports the case of a Zinacanteco woman who was married to a man who drank a great deal. This woman took up employment at the *Instituto Nacional Indigenista* (National Indigenous Institute, referred to as INI) and earned enough money to support her children. Her husband beat her frequently to "control her" but to no avail. Then one day he hit her with a brick, and she was finally able to get a divorce. Independent women in Zinacantán are said to work "like men," and they are often labeled as prostitutes or witches because they have no man over them. Women in Chenalhó also report incidents of wife beating, especially by men who are under the effects of alcohol (Eber 1991:180, 212).

16. See Christine Eber's (1991) study of drinking in San Pedro Chenalhó. She analyzes drinking in ritual and nonritual contexts, including Pedrano interpretations of liquor, problem drinking and its treatment, and the problems drinking causes to families and how families deal with them.

17. See also Lacy (1976:59) for Chamula, and Eber (1991) for San Pedro Chenalhó.

18. Eber (1991:323ff.) reports a similar situation in Chenalhó, especially among Pedranos who have assumed machismo attitudes and behavior from Ladinos.

19. In Chenalhó, a husband is not condemned for killing his wife's lover (Guiteras-Holmes 1961:129). In Zinacantán, the court punishes a woman and her lover through forced labor and the latter may have to return the brideprice to the woman's husband (Collier 1973:192). In Amatenango, a married man commits a serious offense if he becomes involved with a married woman, but the infraction is less serious if the affair is with a single, young woman or a widow (Nash 1985:281).

20. When Pedrano men get drunk, they become jealous and accuse their wives of having lovers; thus incensed, they often beat their wives (Eber 1991:332).

4

In Our Ancestors' Words
Women and Men in Chamula Oral Narratives

Sacred narratives and secular stories in Chamula are omnipresent, publicly accessible, and constantly invoked for teaching purposes.[1] They contain valuable information about how Chamula people envision themselves and their society and how they would like to shape both. In this chapter I examine several oral narratives to determine the symbolic portrayal of men and women in their culture—their different attributes, abilities and weaknesses, rights and responsibilities.

Most of the stories that provide the raw material for this chapter were narrated, in Tzotzil, by Chamula women of various ages. Many of these accounts share themes and stylistic elements with those told by men (an extensive collection of male narratives has been published by Gossen (1974)). Narratives by women compared to those by men are very similar; a gendered perspective of reality does not appear to be reflected in Chamula stories.[2] Since my collection is not as comprehensive as Gossen's, I draw from his material to clarify or expand specific aspects that remain undeveloped in the texts by women.[3]

Three major paradigms or models of the definition of men and women, and the interaction between them, emerge from the analysis of the stories: (1) *jtotik/ jme'tik* (Our Father/Our Mother); (2) First Man/First Woman; and (3) the Earth. Each of these paradigms represents a synthesis of ideas and combines native thought—both ancient beliefs and newer ones developed according to the changing conditions of Chamula life—with Christian and European concepts that Chamulas have creatively woven into their view of the world. Although the degree to which each of these systems of ideas has contributed to any of the three paradigms is difficult to assess with precision, the First Man/ First Woman paradigm seems more European in nature than the other two. The basic structure of the story, namely, the prior creation of Adam, the emergence of Eve from his rib, and the suspicious nature of women from the beginning of time, remains constant. The paradigm contains, however, many native interpretations or additions that make it different from the original biblical account. The Earth paradigm, rooted in an agrarian lifestyle and a close relationship with nature, appears to be the most strongly indigenous; yet, the Earth Lord is a Ladino. I address the prehispanic precursors of each paradigm below.

The paradigms illustrate different aspects of male/female symbolism; the elements in one paradigm may reinforce, complement or openly contradict the others. In considering all three paradigms together, a complex picture evolves that transcends simple dual oppositions. For example, within the Our Father/Our Mother paradigm, the coldness of the Moon/Virgin (and of women) connotes cowardice and frailty; in the Earth paradigm, however, the coldness that connects women to the Earth symbolizes the tremendous constructive and destructive power that the Earth wields. Thus, the Earth paradigm subverts the propositions of Our Father/Our Mother but does not eliminate them; both conceptions remain, side by side, challenging each other dialectically. The symbolic definition of women contains multiple contradictions on various levels that reveal the existence of a profound ambivalence towards women. This conclusion is not a unique finding; researchers have uncovered similar feelings towards women in many societies.[4]

Among the Tzotzil from San Pedro Chenalhó, a drama of ritual humor at the Carnival epitomizes this conflictive view of women. Women are described simultaneously as vulnerable to abduction and rape, and sexually aggressive. In this drama, two men abduct a woman who is the wife or sister of the other character:

> Well, Passion, did you see a woman
> and two men running away?
> My wife (sister) ran away.
> I'm looking for my wife (sister).
> They have sinned.
> They are evil people.
> They abducted the woman.
> They kidnapped the woman...
> (Bricker 1973:141)

The wife or sister is said both to have been abducted by the men and to have run away with them. When the husband or brother finally finds the fugitives beneath a straw mat, the woman lying between the two men, he falls upon all three and pretends to beat the men and rape the woman to punish her for having run off with her abductors.

Gossen and Leventhal (1993) treat the ambiguity towards women as a key to interpret the continuity of Maya religious thought from ancient times to the present.

This ambiguity finds expression in the critical presence of women in transitional space or time, while simultaneously women symbolize permanence and the stability of the status quo. Conservative and dynamic tendencies in female behavior coexist; bloodletting by women symbolized personal and political transitions but was also used to maintain the status quo. In the Popol Vuh, Xmucané (the Grandmother) represents the conservative force, whereas Xquiq' (the daughter of a lord of the underworld, and the mother of the hero twins) marks the transition between the underworld and the earth. Although women live most of their lives on the periphery, their contradictory nature makes them uniquely apt to initiate revitalization movements, which in times of crisis aim to transform the public system at the center. As my analysis unfolds, a multiplicity of images and meanings emerge, combining and recombining to form different constellations that draw their power from the social reality they dynamically reflect and, in turn, attempt to mold.

THE *JTOTIK/JME'TIK* PARADIGM

The *jtotik/jme'tik* paradigm derives from the story of Our Father the Sun/Christ and Our Mother the Moon/Virgin, pivotal deities in the Chamula pantheon.[5] Their lives on earth are recounted in narratives all over the Maya area. The Sun and Moon figures were also the most important celestial gods of the ancient Maya. Thompson (1966:231) has identified sections of this story on an ancient vase. According to the ancient legend, Sun and Moon were the first inhabitants of the world: he was a hunter; she was a weaver. They were the first beings to cohabit, but the Moon was unfaithful to her husband. According to Thompson, Maya scientists tried to reduce the Moon's "erratic ways," but because of her fickle nature, she was always regarded as "capricious, quarrelsome, a prevaricator" (Thompson 1966:230). The Moon's relationship with the day Caban identifies her as a goddess of earth and crops. She was called Lady, Our Mother, or Grandmother.

Thompson notes the ambivalence of the Maya towards this deity, who is depicted as loving and yet unfaithful. This particular type of ambivalence, consistent with the Maya view of deities, seems to have disappeared in the modern accounts of Our Father/Our Mother, perhaps as the Moon assumed some of the qualities of the Virgin. The ambivalence towards the Moon now refers to her simultaneous power and weakness. Her fickle nature seems to have been transferred to the First Woman and to the Earth deity, which continues to represent another aspect of the Moon.[6] By the time of the Spanish invasion, Gossen (1986b:254) notes, these ancient Maya deities had incorporated symbolic associations from the religious complex of Central Mexico. The imposition of Catholic ideas thus added one more layer or aspect to an already multifaceted configuration.

In the contemporary Chamula story, Our Mother was living on the earth, and she was pregnant. The baby had been entrusted to her before she had a husband. Growing in her womb, the child's radiance was already evident, so the forces of evil, the demons, did not want him to be born. They struggled to kill him, but Our Mother fled so that they would not hurt her child. She left with her husband, Saint Joseph. When her baby, Jesus, was born, the earth was lit. The demons tried to prevent the coming of light to this earth, for they thrived on chaos and darkness. They persecuted Jesus and finally caught him. They tormented him and, eventually, killed him. They did not really kill him, however. He went up to the sky, together with Our Mother, where he became the Sun, and she became the Moon (app., text 1).

The Moon/Virgin, Our Mother, exists first. To protect her son from the demons, she employs a typical strategy of Chamula women: she flees so as not to confront her persecutors directly and thereby saves her child. The stories collected by Gossen from male informants explain how the mother's superior power, based on her generational priority, is taken over by the Sun/Christ when he is a child. He tricks his mother and throws boiling water at her face. The water scalds one of her eyes and makes her less luminous and less powerful. Thus, the Sun/Christ overcomes his mother and gains supremacy (Gossen 1974:37), an event which epitomizes the triumph of the gender principle over the seniority principle (see below).

Interestingly, stories narrated by women do not offer an explanation for the lesser power of the Moon. I explicitly asked women if they knew how the Moon/Virgin became less radiant. They did not. For these women, the superiority of Our Father is unquestioned, inherent in his nature, and so apparently is the lesser power and strength of Our Mother. It is men, then, who find problems with the relative importance of the age versus gender principles. Their own ambivalence toward male and female power needs an explicit legitimization. In the words of one woman,

> Our Father is stronger.
> Our Mother obeys his orders.
> It is Our Mother who obeys.
>
> Our Father is hot, we can grow.
> We are happy when Our Father is here.
>
> Instead, Our Mother is cold.
> Everything is dark, we cannot walk far.
> We are scared.
>
> But when Our Father is here we can go far away.
> We walk.

We are not scared anymore.
It is because Our Father has a strong heart.

Instead, Our Mother's heart is soft.
She has a smaller heart.
She is colder. (Tumin C49-68)

According to Chamulas, when Our Father lived on this earth, he let his persecutors kill him instead of his sheep, referring to his children, the people of the world (app., text 2). He proved he had more courage than his mother because he faced the demons directly and sacrificed his own life to spare the lives of his children. On the other hand, Our Father's greater heat makes him less vulnerable to attacks from demons; therefore, he can defend his children better than Our Mother can. Indeed, many stories talk about demons coming to attack Our Mother and threatening to drop her if she does not surrender several of her children. These threats occur when demons cover Our Mother's face in heaven (i.e., when the moon is not visible). When uncovered, she watches carefully over her children during the night. Chamula women make the explicit association between those traits that characterize the Sun/Christ and Chamula men and those associated with the Moon/Virgin and Chamula women.[7]

The metaphor of Sun:Moon :: heat:cold :: courage:timidity :: strength:weakness provides the essential framework for judging a behavior as masculine or feminine. Thus, when a murderer kills his victim with a machete—face to face—he is said to have "acted like a man." But, when he kills with a gun—from a distance or from hiding—he is said to have "acted like a woman." A man who does not want to accept a civil office will also be labeled "a woman." Moreover, a man who does not face his enemies or his problems will be called "cunt" (chap. 7). Because the sexual organs of women are considered cold, they are conceptualized as the loci of women's vulnerability and lack of courage:

But we, the women, don't have as much heat.
In a moment, we'll find a man.
In a moment, we'll find a man who will talk to us.

It is because we're not so strong.
It is because we don't have heat.

Even going from here to San Cristóbal makes us afraid.
Even going to the forest to gather wood scares us.
(Lolen C55-28)

Like Our Mother, then, women are more vulnerable to attacks. Since their heat or strength is limited, they cannot defend themselves; they are less courageous than men. The Moon/Virgin is afraid of demons, but women are afraid not only of demons but also of men. Heat—the source of strength, courage, and wisdom—sustains and legitimizes gender hierarchy within this paradigm.

As prayers and rituals explicitly express, the Sun/Christ established order in the universe. When he ascended to the sky, he generated order out of the existing chaos so that life, light, and heat triumphed over death, darkness, and coldness. These negative forces, of course, were not destroyed permanently. The Sun/Christ with the help of his children, especially the religious cargoholders, continues to battle against them.

For Chamulas, the concepts of time (including day, night, and the seasons) and the spatial divisions or cardinal directions of their universe derive from the trajectory of the Sun/Christ in the sky (Gossen 1974:30ff.). Thus, light and heat, both in the daily and in the yearly cycles, have positive connotations in Chamula thought. They represent the times of greatest strength and influence of the Sun/ Christ. In the same vein, east and north symbolize goodness and life by representing the ascending path of the Sun/Christ in the sky, and west and south are associated with evil and death and the deity's descent into the underworld. Gossen (1974:32) discovered that the positive associations of the right hand and the negative ones of the left hand are also linked to the Sun/Christ's movements; when the Sun/Christ emerges in the east and faces the universe, north is to his right, and south is to his left.

The importance of Our Father the Sun/Christ in the Chamula conceptualization of time and space is overwhelming. The Sun/Christ created most plants, animals and constellations. He provided his children, the Chamula people, with maize, the all-important staple food. Maize came from a part of the Sun/Christ's body, and in prayers it is variously called "a grain of his flesh," "his sunbeam," "his radiance." In contrast, Our Mother the Moon/Virgin gave her children potatoes, beans, squash, and other less important foods (Gossen 1974:40). The symbolism of more important:less important :: higher:lower :: male:female also holds for foods. Maize grows tall, while potatoes and squash grow in and directly on the ground. Beans spread on the ground; they can be forced to climb on the cornstalk, but they remain lower. Every Chamula knows and repeatedly declares in prayers that maize came from Our Father's flesh. In contrast, the idea that beans, potatoes and squash came from Our Mother does not seem to be common knowledge. Many of the women I spoke with were not sure about the origin of these foodstuffs.

In their behavior, Chamula men display symbolic traits associated with the Sun/Christ, while Chamula women display those associated with the Moon/Virgin and the Earth. Thus, in everyday life, women always sit on the cold, feminine ground and walk barefoot, another signal of their connection to the Earth; men sit on small chairs and wear sandals, symbolically accentuating their superior heat and height. Moreover, just as the Moon/Virgin follows her son through his path in the sky, Chamula women walk behind their husbands on the trails. Like Our Father, men must be the main providers for their families, especially of maize. As Our Father defends the Moon/Virgin, men are expected to defend their "colder," more vulnerable wives from demons and other men. Because they have more heat, men are able to go farther away from home and walk alone day or night without encountering dangers; women must stay close to home and must never walk alone at night. Even in daytime, women should walk with other women, and at night they require the company of a man to defend them. Like the Moon/Virgin, who is thought to leave a bowl of corn gruel in the eastern sky for her son to eat, women are expected to attend to their husbands.

Nevertheless, Our Father and Our Mother share the responsibilities of caring for their children. Prayers address both deities consecutively. If one moves beyond the interaction of these deities as male and female and views them in a family context, a pattern of complementarity emerges. Neither *jtotik* nor *jme'tik* alone is considered complete. They complement one another in performing the necessary tasks to guarantee the life and survival of their children.

In addition to social organization by gender, the other basic principle in Chamula society is seniority. Not only people but also saints, topographic features, cargo positions and animal soul companions are ranked as "senior" (*bankilal*) or "junior" (*itz'inal*) in terms of relative age, strength, wealth, size, and other criteria (Gossen 1974:43). Unlike men, women are not explicitly addressed as *bankilal* or *itz'inal*, however, people do rank them in terms of this principle: younger men and women must behave respectfully toward older women, especially those who have held religious positions. Similarly, younger siblings, regardless of sex, owe respect to their older sisters. But unless a woman's age, wealth, or prestige are dramatically superior to those of the younger man, the gender principle often supersedes the seniority principle. The precedence of gender over age is seen in the narrative in which the Sun/Christ dominates his mother. The conflict between gender and seniority occurs with some frequency between men and their older sisters; many women say that a drunken man may beat not only his wife but also his older sisters (see also Lacy 1976:57).

To review, in the *jtotik/jme'tik* paradigm, Our Father the Sun/Christ is the supreme creator and appears at the center of the Chamula universe; by comparison, Our Mother the Moon/Virgin appears dramatically paler. Chamulas believe that their lives parallel this paradigm. Men's control of community government assures that people respect order and tradition so that the Chamula way of life will continue. Women are appreciated as mothers, but the prevailing ideology often slights their contribution to sustaining Chamula society; in fact, as I show in chapters 6 and 7, women's role is critical. Women acknowledge their relative weakness, "just like Our Mother, our heart is soft and small."

THE FIRST MAN/FIRST WOMAN PARADIGM

The creation of the First Man and First Woman is a second paradigm that defines women, men, and their interaction. Chamulas do not invoke this model to explain differences between the genders as often as they do the *jtotik/jme'tik* paradigm; nevertheless, this paradigm is important because it explains the origins of human sexuality and related topics. Although the basic contours of the story come from the Judeo-Christian Genesis narrative, the elements of ambivalence towards sexuality and women seem to have been present in indigenous belief systems prior to the Spanish invasion.

I examine the stories narrated by women first; however, since they are not as detailed as those collected from men, I draw from some of the latter in order to expand the analysis. In the women's accounts (app., texts 3, 4, and 5), a man was on earth first. In text 4, Our Father created the man and put him on earth; in texts 3 and 5, it is not said who created him. In all of these stories, either the First Man himself or Judas removed one of the man's ribs to create a wife for him. Text 4 does not say how the rib was removed, just that it happened:

> It happened that his rib came out and became a woman.
> They were two then.
> A woman.
> A man. (Veruch C62-10)

These versions are not very explicit about the origins of sexuality. In text 3, the man "eats" something and thereby learns how to have sex. Text 4 simply states, "since there were two of them, they had their children." Text 5 is the most explicit on the subject:

> "Do you want to accompany her?" the demon invited.[8]
> "Oh, where did you bring her from?" our First Father inquired.
> He did not realize that the woman had sprung from his rib.
>
> "Do you want to be with her?" the demon asked.
> "Yes, yes, if you give her to me," replied our First Father.
>
> "Well, then, be with her" said the demon.
> "But how is it that I should accompany her?"
> our First Father inquired.
> "Because I don't know how."
>
> "Oh, you don't know?

Well, this is the way you are going to join with her," said the
demon...

It was the demon who taught him.
"This is how you will do it," he said.

Well, he showed him then.
Well, Our Father saw it, and he learned.

That is how people increased.
If it had not been like that,
there would be no people.
We would not be alive. (Antel 64-6)

In all of these narratives, the woman is seen as a part of man, fashioned as a different individual to reduce his loneliness and desolation (app., text 3). In text 5, however, it does not occur to the First Man that he needs a companion until the demon suggests he should have one and gives him the woman. The association of women and wives with the demon shows, again, the ambivalence towards sexuality in Chamula ideology. On the one hand, women have been made from men, for men, to be their companions; on the other hand, women are associated with the forces of evil and must be controlled.[9]

Gossen (1974:43) notes that in Chamula thought, women are considered prone to commit adultery and evil, especially in times of waning heat and light when they come under the influence of the demon instead of the Sun/Christ. This idea, he says, derives from the conception that the demon is the first to have sex with a woman. In the stories I analyze, however, the demon has sex with the First Woman for his own pleasure and to teach the First Man, not for the woman's sake. Women are supposed to be easy victims of rape by demons and men. They can be overpowered physically or tricked into intercourse. The element of superior male cunning is very important and recurs in many stories. In the *jtotik/jme'tik* paradigm, the child Sun/Christ tricks his mother in order to overpower her; in the narrative of the origin of pottery, men "stole the secret away from women" and now make bigger and better pots (Rus 1969).

Among the creation narratives of Gossen's corpus, one is remarkable for its emphasis on the couple's unity before the sexual division of labor. According to this story, before the onset of sexuality, the First Man and First Woman harvest maize, cook food, and make clothing, and their hearts are happy. The demon offers to teach the First Woman how to make children so that she can later teach her husband, but he discovers she has no vagina. He has to open her body with an axe to prepare her for himself and her husband.

In this narrative, male sexuality exists independently, but female sexuality is created by and for men. Sexual interaction determines the asymmetrical relations between man and woman. The woman is portrayed as passive; something is done to her so that her husband can learn about sex and be happy. Women as companions and sexual partners are created for men; therefore, men have the right to control them. Male control over females is clearly represented in a text from Gossen's collection in which the Sun/Christ warns the First Woman that if she seeks another man, her husband will kill her. In contrast, the Sun/Christ tells the First Man that if he gets involved with a married woman, her husband will kill him. The reaction of the unfaithful man's wife is not indicated, and hence unimportant.

The above text presents the idea that men fight with one another for women and for the right to control them. A girl's sexuality is "owned" by her father, and only he has the right to give his daughter in marriage. When a young man has sexual intercourse with a young woman but does not marry her, he is forced to pay a certain amount of money to the woman's father for each instance of intercourse. A man can legitimately buy his wife from her father, or he may "steal" her from her husband or from her father by failing to pay a brideprice (chap. 5). Sex is transformed into a political act that seals a man's claim over a woman or wrests her away from another man. But, sexuality is also valued for its procreational function. Our Father wants his children to multiply so that they will serve him and maintain him through prayers, offerings, and celebrations.

The First Man/First Woman paradigm establishes the superiority and domination of men. The companionship of men and women and their complementarity in family and community tasks tend to be slighted. Text 3 comments only briefly that Our Father wants his children to have a companion, a wife or a husband, because "it is really sad for a person to live alone."

In many other stories, the relationship of husband and wife is referred to in passing as one of companionship.[10] For example, husband and wife go together to pray to the Earth Lord for money. After the money is spent, the couple devise a plan to scare the Earth Lord away in order to escape their obligation of servitude to him. In another story a man cries desperately for his dead wife, wanting to join her in death. In other stories a couple go together to fiestas and distant markets and flee together when the flood comes to punish them for eating their babies. Accounts of the Cuscat rebellion, assert that women joined their men in the battlefront, fighting together against Ladinos.

This companionship seems to derive conceptually from an ideal division of labor, established by Our Father for the first people. In this division, the assigned responsibilities of both husband and wife are indispensable for survival. The man plants corn and brings firewood for the hearth; the woman prepares the food and weaves clothing; both share child-rearing responsibilities. This labor division remains the ideal and is illustrated in the ceremony performed at the birth of a child.

A baby girl is symbolically presented with a spindle, a hand-card and a batten (one of the implements of the backstrap loom); a baby boy receives a digging stick and a hoe. The midwife, who holds the infants, instructs them to employ these tools to earn their sustenance.

After several years of marriage, many Chamula couples develop a strong companionship. Perhaps this perspective is not brought out sufficiently in the First Man/First Woman model because this paradigm supports the ideology of male control over females—an idea that would appear to contradict strong companionship.

It is women's role as sexual partners that is tension ridden and leads to male insecurity. From a sexual perspective, every woman may be seen as a man's potential property. The man must conquer and control the woman to prevent other men from stealing her away. Another series of very popular narratives in Chamula, the *jik'aletik* or black demon stories, also regard women's vulnerability as a consequence of their sexuality. In the following paragraphs, the difference between these narratives and those of Our Mother underscore the link between sexuality and women's susceptibility to attacks.

In origin narratives, Our Mother the Moon/Virgin escapes from the demons who want to kill her child. She saves her son, who then brings light to the earth for humankind. She acts by herself. Although in some of the stories her husband is said to have accompanied her, he does not dominate her. This event happens before the onset of sexuality; her child is not sexually conceived. The important part of the Moon/Virgin story is her role as a mother, not as a sexual partner.

In the black demon stories, which narrate contemporary occurrences, women's sexuality appears at the fore. Many Chamula women say that they will not leave their houses after dark because they might encounter a black demon.[11] The general pattern of the story is as follows: at dawn or dusk the *jik'al* (sometimes portrayed as a bat, sometimes as a bear) carries a woman from her home to his cave. There, he rapes her. Within a few days, still in the cave, the woman gives birth to a child. In the stories that I collected, the child is always a son. This boy becomes an adult in a few days time. The woman remains in the dark cave with her son for a while, but soon he becomes aware of his mother's sadness and asks her what is wrong. Upon learning the truth, he offers to help her leave the cave and return to her husband and children. In some of the stories, he tells her not to worry because he will support her. The boy removes the huge stone that blocks the entrance to the cave and carries his mother home on his back.

Notice the structural similarities between the narratives of Our Mother (Sun/Moon) and the *jik'aletik* (Demon/Woman) presented in table 1. In both stories men are the central characters. In the Sun/Moon model, however, the woman is presented as an active agent, making decisions; in the Demon/Woman model, the woman is an object of an aggression against which she is powerless. In the first example, the woman gives bith to the Sun/Christ, who goes on to save human-

Table 1

STRUCTURE OF EVENTS IN TWO NARRATIVES

SUN/MOON STORY	DEMON/WOMAN STORY
Demons want to kill her son.	Demons want to rape her.
She flees to protect her son.	She is abducted.
She gives birth and thereby brings light to the world.	She is raped in a dark cave and gives birth.
Her son grows rapidly.	Her son grows rapidly.
Her son defends humankind and brings order to the world.	Her son defends her and brings her out into the light.
She follows her son into the sky.	Her son takes her to her home.

kind; in the second, the son metaphorically resurrects his mother by leading her out of the dark, antisocial cave of the demon into the bright, orderly world. Although in the first model the Sun/Christ usurps his mother's power, diminishing her authority and importance, he does not fully control her. On the contrary, in several of the Sun/Christ's adventures on earth, the stories portray his mother as an independent character (see, for example, Gossen 1974:312). When sexuality is an issue, however, men are always in charge of women as fathers, husbands, aggressors, or sons. In the *jik'aletik* stories, the woman's son finally saves her. The black demons, who also symbolize aggressive men, pose a constant threat to Chamula women. Women's sexual vulnerability explains their supposed "lack of courage" and justifies men's control and "protection" of them.

In sum, the paradigms of Our Father/Our Mother and First Man/ First Woman offer complementary views of the natures of men and women. In the Our Father/ Our Mother paradigm, the woman appears first and is independent until her son takes over the dominant position. The son's superior heat qualifies him to create an orderly universe out of chaos and evil. In the First Man/First Woman paradigm, men appear on earth first. Women are created from men, for men, and female sexuality is controlled by men. Women have less heat and courage than men because their sexuality was created for men; therefore, women are vulnerable to male attack.

THE EARTH PARADIGM

The third paradigm, the Earth, reveals a contrasting picture of women. In this paradigm women are depicted as powerful, and this power has both positive and negative features. Women control the fertility of both crops and people but may also cause destruction, poverty, and death.[12] In prayers Chamulas address the Earth primarily as a mother; she carries her children, holds them, and tolerates their walking, sitting and sleeping on her. People ask her forgiveness for making her dirty and malodorous, for filling her with their waste. She is called Our Mother and is conceived as another representation of the Moon/Virgin.

The Earth, like the Moon goddess of the ancient Maya, is also a fertility symbol—a common link in agricultural societies that is pervasive throughout Mesoamerica. In Chamula, the relationship between children and maize is explicitly stated in the prayers for the unborn child. The Sun/Christ is asked to take care of the child as if it were his seed of maize, as if it were his tender shoot of maize. The unborn child is said to be inside its corn husk (*sjojoch'al*), inside the protective covering of bromeliads (*yech'al*). But, as I show below, the female Earth symbolizes not only the motherly aspects of fertility but also the powerful sexual urges that determine fertility.

The Earth paradigm, unlike the other two, is not explicitly developed through a series of stories; it must be pieced together from different stories and beliefs about wealth-bearing objects. Perhaps the Earth paradigm is more obscure and fragmented precisely because it appears to subvert the ideal conceptualizations of men and women as expressed in the other two paradigms. Furthermore, even though the Chamulas talk about Our Mother Earth, the symbols of Ladino male power often conceal the basic female symbols.

In this section, I examine first the stories of *pak'inte'* and of *me' ik'*, followed by the stories of the Earth Lord, his daughter and the *anjeletik*. Finally, I explore the stories of *me'tak'in*, the mother of money, which explicitly associate the female Earth with wealth.

Pak'inte' is one of the most ubiquitous female characters of Chamula oral narratives. She appears frequently in the different hamlets of Chamula, and many of the women have heard her or know men who have seen her. She is a variant of La Llorona, or Weeping Woman, who appears in narratives throughout Mesoamerica. She embodies the female Earth, with her potent sexual urges and her associations with water and mist, gourds, caves, and ravines—all symbols of the Earth. She has many ancient precursors, including the Maya goddess Xtabai, (Landa 1959) who among contemporary Maya bears many resemblances to *pak'inte'*. For the Lacandón, Xtabai is a goddess who lives in the rocks of the forest. For the Yucatec Maya, Xtabai are "demons" in snake form who live in caves. These Xtabai spring out in human form to capture men and to take them to the underworld or to throw them into a cenote (Tozzer 1907:158).[13] There are also strong parallels between *pak'inte'* and Cihuacoatl, the Earth Mother deity of the Mexica. The latter is depicted as a loving mother who appears at night, dressed in white, crying (Sahagún 1956:bk.1:26-27). In one of her aspects Cihuacoatl is Quilaztli, goddess of fertility and crops, with close links to the earth, moon, snakes, water, corn, and other symbols of the Earth. But Cihuacoatl also has an aggressive facet. She is described as an eagle, which according to Garibay (1958:139), defines her as the counterpart of the warring Sun, as his earthly complement. Thus, she is both a terrible and a loving deity.

In Chamula, *pak'inte'* walks alone at night and tries to lure men, especially drunkards, into going with her. She looks exactly like a pretty Chamula woman, dressed in a Chamula skirt and blouse, with a black shawl covering her head. She emerges in the mist from the precipice and invites the man to follow her (app., texts 6-10). "Come here, come here," she says. "I am your wife." She is always searching for a husband. Her intention is to lead the man to the precipice or to a cave and engage in sexual intercourse with him. Many men claim to have followed her for a while until they suddenly realized her identity because she was leading them down trails full of spiny bushes. To overcome her, the man must turn his clothes inside out. Once he recovers his senses, he is able to walk back to the main road and find his way home. Men who have slept with *pak'inte'* say that she is very cold. A clear connection is established here between the "coldness" of women's genitals and the Earth.

Pak'inte' is said to live in the mountains or in the woods. People claim to have seen her fetching water in her gourd. When she finds a drunken man, she lifts his head and addresses him as if she were his wife: "Get up!...What are you doing there lying face up? Let's go home." She asks, "Do you want to drink water?" and pours water on his head to wake him. She takes him to her house where she feeds him and sleeps with him. But *pak'inte'* does not want to kill the man, she is just looking for a husband. Some people say that if a man goes to her house, he will become rich; maybe she will give him a small gourd or some other object. One man was able to seize her gourd; it was very green, and the man became rich (app., text 9).

What are the salient traits of *pak'inte'*? She is a powerful woman who is sexually insatiable and therefore always on the look out for men. She is connected to the wild, antisocial, dangerous aspects of the environment: woods, mountains, cliffs, caves, and precipices. Her appearance in these threatening places symbolizes her wild behavior. She is an anti-woman, for she behaves in many aspects like a man. She aggressively looks for men, initiates conversations with them, takes them with her, and demands sexual intercourse. Moreover, she seems to be an independent agent without a father, husband, or brother to control her. She walks at night by herself. Her behavior completely contradicts the norms of behavior expected of Chamula women. But she is a woman. She has all the physical traits of Chamula women and wears the same clothes they do. She is nurturing in her interactions with men; she feeds them, brings them water, and helps them to stand up when they are drunk. She is a very ambiguous character, who combines male and female elements, and proves by her very existence that women may also be strong and aggressive.

The gourd, as a female, earthly symbol, recurs in stories related to the Earth; in the *pak'inte'* story, it is green and bestows riches. In the agricultural society of Chamula, green is associated with the maize field, the source of wealth and happiness. *Pak'inte'*, then, symbolizes the fertility of the Earth. Through her unbridled sexuality, she also expresses the relationships among female sexuality, procreation, and the fertility of the fields.

Chamula men fear *pak'inte'*. The very idea of a woman conversing with a man and soliciting sex may be frightening because it implies that their own wives and daughters could act in a similar manner. Also, Chamulas believe that men or women who have had contact with a supernatural being will become ill and eventually die from "soul loss," which is caused by fear.

Even this extraordinary woman, however, can be defeated by a man. A man may successfully vanquish *pak'inte'* by turning his clothes inside out. In contrast, the woman who is taken away and raped by black demons only returns to normal life through the assistance of her son. Nevertheless, the powerful statement of *pak'inte'* remains because many Chamula men consider their wives to be potential *pak'inte'*, actively seeking men to fulfill their insatiable sexual needs (Favre 1984:240).[14]

Me' ik', the mother or originator of strong, cold winds, is also portrayed as a woman (app., texts 11-15). Chamulas say that when *me' ik'* dances or lets her hair loose, she unleashes strong winds that destroy the cornfields and even topple big trees. *Me' ik'* also emerges from precipices, caves, or the inside of mountains. Like *pak'inte'*, with whom she is sometimes confused, she deceives men and takes them away. She, too, wants a husband. *Me' ik'* appears as a Chamula woman, lying on the ground, tired and bruised from her journeys; her bruises are caused by the trees and stones that she encounters along her way.

The symbols of the feminine Earth appear again in *me' ik'*: her coldness, her emergence from the Earth's womb, and her associations with *pak'inte'*, the Earth Lords, and the serpent.[15] In accounts of *me' ik'* the Earth's potential for destruction is emphasized. The anomalous qualities of *me' ik'* as a free, independent woman are not without contest. One story relates that a boy, not a woman, originates the wind. Likewise, *me' ik'* is not always a free agent; some people say that strong winds are controlled by Our Father, who sends them to punish his children (app., text 15).

Another narrative, by a Chamula man, illustrates how autonomous women are suspected of being powerful and destructive like *me' ik'* (app., text 16). This man accuses two women in his hamlet of causing the winds. One of the women used to be married; now both live alone. Men approach them, but they are not interested in marrying, neither do they want children. These women are "bad" because they behave like men. They plant their own cornfields; they even fell trees with axes, and chop and sell firewood. The two women allegedly toss their hair about, provoking destructive winds that break the cornstalks. When strong winds blow at night, everyone in the village knows their origin. Indeed, like *me' ik'*, these women represent the ominous and dark aspects of the female Earth and of women in general. Their perceived potential for destruction goes hand in hand with their freedom from male control. On the one hand, they illustrate that women can live alone and support themselves. On the other hand, while they have the capacity for fertility and nurturing, they spurn the traditional nurturing roles of wife, mother, or daughter. People in Nichimtik fear that these women will turn against their neighbors, destroy the cornfields, and thus endanger everyone's survival.

The *yajval banumil* (lords of the Earth) and the *anjeletik* (lords of lakes, rivers and water holes) constitute the third group of figures relating to the Earth. The Earth Lords, including the *anjeletik*, are usually portrayed as Ladino couples, often blond with fair skin (see chapter 3). They represent transformations of the ancient Earth deity that occurred as white intruders appropriated the indigenous lands, which symbolize sustenance and wealth for Chamulas (Goldin and Rosenbaum in press). They express the power that Ladinos hold over material resources. In these accounts, the imposition of Ladino power over the Earth Mother conceals, somewhat, the deep female nature of the Earth. The Earth Lords are married couples who maintain the ideal division of labor in the family; no matter how powerful the female Earth Lord, her husband or father holds the dominant position.

Is it coincidence that the symbol of Ladino power in the figure of the Earth Lord obscures the existence of a powerful, independent, fearless female who is responsible for fertility? Is it coincidence that narratives which assert the primacy of men (such as those of the first two paradigms) contain precise, unambiguous concepts, whereas narratives of the female Earth appear equivocal and piecemeal? A strong male bias acts to overshadow the representation of women as powerful and autonomous. Notwithstanding, the stories of *pak'inte'* and *me' ik'* survive hand in hand with the stories of Ladino Earth Lords. Furthermore, the female nature of the Earth comes through frequently in stories and explanations of beliefs, even in narratives of the Ladino Earth Lords. For example, in a variant of the story of *pak'inte'*, a man dreams about a beautiful Ladino woman who attempts to seduce him into abandoning his wife and marrying her. "Come to me," says the woman; but she is an *anjel*, a female lord of the water. The man throws himself into the lake and perishes because this powerful woman wants to marry him.

The best known account of a female *yajval banumil*, presents her as comparatively tame. Her position closely resembles those of Chamula women as wives and mothers.[16] All men and women are familiar with this story; however, the versions I was able to elicit appear fragmentary. For the purposes of this analysis, I use Gossen's more complete account. These stories make a strong statement about women's contribution to the welfare of the family as well as about the stupid behavior of the many men who mistreat their wives.

A man finds a serpent in the woods. The serpent begs him to spare her life and to take her to her father's home; this the man does. The serpent transforms into a beautiful woman, the daughter of the Earth Lord. The Earth Lord gives her to the man to be his wife. The woman gives birth to two children, a girl and a boy. She magically increases the family's food with a few grains of corn and some beans that she keeps in a gourd. Because she always provides abundant meals, her husband thinks she is exhausting his corn supply. In anger, he strikes her and causes her nose to bleed. As she wipes her nose with a corn cob, red maize is originated. At that precise moment the sky darkens, thunder rumbles, and rain pours down. The Earth Lord arrives to reclaim his daughter from her stupid, abusive husband. Before she leaves, the woman gives her children two clay pots and tells them to touch the pots whenever they are hungry; one pot provides tortillas, the other beans. When the father discovers the children's source of food, he breaks the pots. The mother returns for her children and takes them away. The man realizes what he has done and is devastated.

The associations of women with several elements of the Earth are explicit in this story and include serpents, gourds, clay pots, red maize, and water. The serpent symbolizes fertility and wealth, and Chamulas often directly associate the serpent with money. The *anjeletik* live in the water and are frequently described as serpents or women.

Serpents and the female Earth are definitely related. In another account (app., text 17) a Chamula man finds a beautiful woman in the woods. He immediately asks her to marry him. She accepts on condition that he cease sexual relations with his wife, although he may visit his wife and children and support them economically. The man does not keep his promise. When the woman realizes he has been unfaithful, she tries to leave him. He does not want to let her go, so she transforms herself into a serpent and escapes. There is nothing he can do to stop her because she happens to be an Earth Lord.

The other female Earth associations present in the *yajval banumil* narratives are the gourd and the clay pot. Both gourds and pottery come from the Earth, and both are household items used daily by women for cooking and storing food. The *pak'inte'* and the Earth Lord's daughter carry gourds; the former to hold water, the latter to store and increase the corn supply. The magic pots of the Earth Lord's daughter reproduce food for her children and thus symbolize fertility and abundance. Three gourds and three clay pots are mentioned in the prayers addressed to Our Mother Earth when a baby is about to be born; they symbolize offerings to be given to her. Midwives beg her forgiveness because the child will be "unloaded" on earth and will pollute her with the liquids and blood of childbirth. During the Festival of Games, musicians play three double ceramic pots, conceived as supremely sacred drums. These drums are beaten constantly with the hands and symbolize the plentiful provision of food that the Passion character is expected to give the Chamula people. Appropriately, Chamulas jokingly call these pots "breasts" (Gossen 1986b:235).

Gourds, pots, and serpents, then, are linked to women's powers of fertility, which often are expressed as material wealth. There are many interesting accounts of magical objects, usually found in the ground, that have the property of bestowing wealth. These objects are generically called *me'tak'in*—mother or generator of money. These accounts are not "stories," rather they are true narratives about the discovery of such objects. Many people say they would like to dig in certain locations because they might find a generator of money (app., text 18). People sometimes refer to money directly, believing that it has been left in a particular place by their ancestors; but mostly they discuss objects that are associated with the Earth and are thought to be capable of "creating" wealth, either in the form of money or of plentiful crops and large livestock.

In text 18, Maruch talks about finding a serpent, or a little statue of a saint, or a basalt pestle that is used to grind corn. The stone grinder and the statue are said to be green, like a cornfield. Small clay pots, small porcelain jars and gourds may also be money generators. People who find such an object believe it will make them wealthy; corn, together with anything else they plant, will yield splendid fruits. The serpent, too, is a "mother of money." Sometimes the serpent transforms into a small green stone; people take this stone to their homes, burn incense to it, and keep it in a box. Every month the serpent will shake off its "children" (i.e., money). Wealth is inextricably linked to the female Earth and the production of corn. The adjective used to describe the color of the pestle, the stone, and the little saint is *yax-balan*, the same term that is applied to a green cornfield.

The Earth paradigm endows women with awesome power. Women symbolize abundance, as exemplified in the story of the Earth Lord's daughter. As I mention above, Chamulas say that a wife brings *skuerte* (from the Spanish *suerte*, meaning good luck) to her husband; if he stops drinking and works hard alongside his wife, he will become wealthy. A patient and intelligent woman has a positive impact on her husband's lot. If left uncontrolled, however, a woman's power may run rampant, as illustrated by the insatiable sexuality of *pak'inte'* and the cold and deadly *me' ik'*.

SUMMARY

The picture of men and women in Chamula ideology is complex. In the paradigm of Our Father/Our Mother, the difference between men and women is defined in terms of heat. Women possess less heat than men, either as part of their nature or because they permanently lost heat when Our Mother's eye was blinded. The Moon/Virgin's role as mother is exalted; by protecting her unborn son, she guaranteed the light required for human existence. Our Mother initiated the chain of events that led to the creation of an orderly world. Our Father, the supreme creator, is responsible for order and morality and for the continued existence of life and crops. In this instance, the male appears overwhelmingly superior, projected in the image of a benevolent father who protects his wife and creates the best possible environment for the development of his children. The wife remains generally submissive within a complementary division of labor.

In the second paradigm, First Man/First Woman, the role of women is defined in terms of sexuality. Women are made from and for men. Sexuality makes women vulnerable. Because the demon taught the first woman how to have sex, attitudes toward sexuality are ambivalent. Where procreative aspects are emphasized, however, the roles of men and women as fathers and mothers assume a divine dimension because Our Father wishes to have many children to honor him.

The Earth paradigm portrays women as extremely powerful, but potentially wild. The female Earth is a fundamental source of sustenance, producing children and crops. Independent of male control, however, female energy may destroy the system. Under the aegis of men, women symbolize wealth and abundance. In contrast to the first two paradigms, women are controlled, not because they are weak and may be hurt, but because they are powerful and may become destructive or assert control over men. Nevertheless, in his exercise of control, a man may be foolish and ruin everything, as happened to the man who lost his family in the story of the Earth Lord's daughter.

The analyses in this chapter have examined fundamental aspects of gender ideology in Chamula. These stories are not the exclusive domain of a few specialists; most Chamulas know them, narrate them, and use them to instruct others in specific situations as well as for entertainment purposes.

The *jtotik/jme'tik* (Our Father/Our Mother) paradigm may be invoked with more frequency than the others and is the most clearly delineated in people's minds since prayers and rituals make constant reference to it. This paradigm is the most "official" view of gender. The second paradigm is invoked mostly in the context of discussions of male and female sexuality and the interaction that ensues on this basis. Jokes, insults, and derogatory statements about men and women often revolve around the images and meanings this paradigm constructs. The Earth paradigm may not be structured as explicitly or brought up as routinely as the Our Father/Our Mother or First Man/First Woman paradigms, perhaps because it undermines the statements of the other two. I would argue, however, that because of Chamulas' dependence on nature for sustenance, the Earth symbolism erupts repeatedly, reminding people of the power women exercise by virtue of their connections to the Earth.

Some of the mutually conflictive traits that describe women in different Chamula narratives are the following: vulnerable and aggressive, weak and strong, fragile and suspicious, sexually assertive and victimized by rape, independent and controlled by men, nurturing and hostile, fertile and destructive, bearer of life and bringer of death. Women's relationships with men are variously characterized as hierarchical (with men dominating), interdependent and complementary (based on companionship), and conflictive. The different characters and their behavior function like dynamic prototypes that originate in the social arrangements on the ground but, at the same time, continuously reshape the social patterns. Because they present such diverse and contradictory possibilities, these paradigms provide the setting for a multiplicity of arrangements between men and women. The religious cargo system, for example, encourages complementarity and companionship of husband and wife. The economic system requires interdependence and complementarity, but because of the extremely difficult economic conditions, these ideals are not often achieved. In the political realm of the civil cargos, however, women are invisible. Court judgements systematically reinforce the ideas of women's weakness, vulnerability, and need for male control. Men's deep ambivalence towards women often underlies male/female interaction and manifests itself in suspicion and fear of women, and concomitant feelings of inadequacy. These feelings may lead men to act in despotic ways.

NOTES

1.   The narratives explored in this section belong to either of two categories of Chamula native exegesis (Gossen 1974:50): *batzi antivo k'op* (true ancient narrative) refer to events that happened a long time ago during the first, second and third creations; the more recent stories *batz'i ach' k'op* (true recent narrative) refer to events of the fourth creation, including the narrator's own experiences or occurrences during the narrator's life.

2.   In his study of myths in two Nahuat communities, Taggart (1983) observes that individuals' positions in the social structure—within the family, the community and the wider world—affect the way they portray characters and develop plots in the stories they narrate. In the case of men and women within the same community, however, this does not seem to hold, at least at the level of general themes and characterizations. In societies like Chamula, where oral tradition is still a central tool of knowledge and socialization, stories define and legitimize a culturally sanctioned reality and instill essential values and desir-

able behaviors. The goal of narratives is to shape a general definition of reality and moral behavior that people will share, just as they share a common language. It is possible, however, that a more microscopic analysis of the stories might uncover differences in men's and women's versions.

3.   The stories narrated by women appear to be fragmentary in comparison with those collected by Gossen from male informants. It is possible that, as Chamula men say, men are more experienced storytellers than women. The oral narratives in my corpus were elicited from women whom I interviewed because of specific characteristics of their activities or life experiences, not for their storytelling ability. Therefore, I may not have dealt with women who have recognized talents in this area. It is important to stress that although the stories presented here may appear fragmentary, most Chamula women are familiar with the stories, their ideas, and the unfolding of the plots.

4.   For example, Brandes (1981); Paz (1959); Shore (1981); and Taggart (1983).

5.   Sun and Moon deities are recognized everywhere in the Chiapas highlands as Our Father and Our Mother, but in the other communities they are not the main deities. The ancestors, *totilme'il* (fathers-mothers) in Zinacantán and *me'tiktatik* (mothers-fathers) in Amatenango, are at the center of the pantheon in these communities. In both Zinacantán and Amatenango, the ancestors were men endowed with superior powers, who destroyed monsters and enemies of the people. They now abide inside the surrounding hills, with their wives, who live in different "female" mountains (Vogt 1969:299). The story of the birth of the Sun from the Moon and their ascendance to the sky is common everywhere in the highlands. In Amatenango, the Sun, Our Father, behaves like a caring and punishing father; the Moon, Our Mother, fights with her son to prevent his wrath and thus protects humankind (Nash 1985:201). In Chenalhó, the Sun is an all-beneficent deity that helps his children, and the Moon is considered a blessing in her identity as a lake (Guiteras-Holmes 1961:292). In this community, however, male and female principles are epitomized by a Sun/Earth duality; the supreme force of the universe is not the Sun, but the Earth, Our Mother. The Sun dispels night and darkness and thus fights the Earth's evil creatures, who threaten human life. The Moon also protects her children, but because her light is much weaker, she cannot completely ward off the forces of evil (Guiteras-Holmes 1961:287).

6.   For an interesting discussion on how the incorporation of European ideas has dichotomized ambiguous characters into more rigid, unidimensional ones, see Taggart (1983) and Hunt (1977).

7.   The Nahuat of Taggart's study also identify men with the sun, heat, and light, and women with the moon, cold, and dark. While Chamulas emphasize women's weakness as a result of their being "cold," Nahuat people underscore women's association with the "dark" (i.e. their dubious moral character and their ability to undermine the moral order (Taggart 1983:176)). Everywhere in the highlands of Chiapas, men are conceived to have superior heat and its associated qualities. Women are defined as "cold," but their association with the Earth makes them powerful: they can "tame" or "cool" objects that are connected with male heat such as bulls and guns (Bricker 1973:10; Guiteras-Holmes 1961:55). In Amatenango, water used to wash women's genitals is considered to be so cold that it is used to cure snake bites (Nash 1985:272).

8.   Throughout this work, I have rendered the Tzotzil word *pukuj* as demon. *Pukujetik* are the evil supernaturals most frequently mentioned in Chamula. They are described as black and hairy creatures that live in caves and the passages of the underworld. A *pukuj*

taught the first people how to have sex and to this day continues to kidnap and rape women. These evil beings are also responsible for killing the Sun/Christ since they represent the forces of darkness that the Sun/Christ tried to crush (Gossen 1974; Blaffer 1972).

9.   Taggart (1983:175ff.) discusses Nahuat stories of the creation of human beings in similar terms. The fact that the stories place Adam before Eve, who was created for his sake, expresses the general primacy of men. Taggart finds that the stories from Huitzilán— a town where women have a more submissive position in the family—portray Eve as suspicious, sexually voracious and morally weaker than Adam. This depiction legitimizes male control over women. In Yaonáhuac, where women have more influence in family affairs, Eve appears in a different light. She does not appear as deviant or dangerous to the social order.

10.   These stories are not analyzed in detail here because they deal only tangentially with male and female interaction.

11.   Blaffer (1972) notes that *jik'al* stories, which are widely known in Zinacantán, link cowardice and vulnerability with women, and courage and strength with men. These versions depict the *jik'al* as a symbol of male hypersexuality: he has a very long penis with which he not only rapes women but kills them; the locus of men's power and women's vulnerability is pinpointed. In one version, it is not the woman's child who saves her, but a passing hunter. In another version, two men are traveling together and confront the *jik'al*, who has abducted a girl and carries her rolled up in a straw mat. The most courageous man saves the beautiful girl and marries her. Thus, brave men protect and save women and are rewarded for their actions. There are other *jik'al* stories, however, in which the repugnant creature approaches a group of women who then throw scalding soup on him (Laughlin, personal communication). Perhaps stories such as the latter intend to call attention to the collective strength of women.

12.   A similar idea prevails in neighboring San Pedro Chenalhó, where the Earth is the giver of all life (animal, human, and plant) but is also the grave. The Earth is a wrathful female deity, associated with the wilderness of forests, caves, and sinkholes. Pedranos also establish a connection between the Earth and cultivated fields and houses: before planting or building a house, they propitiate the Earth deity so as not to provoke her destructive wrath. She manipulates cosmic forces (earthquakes, rain, fire, and wind) to punish her children (Guiteras-Holmes 1961:289).

13.   In a collection of stories from Yucatán (Pachecho Cruz 1947), the Xtabai appears as a beautiful woman who comes out at midnight from the ceiba tree, calls to a man, and asks him to go with her. When the man approaches, she disappears. Her apparition is regarded as a bad omen.

14.   The idea of sexually aggressive women who search for husbands is found in other highland communities as well. In Zinacantán, the character is well known (Blaffer 1972:14). A man with an oversexed, powerful wife is considered a potential cuckold. For example, when a cargoholder fails to show up for an important celebration, he is made fun of by the blackmen impersonators; they proclaim in public that he has an oversexed wife who keeps him busy at home and, furthermore, that she lies on top of him (i.e. a reversal of the sexual and, by association, the power positions of men and women (Blaffer 1972:106). Everywhere in the highlands, women are seen as posing a threat to the virility of men. In Amatenango, a woman who steps over a man's feet or clothing is believed to affect his virility (Nash 1985:272; see also Tax 1966:305; Blaffer 1972:105; and Guiteras-Holmes

1961:203). Ideas of women's insatiable sexuality are common also in Nahuat stories (Taggart 1983).

15. Nahuat stories also establish an explicit connection between women, sexuality and the bounty of the Earth. Women often appear as snakes; they bestow riches on men who find them in the forest and have sexual contact with them. Their power is ambivalent, though, for it may become a threat to the moral system. The relationship between the fertility of crops and that of humans is stated explicitly by Nahuat people when they say that a woman's vagina is her husband's milpa, and pubic hairs are the plants that grow in the milpa (Taggart 1983:59, 171).

16. In Chenalhó, the Earth Lord's daughter is called *xob* and is considered to be a virgin, like the Moon. More importantly, she is the spirit of corn. The relationship of women to the fertility of crops is revealed in several practices. Women may be asked to step three times over the basket where the grains of seed corn are kept; this practice is said to protect the harvest. Also, a wife places her comb and spindle in the basket, sometimes twirling the spindle among the grains as if spinning corn (Guiteras-Holmes 1961:43). In Chenalhó, the *anjel* is a male force who cares for the milpas. The *anjel*, however, is subservient to the female Earth and more limited in power (Guiteras-Holmes 1961:291). Zinacantecos also perceive the Earth as a powerful deity in a "tame" form, either as the daughter of the *anjel* or of the Earth Lord (these figures are sometimes considered different aspects of the same deity and sometimes as separate deities) (Laughlin 1977:165, 238). In Amatenango, the spirits that inhabit springs and caves are petitioned for fertility; some springs are thought to have a female spirit (Nash 1985:12).

5

The Other Eye, the Other Side of One's Face
Courtship and Marriage

The ritual of petitioning for a wife in Chamula lasts only a few weeks, but it is a complicated affair.[1] The process unfolds in regulated stages, from the moment the young man decides he wants to marry a young woman, to the time when she finally leaves her parental home to go with him.[2] Each stage contains rich symbolic information on the interaction between men and women, usually in terms of ideals. By examining the social contexts and related behaviors of specific cases, one can piece together a dynamic picture of courtship. Although men appear to dominate the process—and often do—women are able to maneuver within a range of possibilities to gain leverage and control over their own lives.

Marriage establishes ties, not only between bride and groom, but also between their families. According to common Chamula wisdom, if the couple's parents become friendly with one another and advise their children well, the marriage is more likely to succeed. In Chamula, as in other indigenous communities of Highland Chiapas, marriage is a formal arrangement between patrilineal groups in which the groom's group directly petitions the bride's group for her hand. The bride is then transferred from her father's household to that of her in-laws. This procedure may have survived from an earlier time when patrilineages were stronger. Today, patrilineal groups have been weakened substantially by several factors, the most important being the loss of their land base. As population increases and a growing number of men depend on tenant farming or wage labor for their livelihood, patrilineages break down; however, some of the organizational and ideological aspects of the patrilineal system may remain.

In an interesting, longitudinal study of stratification in Zinacantán, Collier (1989) finds that dramatic transformations in marriage patterns take place as the nature of the local stratification system changes in response to general trends in the Mexican economy. In the 1950s, as a result of agrarian reform favoring labor intensive milpa production, Zinacantecos developed a long and expensive system of courtship to control the labor of their offspring. This bridewealth system replaced an earlier system of brideservice. In the bridewealth system, a young man became indebted to his father, who financed the marriage gifts. Thus, a father acquired rights over his son's labor for several years. The economic boom of the 1970s, however, opened construction jobs at a time when rapid population growth was taxing the ability of agriculture to support the community. Many Zinacantecos became semi-proletarian workers. Wage work enabled a young man to gain economic independence from his father. Soon, elopements became the preferred route to marriage, and the system of indebtedness was undermined. A young man today spends a smaller amount of money to appease his bride's family following elopement than he would have spent in a costly courtship.

More information from Zinacantán is needed to assess whether this transformation in marriage patterns, which also gives women more choice in selecting a mate, leads to other behaviors that could further undermine patrilineal groups, such as changes in residence patterns and a stronger bilateral orientation. If, indeed, these changes are taking place, the lives of Zinacanteco women unquestionably will be affected. Women who marry into a group of patrilineally related men appear, at least in the beginning, as outsiders, and the authority of husbands is reinforced by the support of male relatives living close by. In nuclear, bilateral families, women tend to be more independent, and the authority of men diminishes as both husband and wife get moral support from their families. Nash (1985:55), for example, finds that young women in Amatenango used to learn pottery-making from their husband's mother. Mother-in-law and daughter-in-law worked as a team. Now women marry at a later age and learn work skills from their own mothers. A woman often insists on living close to her mother so that the two can continue working together. Elopements are increasingly common in this community as well (Nash in press). Furthermore, the monetization of the "brideprice" that is paid to the bride's family after an elopement is transforming the symbolic view of women as treasures toward a view of women as commodities.[3]

The case of Chamula contrasts with the patterns I describe above. Chamula men have depended on wage work for many decades. At the time of my research in the 1980s, however, the economic independence of young men from their fathers had not led to a significant increase in elopements. Although the groom pays for all the courtship and wedding expenses himself, the form of the petition process has remained basically unchanged for the past 30 years. Chamulas have always been poorer than their neighbors, and Chamula courtship today is much shorter than the "traditional" Zinacanteco courtship. Modern Chamula courtship, however, remains about the same length as courtship during the previous generation. Virilocality is still the preferred form of residence, as it was for the previous generation. Thus, even though patrilineages in Chamula have no strong material bases, many aspects of a patrifocal ideology linger on and are reflected in the process of obtaining a wife.

In addition to the marriage petition, this chapter also covers the process of separation and reconciliation, elopements, and the monetization of the marriage transaction.

JAK'OL: THE MARRIAGE PETITION

The Beginning of Courtship

When a young man reaches 17 or 18, he may initiate a courtship.[4] A young woman is considered to be ready for marriage at roughly the same age, although she may be one or two years younger or older. Most Chamulas marry between the ages of 15 and 18. When a young man notices an attractive, nicely dressed, young woman, he observes her at a distance to make sure that her behavior is appropriate—that is, she does not laugh excessively, talk to men, or walk alone. It is important that no men meet her outside of her house when she fetches water, carries firewood or cares for her sheep. Once he decides that this woman suits him, the young man communicates his choice to his parents.

Although a young man is not permitted to talk to a potential mate—especially outside of her home, on the trails, or in the pasture—the young woman may signal that she likes him by looking at him and smiling when he is watching her. In this way, he has some assurance that she will accept him when he asks for her hand. If their parents are relatives or friends, some conversation may take place between the young people when they accompany their parents on visits. Since most marriages occur within the limits of the hamlet, the young woman often knows or has seen her suitor, but normally little or no interaction has taken place between them.

The young man's father and mother may suggest a match to their son—usually the daughter of a friend or a relative. In this situation, the man's parents play a more active role in the courtship. They talk to the parents of the potential bride and present them with gifts of food and liquor in order to show interest in their daughter and to reinforce the bonds that already exist between the families. The man's parents try to convince the woman's parents that their son is a worthy candidate. The woman's parents, on the other hand, do not actively encourage the courtship.

On occasion, the young woman's parents take the initiative, and in a few instances a woman has directly initiated courtship. Significantly, in two cases in which the young women took the initiative, the young men felt that their role had been preempted. A man is expected to "conquer" a woman either by talking to her on the road or through a formal petition. Chamulas say that the woman who offers herself like a gift to a man is worthless:

> Well the girl liked me, let's say. She talked to my sisters when they were watching the sheep.
>
> "Oh, your brother is very nice," she said.
> "Do you want to marry him?" my sisters asked.
> "If he wants me, I'll marry him," she said.
> Then my sisters told me, and I went to look for her. I embraced her. She liked it, she smiled.
>
> "How much do you want me to pay for you?" I asked her.
> "I want 500 pesos [$4.00]," she said. "Let's run away to hot country," she said. "Just give 500 to my grandmother" [her parents were dead].
> "Well, but 500 is too expensive," I said. [It really was very inexpensive since Xalik paid 3000 pesos ($24.00), in addition to brideprice goods, when he acquired his wife the traditional way.]
> "Well, then only 200 [$1.60]," she said.
>
> She came to my house and offered sodas to my parents. She thought we would go to petition for her. She got very angry when I went to ask for Vel's hand and married her instead. (Xalik C40)

The high brideprice and the man's great effort to acquire a wife symbolize the bride's value. Furthermore, the man who accepts a woman who has offered herself to him is himself considered useless, for he is seen as unable to sustain the effort and expense of getting a wife in the traditional way. A worthy man works hard and earns money to pay for his wife, and a valuable woman waits for a suitor to ask for her hand.

The young man, under his parents' supervision, likes to be in charge of the situation. With two liters of liquor and some meat, he begs his parents to help him with the petition. He lets them know that he has selected a wife. The parents ask if he has enough money for the petition, and he reports on the state of his savings. Next, they tell him to recruit additional petitioners, preferably people who will speak forcefully and will not tire or give up easily. From this moment on, the young man submits to his parents' advice regarding the traditional way to ask for a wife. Even though he makes the initial decision to seek a particular woman's hand and pays all the expenses, his parents control the petition process.[5]

The young man presents the liquor and gift of meat to his parents to thank them for their promise of help. With the gifts in their hands, the parents pray, addressing Our Father the Sun/Christ, San Juan, the Holy Earth, and many saints. They tell the deities of their intention to ask for the woman's hand and remind them that this action fulfills the wishes of Our Father, who established that people should marry and that courtship should take place through petition. The prayer invokes tradition by stating that the very first people married through petition, and therefore it is the proper way for courtship to proceed. Finally, the parents plead with the deities to precede them to the young woman's house and to convince her and her parents to accept their son. The deities are also asked for protection against violence from the woman's father.

After praying the parents thank their son for his gift, and all family members who reside in the house partake of the liquor and meat. The parents suggest candidates to be the other petitioners, frequently one of the father's brothers and his spouse, either set of grandparents, or relatives of the mother. Usually a pair, husband and wife, are recruited as petitioners. For purposes of this discussion, I assume the petitioners are the man's uncle and aunt.

During the next day or two, the young man, accompanied by his parents, visits the prospective petitioners. He brings two or three liters of liquor and meat as gifts. The parents speak on behalf of their son. Once a couple agrees to help, the young man presents them with the gifts. The uncle prays by the hearth, holding the liquor in his hands: he appeals to Our Father, Our Mother, and the saints to intercede on his nephew's behalf and to persuade the young woman and her parents to accept her suitor. Then everyone drinks in order of rank: the male petitioners (uncle and father); the female petitioners (aunt and mother); and, finally, the children.

Father, mother, uncle, and aunt accompany the hopeful groom to church that same afternoon or the following day. They place candles at the feet of Our Mother the Moon/Virgin (me' vinajel); Our Mother Rosario; San Juan; San Mateo; Our Father in Heaven; Our Mother Santa Rosa; and Our Mother Asunción. The young man fastens the candles to the floor and lights them in the same order. Then, the party stands in front of Our Mother the Moon/Virgin, and everyone but the young man prays.

The prayers are directed mainly to Our Mother the Moon/Virgin. Chamulas believe that the prospective bride is the earthly representative of Our Mother, and therefore Our Mother has influence over her. Our Mother is asked to go to the young woman's house and convince her to accept the suitor. She is asked to tie the hands and feet of both the woman and her parents so that they do not respond violently to the petition and to cover their mouths so that they do not insult the petitioners. Then, the group addresses San Juan, the patron saint of Chamula. They tell him that they are striving to follow Chamula tradition by marrying their own kind, instead of joining with people from different lands. At the end of the prayer, the protection of Our Father, Our Mother, and the saints is invoked against the wrath of the woman's parents.

Following the prayers, the petitioners go to the young man's house and drink liquor to become "heated" and to gather courage to start the *jak'ol* or formal marriage petition. On the way to the woman's house, the young man carries two more liters of liquor to offer the petitioners so that their words may be strong.

In the above description, the young man does not initiate courtship until he is able to earn a living. Economically, he is an adult, but socially, until he has a wife, he cannot fulfill his obligations as an adult member of society. He must convince both his parents and the young woman's parents that he is capable of supporting a family. He demonstrates that he is a hard worker through his ability to obtain the money needed for the marriage petition. Although formally his parents are petitioning for the wife, who in the past would have become part of their economic unit, in reality the young man is economically independent. The newly married couple moves into the house of the groom's parents but usually remains there only a year or two.

The young man is guided through the petition process by his parents. He pays respect to the older generation, who knows how to do things properly; in so doing, he upholds the values of his people. As the prayers suggest, he follows the example of the first Chamula fathers and mothers. An interesting aspect of the prayers is the invocation for protection against violent reaction by the woman and her parents. This invocation reveals the importance of acquiring a wife in Chamula society. The young man, his parents, and his petitioners must humble themselves and patiently withstand insults and even blows. The potential wife-givers appear powerful. Although the prayers repeatedly mention the woman's parents, especially her father, they also indicate that the young woman has a choice in the matter. She may take an active part in insulting and even striking the petitioners, and her response is feared. From this perspective, she is not as passive as the formal aspects of the marriage petition may suggest.

The petition at the bride's house. The young man does not accompany the petitioners all the way to the woman's house, but hides nearby. Upon arriving at the woman's home, the rest of the group greet her father first:

> "Good evening, older brother, are you there?" ask the petition-
> ers.
> "Yes, I am here. What is your business?" asks the woman's fa-
> ther.
> "Nothing, I just came to visit you and your gift, the fruit of your
> efforts," a petitioner replies.

At this point the group kneels and begins to pray. The father immediately realizes the visitors' intentions and closes the door. The petitioners are forced to remain outside, but within the house, the woman's family listens to their prayers as they address her parents.

The petitioner tells the parents that the group has come to talk to them about their "gift," their "travail" (i.e., their daughter), who was bestowed on them by the Mother of Heaven. The petitioners humble themselves. They acknowledge that they have come on an errand that brings headache and pain but declare that the woman's parents have the responsibility to marry off their daughter at the feet of the great San Juan and not to let her go to a distant land. The woman should not die in her parents' house, the group contends, rather she should join a different household. They reiterate that Our Father and Our Mother created and gave this daughter to her parents; therefore, they assert, she will give in to the request, little by little, without coercion:

> Our hearts will not be satisfied,
> our blood will not be satisfied,
>
> until we father them together,
> until we mother them together,
>
> until they marry,
> until they join,
>
> our children,
> our offspring... (Xalik, from Gossen's files)

Inside the house the young woman, her parents, and her siblings listen, and when the group has finished, her father responds. At first, he attempts to discourage the petitioners by denying he has a daughter or by claiming his daughter is already married; he may threaten the petitioners to see if they will leave.[6] Frequently, the woman's parents try to sneak out the back door so that the man's party will think no one is at home and leave. For this reason, the man seeks strong petitioners who will persist no matter how difficult the task. The petitioners may wait for hours until the woman's father returns from work, or they may arrive in the early morning before he leaves. Petitioners return to repeat the same words as many times as necessary—eight, ten, twelve times—in order to wear down the resistance of the woman's family. They always reply in formal, respectful language to whatever objections her family raises. Even when treated roughly, they must continue in the same calm manner, constantly asking forgiveness for the inconveniences and pain their words cause.

I have come to ask you,
I have come to knock at your door,
for your gift,
your travail.

I have come to give you a headache,
I have come to give you a heartache.

I have come kneeling,
I have come bowing low,

with my dog [the young man],
with my pig,
with my lazy one,
with my indolent one... (Xalik, from Gossen's files)

The woman's parents raise objections about both the man's behavior and that of their daughter. They may claim that the man is a drunkard, that he does not know how to work, that he has other women, or that he is well known for his bad temper. The petitioners must answer all these accusations with poise, arguing that he does not have other women, that he is learning to work with his father, that he will mature and change once he has a wife, and so forth. Often, the woman's parents try to discourage the petitioners by pointing out the undesirable qualities of their daughter. They tell the petitioners she is lazy and does not possess the skills of a housewife. The petitioners reply:

Well, she will grow up,
she will get her spirit,
she is young yet,
she is little yet.

Look, we grew up the same way,
we matured the same way,
we were also little,
but our spirit finally came to us,

she will get her spirit,
little by little,
just the way we got ours,
just the way we learned how to work. (Loxa C32)

Persistence sometimes works. After several sessions of prayers, with petitioners kneeling outside her house for hours, twice a day in some hamlets, the woman and her parents accept the petition. On occasion the parents alone accept. They then attempt to obtain their daughter's cooperation, or they may force her into the marriage.

If the woman or her parents do not like the young man, they refuse him. They tell him not to continue spending his money, or they scold the petitioners. The man may look for another bride immediately and start the process over. If he persists after the woman and her parents have clearly rejected him, her family has recourse to the court and may ask the president to stop the petition. Sometimes the man ceases the petition process because he loses interest or cannot afford to continue.

A suitor may be refused for a number of reasons. If he lives in another hamlet, the parents may object on the basis that they want their daughter to live nearby. Sometimes the woman is too young, or the man is too old. A man who already has children is likely to be rejected by the woman.

Accepting the words. The more frequently the petitioners go to the woman's house with their words and prayers, the more money the young man must spend on offerings of food and liquor. They may go less often (e.g., every two days) to press their cause for fear that more frequent visits will increase the family's anger and provoke yet more scolding. But in the hamlet of Tzajal Vitz, petitioners go twice a day, at sunrise and sunset. Each time, the woman's parents insist that no woman is there and reiterate that the petitioners have been told to seek a bride elsewhere; the group replies that they know the couple has a daughter. The petitioners' task is especially difficult. Not only must they stay calm and answer correctly, but they must go often, praying and speaking for a long time on each occasion, despite rain, intense cold, and mud.

When the woman and her parents finally accept the petition, they open the door and invite the group, including the young man, to enter. The man's party offers two liters of liquor as a gift, and the petitioners thank the parents for accepting their plea. All parties drink together in the following order: the young woman's father, her mother, the young man's uncle, his father, his aunt, his mother, himself and, finally, his bride. The woman's parents question the man, who listens thoughtfully. Is he happy that he will marry their daughter? Is it true that he has no other woman? Will he support her? Will he refrain from scolding and beating her? Will he be nice to her? Will he provide the food she needs? He bows and responds that he will treat her well, that he does not like to drink (or will not drink anymore), and that he is a hard worker. The woman's parents set a date for the blessing ceremony (*ak' riox*).

Decision making in the young woman's house. What occurs in the woman's house during the petition process? How does the family reach a decision? The scenario differs and depends primarily on the relative power of husband and wife, but also on how much the daughter is allowed to influence her parents' decision.[7]

Sometimes the parents make the decision and then try to persuade their daughter to accept it. Maruch's parents told her that so many petitioners had come already, and others would only continue to come. They suggested she marry her current suitor because he lived nearby, and they would be able to visit her frequently to see if she were happy and if her husband were kind to her. They promised to defend her if her husband were to mistreat her. They also argued that if she were to marry, she would no longer have to go to the hot country with her father; her suffering there would be over. Convinced by these arguments, Maruch accepted.

Dominga's case was similar to that of Maruch. Many suitors came to her door, but she did not like any of them. When they came, she always told her parents, "If you will prepare his food and sleep with him, then accept him, because I will not!" Her parents had to face the petitioners and tell them that their daughter did not approve of the suitor. One day they got fed up with petitioners coming and going, and praying for hours in front of their house. They scolded Dominga because she would not accept anyone; they were afraid that sooner or later one of the angry, rejected men would use witchcraft to afflict them with a disease. Finally, Dominga's mother accepted a suitor for her on condition that the pair wait six months to marry so that her daughter could get used to the idea (Dominga's father had died in the meantime).

In other cases, the woman's father alone makes the decision and proves his power by forcing his daughter to marry. Dominga's husband, for example, told each of his daughters that he would sell her before she could find her own husband and bring shame to her family. Frequently, a father tells his daughter that since he has chosen a husband for her, she can count on him to defend her should her husband scold her constantly or beat her. The father might send his son-in-law to jail or physically beat him. If the young woman embarrasses her parents by choosing her own mate, however, the father threatens to do nothing should her husband makes her miserable. The mother may agree with her husband, but a despotic father often abuses his wife; therefore, she generally sides with her daughter.

The gifts or brideprice also influence decisions. Sometimes money is given in addition to the goods of the brideprice. The money is in lieu of the year or two of work that the new husband is supposed to give his father-in-law following the marriage. Many Chamula parents are extremely poor, and occasionally they give their daughters away for the liquor, good food, and money that they receive from the marriage.

The woman's parents may accept liquor at the insistence of a man who comes to ask for their daughter's hand. The parents may be under the influence of alcohol or in the midst of a seemingly innocent conversation, but once they accept the liquor, they have accepted the petition. Their daughter must marry the man even though she may not have known she was being petitioned. Antel was told by her parents that, in her absence, they had accepted a liquor gift because the petitioners continued to petition for her "as if they had no ears to hear refusals." Antel angrily told her parents she believed that the truth was they no longer wanted to support her. She said she would leave and support herself. Nevertheless, she had to marry the suitor.

Tumin's parents accepted a petition because her suitor told them he had already talked to her and made a deal with her along the path. They believed him and received his liquor to legitimize the situation and to avoid being shamed by their daughter's behavior. Tumin, however, insisted she had not spoken to him. With the support of her aunt and grandmother, she summoned both her parents and the man to court. He confessed he had lied; she had scolded him but had not made a deal with him. Tumin's parents did not force her to marry him. But according to Tumin, the man was a witch and later "threw" a disease upon her that almost killed her.

Women are expected to refuse their suitors. Frequently a woman cries and gets angry at her parents when they accept a petition.[8] According to Lukax, an experienced father of several daughters, a young woman never explicitly says that she wants to marry a particular young man, but when her parents ask her whether she likes a suitor, she remains quiet and thoughtful. By not rejecting him loudly, she indicates her acceptance of him.

Often when the petition finally is accepted and the young man enters the house with his petitioners, the woman behaves angrily. Her parents insist that she drink the liquor, but she responds by covering her mouth with her shawl. If her parents remove the shawl, she throws the liquor away.

> "Drink your soda," the parents order.
> "No, I don't want any of your soda. I can buy my own," she retorts.
> "Don't behave like that, you can't do what you want," they tell her. "We brought you up until you grew tall, until you talked. If you don't accept willingly, go away, out!" (Manvel C47)

Finally, the woman takes the liquor, but she cries and demonstrates her dissent. This type of behavior is almost expected from the moment the petition is accepted. A woman who has been taught to avoid any sign of interest in men and to respond aggressively when men attempt to talk to her on the road acts rebelliously, sometimes even violently, toward the petitioners. Even should she approve of her suitor, she does not openly express her wish to marry lest her enthusiasm reveal that she already has spoken with him.

When Loxa was 11 years old, the first petitioners came to ask for her hand. They entered the house and began to pray by the hearth. Loxa's father insisted that she was too young to marry, but the petitioners continued to pray and talk. Loxa took matters into her own hands and hit the man's parents with a stick saying, "What do you want from me? Do you really think that I can support your son?" The parents were kneeling when she hit them, and they fell over. They left the house, but just outside the door, they began to pray again:

> Well then, Our Lord,
> well then, Holy Father,
> her foot has descended [on us],
> her hand has descended [on us].
>
> Well, Our Lord, Holy Father,
> make her get it into her head,
> make her get it into her heart,
>
> may she decide in her head,
> may she decide in her heart,
>
> that one cannot live alone,
> that one cannot be alone,
>
> with only one side of the face,
> with only one eye.
>
> Because it is you who left it thus,
> it is you who decided,
>
> that there should be two eyes,
> that there should be two sides in a face,
>
> of our gifts,
> of our travails. (Loxa C32)

Thus, although men appear to be in charge of the formal petition, the prospective bride frequently has an important say in the decision. Today women have more income potential, which gives them more leverage in marriage decisions than in the past. Although women have always had income from the sale of firewood, chickens, eggs, and woven goods to their neighbors from Chenalhó and Tenejapa, today their products are in demand by the Ladino population and tourists.

Parents, especially fathers, still have a great deal of power over their daughters, however, and a woman may be "sold" against her will. Aware of the difficulties that wives may experience, a mother frequently sides with the daughter and pressures her husband to leave their child alone. In extreme cases, daughters may threaten to kill themselves or flee if their parents pressure them to marry. Sooner or later a woman must marry; if she does not strongly reject the suitor, her parents talk her into the marriage.

Without exception, the married women who I interviewed said that they were not interested in marrying when young. They liked being relatively free and did not want to take on the responsibilities of a wife and mother. Chamula girls who have reached a marriageable age resist marriage with arguments that men frequently scold and beat their wives and that they restrict their wives' mobility and activities. When in a group, however, these young women compare the qualities and behavior of different marriageable men. Moreover, I saw several young women looking with interest when they encountered a young man on the path. Therefore, a woman's insistent rejection of men seems more a performance to divert community criticism than an actual disinterest in men. To be accused of actively seeking a husband is a major transgression for a young woman in Chamula. Trained to respond aggressively to men's propositions, a woman is almost expected to respond with anger when a man is finally accepted.

Young women suffer a great deal of anxiety concerning marriage. They know that early marriage is stressful because they must live for some time with their husband's parents, particularly as brideservice becomes less common and of shorter duration. In the best situation, the woman knows she will have to work extremely hard to prove her worth, and in the worst case, she may face constant battles with her in-laws over different ways of doing things. Women also fear marrying a heavy drinker. They believe that such marriages lead inevitably to poverty and probably to abuse. In Tzajal Vitz, a hamlet of about 150 families, only a few marriageable men were considered potentially good partners. These young men worked hard and did not drink. Several young women expressed the hope that one of these young men would petition for them!

The prayers of the marriage petition always emphasize the companionship of husband and wife. This companionship is seen to be basic, as natural as the fact that a face has "two eyes and two sides." The prayers stress egalitarianism, complementarity, and sharing; a person alone, without a spouse, is truly an incomplete person.

Ak' riox: The Blessing Ceremony

The blessing ceremony (*ak' riox*) precedes delivery of the bridal gift. It is called "the small one" because only some of the woman's relatives attend and there are fewer gifts than in the *ochel ta na*, the final ceremony of the petition. The *ochel ta na* is called "the big one" since many of the woman's relatives gather to receive the gifts brought by the groom.

On the day the groom is accepted, the bride's father sets a date and time for the blessing ceremony. He announces that should the groom and his party arrive late, the engagement will be broken. The petitioners arrive on time, and several assistants help the groom carry the gifts: 12 liters of liquor, beer, four crates of sodas, and cigarettes. The bride's family opens the door, and the two groups align themselves on either side of the entrance. The bride's family remains indoors; the groom's group stands outside. Some people claim that only the men pray and that the women stand silently behind their husbands. Others say that both the fathers and mothers of the couple pray.

The *ak' riox* prayer confirms the commitment of both families to the marriage. It restates Our Father's desire for his children to be complete through the taking of a spouse. The prayer also emphasizes the continuity of Chamula tradition; the couple will be wed at the feet of the great patron saint San Juan in the same manner as the first Chamula fathers and mothers. The ancestors of both families are called to share in the sacred liquor that will bless the married couple. This address to the ancestors differentiates the *ak' riox* prayer from the other prayers of the marriage petition.

> Those of the white hair,
> those of the white corn silks,
> our first fathers,
> our first mothers,
>
> may they still come to share,
> may they still come to enjoy,
> the water from heaven [liquor],
> the grace from heaven.
>
> May it not be only we who share it,
> may it not be only we who enjoy it,
> ancient father,
> ancient mother! (Xalik from Gossen's files)

Immediately following the prayer, everyone drinks, the groom's representatives still standing outside the door. This prayer affirms that an arrangement has taken place that will join the two families, including the ancestors on both sides. The ancestors have contributed to the marriage both by maintaining a tradition and by bequeathing land and other resources.

After this prayer, the groom and his family enter the house, where chairs are set out for them. The bride's father distributes the liquor and cigarettes among all present. The young man pours liquor for everyone. The men are served first, in order: the bride's father, the groom's uncle, and the groom's father. The women are served next, as follows: the bride's mother, the groom's aunt, and the groom's mother. The bride and groom do not drink. The couple's fathers converse in one part of the room and their mothers in another; the bride sits on the ground with the women. Once again, the groom serves liquor to everyone. When the liquor is consumed, the young man's father discusses the date for the *ochel ta na.*

Ochel ta na: The House-entering Ceremony

In preparation for the house-entering ceremony (*ochel ta na*), the culmination of courtship, the groom's father and the petitioners advise him on the purchase of the food (*matanal*) for the brideprice. The *matanal* may consist of a large basket of bread, two packages of dark sugar, 100 bananas, 100 oranges, a *garrafón* of liquor (approximately 20 liters), four to six crates of soda, five crates of beer, two dozen cigars, one kilogram of chocolate, one kilogram of coffee, one package of cigarettes, and a cloth napkin to cover the bread. The groom also buys about 12 kilograms of fresh meat over half of which he takes to the bride's house; the remainder is a gift for his own family. He also buys some dried beef. These quantities vary depending on the economic situation of the young man.

The groom enlists the help of his immediate family to carry the gifts. Brothers, sisters, cousins, and their spouses all help, but the groom must carry the most important and heaviest gift, the liquor. His parents and the other petitioners do not usually carry the food, but this practice varies.

On the Sunday of the *ochel ta na*, the groom, the male members of his immediate family, and the male petitioners gather at his house to count, assemble, and pack the gifts. The older men instruct the groom and the other young men on arranging and packing the goods. Meanwhile, the women in the family prepare a large stack of tortillas to be eaten when the groom's party returns from the bride's house (Vogt 1970, personal communication to Gossen). Before the retinue leaves, the items and their prices are carefully recorded. This step is crucial, for if there are problems in the first months of marriage, and the couple separates permanently, the man will ask that the monetary value of the brideprice be returned to him so that he can petition for another woman.

The groom's party arrives at the bride's house at the prearranged time. The group kneels three times on the patio and repeats the "*ak' riox*" prayer, some say, three times. The ceremony lasts about an hour during which the groom's helpers must not put down the gifts they bear on their backs. The groom's group remains outside the door, the bride's group inside, as all parties pray in unison and exchange ritual drinks. When the prayers end, the gifts are brought in. One by one the burden bearers approach the doorway and turn their backs so that both fathers and their helpers may remove the loads. The groom goes first with the big bottle of liquor, followed by the bread, the bananas and oranges, the meat and the sugar, and finally the sodas. One person told me that the gifts are received by the father and uncle of the bride; another said that the woman's father and mother receive them.

The groom's parents, the petitioners and, finally, the groom enter the house on hands and knees, their foreheads touching the earth floor. They thank the father of the bride then lower their heads to the floor once more to thank her mother. The groom, his parents and his petitioners thank the bride's parents for their kindness and for not beating, scolding, or rejecting them. They reassure her parents of the groom's happiness and his desire to be a good husband. The bride's parents request that the group rise from their humble position and go on to say that they and the groom's parents are united as parents-in-law and should sit together. The rest of the groom's party enters. The fathers of the groom and bride sit together; the mothers sit together apart from the men. The wife-givers, the most powerful and prestigious group in the gathering, sit toward the east side of the house, considered the most positive location (Vogt 1970, personal communication to Gossen).

The woman's family serves a meal, usually black beans and tortillas, to all but the groom. This meal is customary, but not required. It is a nice gesture that shows "a kind heart." If the bride's father is generous, he serves two or three liters of liquor from the groom's gift. The groom distributes the liquor to everyone present. First, the men are served as follows: the brides's father, the groom's uncle or other male petitioner, the groom's father, and the rest according to age, including the male children. Next, the women are served in order: the bride's mother, the groom's aunt or female petitioner, the groom's mother, the bride's aunts, and the other women and female children according to age. When all are served, the groom presents another glass of liquor to his father-in-law as a gift, but the latter takes only a sip and passes it on for all present to do the same. Then, a glass is served to the bride and passed in the same manner. A final glass is served to the groom. He drinks exactly half and hands the other half to the bride, who finishes it. Drinking from the same glass expresses the unity established between the families through the marriage. The bride and groom partake from the same glass, in exactly the same proportions, to symbolize the ideal of sharing everything throughout their life together.

When the meal is over, the groom's relatives leave. At the door, both sets of parents again pray, restating their commitment to guide and to care for their newly married children. After his parents leave, the groom serves liquor to everyone in the group, beginning with the bride's father and mother. Everyone drinks two or three of the small glasses, and then the gifts are examined. The bride's parents first count the liters of liquor in the large bottle and then the remaining gifts. Except for the meat, which is a gift for the bride's immediate family, all of the *matanal* is distributed among family and guests. Every relative of the bride who attends the party receives a portion of the gift, even the children.

What does the groom do while the bride's parents count the brideprice? In the hamlet of Nichimtik, the man customarily visits his parents. In Tzajal Vitz, the groom is expected to take care of the bride's relatives, who usually drink a great deal and may need assistance, and to wait on them, serving them anything they want of the food and liquor.

Often the bride's relatives are rude to the groom. They observe him carefully. Should he spill some of the liquor while serving it, they scold him. Should he forget to give liquor to anyone in the room, they scold him. They do not let him rest or sit for an instant, and if he does, they reprimand him again. Sometimes they physically abuse him, as one woman recounted of her sister's wedding:

> My mother got drunk and started scolding Sebastián, my sister's groom. When they counted the gift he had brought, she started saying,
>
> "It wasn't much money that he spent, I can get my daughter back if he doesn't treat her well. If he beats her or scolds her, I will return his money right away. I will make her come back," that is what she was saying.
>
> Then my mother's brother wanted to go outside to relieve himself, but he was drunk and couldn't walk, so he asked my sister's groom to take him out. The old man could not open his trouser zipper.
>
> "Open it, open it!" he yelled. But Sebastián could not open it either.
>
> "It's stuck," he reported worried. "It doesn't open."
>
> So the old man got angry and punched Sebastián's face. Blood started flowing from his nose. Oh, my sister did not say anything, she just laughed. Poor Sebastián was crying, his handkerchief full of blood. The old man had broken his nose. (Veruch C26-34)

Apart from the token half-glass that she ritually takes with the groom, the bride is not supposed to drink that night. She helps her new husband take care of her relatives so that they will not hurt themselves while inebriated. Although some people mention that the bride's parents may be nice to the groom and allow him to sit and rest, in general, this is a hard night for him, left alone with the drunk, aggressive relatives of his new wife.

Around six o'clock in the morning, once some of the relatives have left and the others lie sleeping, the groom goes to the field to get a load of firewood for the bride's parents. The bride cooks tortillas and meat for her parents, her grandparents and her husband. The groom acts embarrassed when the bride hands him his portion and often does not eat it; the bride also reacts shyly when she receives her portion.

The groom remains at the bride's house anywhere from three or four days to a year, depending on the arrangement with the bride's parents. Whatever the length of his stay, the groom is supposed to work with his father-in-law, hoeing, planting, weeding, and harvesting the milpa, fetching firewood, and so forth. Today the groom commonly negotiates a sum of money, which he pays his father-in-law in lieu of service. Where additional labor is necessary to plant the land, brideservice makes sense, but since most lands in Chamula are small and men work for a wage several months of the year, monetary compensation may be a more practical solution.

Many Chamula men speak of the discomfort and embarrassment they experience while residing with their in-laws. Accustomed to their independence, young men resent living and working under a father-in-law's supervision. Men feel that the woman gains power within the marriage because of support from her parents, and thus she does not obey her husband as she would if the couple lived at his parents' house or in a house of their own. One man said that when he lived with his wife's parents, they or his wife herself often told him, "If you don't like it, leave!" Living with in-laws, then, seems to limit the young husband's authority over his wife.

The couple sleeps in the same room as the woman's parents and siblings. Therefore, the marriage is never consummated the night of the *ochel ta na* and sometimes not until the couple move to the husband's house. In many cases, the young man, who has spent much money to acquire a wife, leaves a day or two after the wedding for the plantations in order to earn money to pay his marriage debts. Not infrequently, he leaves his new wife, still a virgin, at her parents' house. Most Chamula women say that at the beginning of married life, they were embarrassed and frightened at the prospect of sex, but after a few weeks, they learned to enjoy it.

When the pair leave for the groom's house, the bride's father always instructs the new husband to be good to his daughter, to work hard, and not to beat her. He tells his son-in-law that he will be observing the young man's actions and will take his daughter back if she is unhappy. He also tells the groom to instruct the bride as to his preferences. The bride's mother advises her to weave the wool for her husband's clothes, to have his food ready when he returns from work, and so forth. Every so often, the couple visits the bride's parents, bringing liquor and food gifts. Occasionally they sleep at her parents' place.

The preceding pages reveal that a wife is seen as precious, someone for whom great expense and ordeals are demanded. The groom and his petitioners brave the weather and spend long hours waiting for the woman's parents to return home or to acknowledge their petition. The groom must withstand abuse and humiliation from the woman's relatives the night of the *ochel ta na*. Courtship involves a great deal of effort and courage on the part of the groom—attributes considered important in a man. Through his gifts, perseverance, and humility, the young man proves he is deserving of a wife. He learns that obtaining a wife is an exacting task and that he should try to keep her happy so that she will want to remain with him.

A wife's excellence is symbolically expressed in the *matanal*, the gifts of the brideprice. The liquor, beer, meat, cigarettes, and cigars represent the giving of heat, which stands for life and strength. The fruits, breads, chocolate, dark sugar, and coffee are all considered luxury items, very desirable treats. A Chamula groom lavishes these valuable gifts on his in-laws and the bride's other relatives to recognize his wife's worth and to show his intention to establish good relations with her family.

The woman's household loses a productive member; at this age, a daughter contributes fully to the family's economy. She works in the fields; assists at home; produces clothing for herself, her parents, and her siblings; and frequently makes some income on the side. The brideprice compensates symbolically for the loss of the woman's economic contribution to her family and for their investment in raising her.

The husband is the new beneficiary of his wife's productive and reproductive capabilities. She cooks for him, makes his clothes, and bears his children. She works to help him support their household. The husband's sexual rights are an important component of the marriage transaction. In Tzotzil, sexual intercourse without marriage is called *moton*, a gift, because the man has not acquired the legitimate right to sex through payment of a brideprice.

The prayers and the couple's sharing of liquor from the same glass emphasize marriage as companionship. From the *ochel ta na* on, the couple will support and take care of one another. The idea of spousal companionship is sanctioned by the deities; Our Father the Sun/Christ instituted marriage at the very beginning of human life. Through marriage, Chamulas continue a cherished tradition of their ancestors, namely, to join at the feet of San Juan.

Although a wife is considered precious, an idea clearly portrayed in both the marriage transaction and in some of the narratives presented above, the image that she is acquired through a commercial exchange sometimes gains salience. In the marriage transaction the woman is said to be "sold" and "bought" (in Tzotzil, *chon* and *man*) like any other commodity; the concept that she becomes a man's property when he pays for her adds further tension to the relationship between husband and wife. Therefore, the view of women as companions, of a woman as the other side of a man's face, is distorted.

SEPARATION AND RECONCILIATION

Husbands and wives separate for a variety of reasons. Early in the marriage they may quarrel for a trivial reason. The man may tell his wife to go, or she may decide to leave. If she leaves unimpeded, the husband soon goes to his in-laws house to discuss the problem with her father or both parents. He tries to persuade her to return. The woman's father tells his son-in-law that if he does not want his wife back, she may remain with her parents. He, the father, will "tolerate her stupidity and her laziness."[9]

Often, however, the separation is caused by more serious problems—the man beats his wife, or he drinks too much and does not work. In these cases, the husband has more difficulty gaining his wife's forgiveness, and sometimes they separate permanently. No procedure is required for "divorce." If there are children, however, the man must compensate the mother with a one-time payment for child support. Most children leave with the mother, but one or two, usually boys, may remain with the father. If the wife is lazy, her parents must return the brideprice so that the man will be able to petition for another woman. But if the husband is at fault, he will not be able to recover the brideprice. In any event, the families involved negotiate the divorce. Usually the husband, alone or with his parents, goes to his in-laws' house and discusses matters with her parents. The issue is only taken to court if there is no agreement on the return of the brideprice or in order to enforce the child support payment.

At court the president and his assistants judge the situation according to Chamula tradition. Often the courts side with the wife; perhaps because the majority of the problems leading to divorce stem from the man drinking excessively, mistreating his wife, or finding another woman and abandoning his wife without resources. The man is scolded, jailed, and money is demanded from him for his children. If a married woman commits adultery, the court sends her and her lover to jail. If a woman is lazy and is sent back to her parents by her husband, the court demands the return of the brideprice.

If husband and wife have been separated for some time and the husband wants to reconcile, he goes to his in-laws' house and tries to appease both his wife and her parents. The reconciliation process is similar to the petition process because the woman's parents, especially her father, control the situation. A woman is never an independent agent, unless she is an older widow. As a widow, she is not subject to familial control although her sons and daughters may help her economically. If her parents are dead, but she is still relatively young, she may be in the custody of her brothers.

A man most frequently directs his pleas for appeasement and reconciliation to the woman's father, who may scold and even beat his son-in-law if the latter has mistreated his daughter. For example, Maruch's husband sent her back to her parents' house. There she gave birth to a child who died after a few weeks. Her husband never saw the child; he had been busy petitioning for other young women. Everyone in the hamlet knew his wife was blameless for the separation, so his petitions did not meet with success. Finally, he went to his in-laws and requested they return the brideprice to him since their daughter's child had died. His father-in-law became terribly upset, scolded him, and threatened to take him to court:

> Ah, if you want your money back,
> if you want your penny back,
> we will go to Chamula
>
> and talk to the president,
> and talk to the judge,
> and we will see whose is the money.
>
> What is it?
> Are you not a man?
>
> Or is it that I told you,
> "Marry my daughter. Here she is!"
> No, you came here on your own!
>
> Look, I am still alive on this earth.
> I will support my daughter! (Maruch C29-21)

Maruch's father began to beat his son-in-law. The young man was kneeling and did not attempt to stand up or hit back. When his father-in-law finished beating him, Maruch's husband took out two liters of liquor he had brought with him as a reconciliation gift for his in-laws. He considered that having been beaten, his crimes towards his wife had been expiated; his guilt had vanished.

In another case, Xunka returned to her mother's house (her father was dead) following a beating by her husband. He had beaten her when his mother informed him that Xunka was rebellious and lazy. When Xunka's husband brought gifts of liquor to reconcile with her, he was reprimanded by his wife's mother and older brothers. They told him that he should behave like a man, stop living at his mother's house, and build his own house so that his mother could no longer torment his wife. He promised he would do as told, and Xunka returned to him.

In most cases of reconciliation, the father deals with his son-in-law because men are thought to possess the necessary "heat" and strength to handle difficult situations. When a conflict arises, the father visibly exercises his role of protector of his daughter. Depending on the mother's self-assurance, she also may participate in the reprimand.

On occasion, the mother may control the reconciliation process. Xmal, a curer and midwife in the hamlet of Tzajal Vitz, talked to a group of petitioners herself. The petitioners had come to plead with her to allow her daughter to return to an abusive husband. This man beat his wife, then left her and their baby because she did not want to move to his parents' house. He married twice during the next year and a half, but these marriages did not work out. Finally, he decided to repetition for his first wife. Xmal was furious at him because for two years she and her daughter had struggled to keep the baby alive through many illnesses and not once did he help them with food or money, nor did he visit his child. When he arrived with his petitioners, Xmal hit him and told the petitioners she would not even consider reconciliation. She asked one of the petitioners why that woman did not give him her own daughter, instead.

The next day, Xmal was summoned to court by the president and compelled to honor the request of her son-in-law. The president and the judge determined that he had satisfied the requirements for appeasing his in-laws and therefore should have his wife returned to him. Although Xmal's daughter did not want to return, she remained silent. The court system, comprised exclusively of men, has the final word in disputes of this kind. Cases like this one give public sanction to the idea that women are ultimately controlled by men.[10]

Xmal's case is interesting because her husband did not handle the reconciliation. She says that he has a "very kind heart" and would have given in right away. He is well known in the community for being mild and friendly. He often accompanies and assists his wife on her curing trips to different houses or on her prayer rounds to the church in Chamula Center and to churches in San Cristóbal. Xmal became more involved than her husband in facing the petitioners because she strongly sympathized with the suffering of her daughter and her grandchild and was not ready to forgive.

TRATO TA JUERA: THE DEAL OUTSIDE THE HOUSE

As I mention above, young men and women are not supposed to talk to each other, especially outside the woman's house. A woman is not supposed to choose a man and make an arrangement with him. Such behavior is considered a serious violation of Chamula mores.

Sometimes a man talks to a woman on the path because he likes her and wants to know if she has some interest in him. If so, he may initiate a formal petition. Given the great amount of money and effort spent on the petition and the brideprice, a young man tries to get some assurance beforehand that his petition will succeed. Therefore, when a woman is approached by a young man that she likes, she simply tells him to talk to her parents if he wants to marry her. In some instances, however, the man is able to engage the woman in conversation. When this happens, it may lead to further meetings and, eventually, a sexual liaison. This type of arrangement is called *trato ta juera* or making a deal out of the house. The "out-of-the-house" element is revealing, for it implies that this is a wild, anti-social way to do things. Inside the house means tradition, supervision by adults and family. Out-of-the-house means independence and rebelliousness. Out-of-the-house deals do not happen very frequently in Tzajal Vitz or Nichimtik, but Lacy (1976:34) reports many occurrences in Chamula Center.[11]

Why would a young woman choose this alternative when she knows it will cause her a great deal of trouble with her family? In some instances, the woman may be rebelling directly against her parents in order to prove she is capable of choosing her own marriage partner. In other cases, she probably yields impulsively to temptation. In yet other instances, the young woman may be formally engaged to a man she does not want and decides to elope to avoid marrying her parents' choice.

A *trato ta juera* provokes a major conflict between the woman and her parents, who are terribly shamed. The father says to his daughter:

Why did you do this?
Why did you not say a word?
How do you explain it?

Is it that I am not your father?
Is it that you brought up yourself?
Is it that you supported yourself all this time?
Is that why you decided to go with the man?

Was it not with my corn you grew up?
Was it not with my beans?

Is it because you do not owe obedience to anyone?
Is it because I am not in your heart anymore? (Xun C59)

"Making a deal outside" bypasses parental control as if the daughter did not owe her parents any loyalty for raising her. The daughter's father, in particular, loses face in the community. Unable to control his daughter, his authority suffers considerably; people comment that he has no power. In contrast, when a son tells his parents he has made a deal with a woman, they advise him on how to reconcile with his new in-laws.[12]

In an outside deal the couple try to appease the woman's parents by bringing gifts of liquor and soft drinks and by offering to pay the brideprice. Often the groom sends petitioners to formally present an apology to the woman's parents. After many petitions, the parents may acquiesce, forgive their daughter and her husband, receive the brideprice, and drink together to initiate a new relationship. If they do not give in, the man takes his case to court because he does not want to remain in conflict with his wife's relatives. In court, the president convinces the parents to accept the apologies and receive the brideprice from their son-in-law who has done everything possible to appease them.[13] The woman cannot return to her house and wait for the man to go through a formal process; the marriage is a fait accompli. If the woman and her husband remain in conflict with her parents, the stability of their marriage is threatened. Especially at the beginning, a marriage depends on the mediation of both sets of parents. The conflict also imperils the woman; once she severs her ties to her parents, should she have a problem with her husband, they may deny her any support or even admittance into their house.

A man may be attracted to "make a deal outside the house" because the cost of elopement is less than the cost of courtship. In 1984, the total expense incurred by a man to "buy" a wife through formal courtship was approximately 10,000 ($80.00) to 12,000 pesos ($96.00), or about 60 days work at a daily wage of 200 pesos ($1.60). The expenses of an elopement were much less, about half those of the formal courtship, plus the cost of some liquor and soft drinks. In an elopement no gifts of luxury foodstuffs are required for the bride's parents, nor are repeated presents of liquor and food made to the man's parents and petitioners. Nevertheless, elopement remains rare in Chamula because of the tremendous risk it implies for the woman.

If a woman converses with a man, she may be in for a great deal of trouble. Malicious gossip destroys her reputation and that of her parents, who are accused of being unable to control their daughter and of failing to teach her respect. Furthermore, the man may be deceiving her and have no intention of marrying her. A man whose ultimate goal is not marriage, but a conquest to boast about to his peers, informs his friends that this woman likes to engage in conversation with men. Because she has transgressed the basic prohibition against such conversations, many men will approach her to try to obtain her favors, including married men. A woman who talks to men outside her house is automatically devalued. A good, hard-working man will never petition for such a woman. Married women severely criticize such behavior because young women are expected to aggressively reject the men who talk to them and thereby discourage married men from looking for other women.

Most Chamula women have a reputation for being ill-tempered and for responding angrily when men try to engage them in conversation. Men tell their friends about these young women, and no man tries to approach them on the path.

> "Go talk to my father and mother, don't talk to me," the young woman says if a man talks to her.
> "But can't we make a little deal? Can't you accept me, just between us?" asks the man.
> "No, I can't. My father is still alive, my mother is still alive. If my father were dead, if my mother were dead, I would decide all by myself. But they are living. And I also have older brothers. They are very ill-tempered and mean, they would kill you!" she says. (Manvel C55)

A man who reacts angrily to the rejection of his marriage petitions may decide to ruin the woman's reputation. If he lies, claiming he has seduced a woman, soon the whole hamlet is commenting about her behavior. Her situation is precarious; her risks are great. She is less vulnerable if she does not take any chances and plays the role of a hard-working, obedient daughter who leaves her parents in control. From inside the house, she can try to influence the choice of her partner.

ACQUIRING A SECOND WIFE

The procedure for acquiring a second wife to live with polygynously is no different from that of a single man and woman "making a deal outside," especially if the married man is relatively young. When a young married man finds a woman who is willing to converse with him a few times on the path, he brings her to his house where his other wife lives. Afterward he must appease the new wife's parents. Sometimes an older man has an affair with his wife's sister and acquires her as second wife, probably because there are more opportunities for approaching these women.

Both sets of parents react strongly to polygynous arrangements. When his son told him that he had acquired a second wife, one man's father had this reaction:

> My son came to me and said,
>
> "Damn! Dad, I talked to a woman."
> "Did she accept?" I asked him.
> "Yes," he replied.

"And do you intend to live with her?" I asked.

"Yes," he said.

"Well, all right, live with her, but you will have to go pay for her by yourself. I cannot go with you because you have a wife already," I told him, "because that is your real wife let's say. When it is your first wife, if you don't have a wife already, I will always go," I said.

Since it is his second wife, and there is already one, Tumin [the first wife] will be very angry.

"Bastard!" she will say. "His father advises him to look for another woman. The son just comes tagging along. First he came to my house to pray when he came to ask for my hand, and now he is looking for another wife for his son," she will say. I would be embarrassed.

Then my son went to pay. He looked for a companion to go, my brother Juan went with him. The girl's father and mother asked my son if his mother and father were coming, and he said,

"No. They are not coming because they are embarrassed and because they have performed religious duties in the community. Moreover, getting another wife is not a tradition. There is not a law that says that I should look for two wives. I just talked to your daughter, and we made a deal outside," that is what he told them.

He paid about 1500 or 2000 pesos [$12.00 or $16.00], I'm not sure, and he took her to his house. (Manvel C53)

This example does not describe the usually explosive reaction of the woman's parents toward both their daughter and the married man. The woman's parents usually feel insulted and betrayed, as described in the "deal outside." This quote, however, does illustrates the powerful feelings monogamy elicits. Monogamy is considered the correct and traditional way to live. However often polygyny may occur, it is felt to be an infraction of society's laws. But, the authorities in Chamula do not condemn polygyny.[14] They only punish a man who has more than one wife if one of the wives complains of mistreatment or general irresponsibility on the part of her husband toward herself and her children.

The reaction of the first wife, the struggle between the two wives, and the sharp criticisms to which the second wife is subjected are discussed in chapter 3.

The case of an older man acquiring his wife's sister as second wife is even more conflictive because his in-laws regard the behavior of both their son-in-law and his new wife, their daughter, as outrageous (see also, Lacy 1976:32).

Xun made a deal with his wife's younger sister, a divorced woman. They planned to run away together to the hot country. He went to her mother's house to pick her up:

> "Is your daughter here?" the man asked his mother-in-law.
> "Yes, she is here. We were sleeping," her mother replied.
> "Hurry up, wake up. Aren't you coming with me to the hot country!" he told the younger woman. Up to now the mother-in-law had not realized something was going on.
> "Ah, what is it, what kind of deal do you have?" she asked her son-in-law.
> "Nothing, we have no deal, only that we're going together to the hot country," he said.
> "Oh, *porquería* you are an evil woman. Get out of here, I do not want to see your face," said the old woman.
> "Well," he said, "you did not realize that we talked because you were drunk."
> "No, I saw nothing," she replied.
> "Are you going to insist on being angry?" he asked. He had taken a liter of liquor to her mother when he went to pick up the woman.
> "I do not want to drink your liquor," retorted the old lady. "Get out of here, you are disgusting! Do not come close to me, do not touch me!" she exclaimed angrily. (Tumin C31-59)

Thus, Xun offered his mother-in-law minimal compensation, a liter of liquor given in a hurry. This situation was particularly difficult because Xun had beaten his first wife. He had to leave quickly before she could arrive in Chamula to denounce him and have him jailed. Appeasing his mother-in-law was not one of his major concerns. It is interesting to speculate whether he would have been able to get away with such behavior had the sisters' father been alive.

THE MONETIZATION OF THE MARRIAGE TRANSACTION

In the "deal outside the house" there is no *matanal*, only liquor and sodas are given as appeasement for the trouble that the man has caused the woman's parents. In this sense reconciliation is no different from the usual process of asking for a favor or for forgiveness. Also, a monetary payment symbolically compensates the woman's parents for the expenses of raising a daughter. In the monetization of the transaction, the woman even more closely resembles a commodity, the property of the man who buys her. A man may have as many wives as he can afford.

A gift of a whole array of luxury food items is qualitatively different from "paying" for the woman with money. The brideprice epitomizes a situation in which an individual seeks the goodwill and help of another person or group of people. Thus, it is related to the gift-giving that characterizes the recruitment of petitioners or cargo helpers, or a request for a loan or for help to build a house. The brideprice differs from other gift-giving practices, however, in that many more gifts are presented, particularly, in the form of food.[15] When money is the main vehicle, however, the exchange takes on the appearance of any other commercial transaction.

The foodstuffs of the brideprice are established by tradition. There does not appear to be any discussion of what items to include or how much to give. Informants say that the greater the variety of goods, the happier the bride's parents will be and the better they will relate to their son-in-law; but the quantity of each item seems relatively fixed according to the groom's economic situation. Where money is the medium, however, haggling takes place over the amount to be paid, once again the exchange turns into an economic transaction.

The difference between the brideprice and monetary compensation is not lost on Chamulas themselves.[16] When Manvel was married, his petitioners asked his father-in-law whether he wanted gifts of food or money:

> "No, may the tradition of our grandfathers and our grandmothers, of our fathers and our mothers not be lost. Will I receive money? No, I am not an animal. I am not an animal to receive money, I want *matanal*," he said. (Manvel C47-14)

Manvel's father-in-law explicitly distinguishes between *matanal* and money. As one of a people with traditions and feelings, he cannot give his daughter away for money. For him to accept such a transaction is tantamount to behaving like an animal.

When Xalik was married, however, following the *ak' riox'* ceremony, his father suggested that they pay for the woman immediately rather than return in eight or fifteen days as tradition demands:

> "Why should we leave it for a week or two?" my mother suggested.
> "But is it possible?" they asked.
> "Yes," my parents said. "Tell us right away, we will pay it now."

"Well, all right," Dominga's mother said.
"How much [money] is her 'substitute'?" my parents asked.
"Oh, I will not be able to pay it back in case my daughter is no good," her mother said. "Give me around 3000 [$24.00]."

Then they gave her the money. Well, my father gave her 3500 pesos [$28.00]. He passed it to Dominga's older brother.

"He gave me more money," he said.
"Give it back," Dominga's mother demanded.

And he did. Exactly 3000 pesos. They drank liquor, they drank beer. And that was that. (Xalik C40)

Had Dominga's father been alive, a more elaborate ceremony might have been required. Xalik's parents insisted on rushing the process, however, and Dominga's mother gave in. Interestingly, the actual monetary exchange was made between men: Xalik's father and Dominga's older brother. Men control the formal aspects of the marriage process. The president of Chamula had talked to Dominga's older brother, who had opposed the marriage. The president told him not to bother his younger sister but to "sell her in a good way." He knew that Dominga still had a mother, but he did not instruct the brother to assist his mother's decision, rather he told the brother to sell his sister without causing trouble. Nevertheless, the tenuous nature of this metaphoric exchange of women by men is clearly revealed: the older brother may have received the money at the moment of exchange, but the mother controlled the amount and did not allow her son to accept more. Moreover, she kept the money.

The above case epitomizes the central ideas of this chapter, namely, that although men wield definite control over women's lives, their power is not monolithic and does not go unchallenged. Because patrilineages have no substantial economic base, the authority of the father is considerably weakened, as demonstrated by increases in elopements in Zinacantán and Amatenango. A father's authority seems to depend more on loyalty, reciprocity, and tradition than on the manipulation of inheritance. The long and involved marriage process stresses the concept of a wife as precious—an invaluable companion who makes a man complete and for whom he must set forth his best efforts. The considerable economic and social investment a man makes to acquire a wife help to curb his excesses.

In contrast with women, men have the right to choose their mates. Nevertheless, despite the many cases in which fathers exercise despotic power over the selection of a daughter's mate, in most instances, mothers and daughters contribute to the marriage decision. The new economic leverage of young women strengthens their voice in the decision. Men behave as their daughters' "protectors," but a strong woman may override her husband and defend the daughter. Where men's power seems insurmountable is at the all-male court, the ultimate expression of male domination. As I discuss in detail in chapter 8, this governing body acts like a benevolent patriarch who has the right to make final decisions over a woman's fate, often against her will.

NOTES

1.   The energy and money expended in marriage transactions, the excitement they generate, and the enthusiasm with which people talk about them reveal that marriage represents a fundamental moment for the simultaneous negotiation of practice and meaning—as Yanagisako and Collier (1987:44) contend, a moment of "systemic reproduction."

2.   Today, marriage in Chamula does not include the *nupunel*, a final marriage ritual. The *nupunel* was usually performed several months or years after the couple had begun life together and had saved enough money to pay for it. This ceremony is still performed in other indigenous communities in the highlands (see Collier 1968). In Chamula the *nupunel* involved a church wedding, followed by a special dance and meal. The main objective of the *nupunel* was to protect the souls of husband and wife and to insure that they would meet again after death (Warshauer 1969). The great expense of this ceremony seems to be one of the main reasons why it is no longer celebrated. Also, for many years Chamulas have had conflicts with the Catholic priests in the area, and these weddings were performed in the Church by a priest. It appears that Chamulas had to receive lessons on Catholic doctrine and learn Catholic prayers; the priests acted impatiently, intimidating them. Antel relates that on one occasion the priest became so furious with his class, because they had not learned the doctrine, that he yelled at them "to leave right away and go find leaves of corn to eat, for they were no better than animals."

3.   The loss of patriarchal protection, in cases where the basic ideology of male dominance remains intact, makes women extremely vulnerable. In the urban colonies established by Protestant Chamulas who have been expelled from the community, there are many cases of single mothers and abused women. These women, in the anomie that characterizes the new setting and without the safety net of a father's protection, have nowhere to turn (Garza Caligaris and Ortíz in press; Nash and Sullivan 1992). In Chenalhó, too, ladinoized Pedranas who refuse to conform to traditional institutions (such as marriage with parental mediation) become victims of abuse as a result of their ambiguous status (Eber 1991:327).

4.   Unfortunately, I did not observe the petition process firsthand. This subject, however, is one that Chamula women and men enjoy talking about, discussing it in detail and at great length. For the most part, this chapter is based on Chamulas' extensive descriptions of the various stages leading to marriage. The formal petition process in Chamula is similar to the petition processes found in Zinacantán, Amatenango, and Chenalhó, although courtship may take longer in Amatenango (six months to a year, Nash 1985:125ff.) and Zinacantán (up to two years, Collier 1968). Gifts of luxury foods and liquor accompany praying and

pleading sessions everywhere (see also, Eber 1991:91). In all four communities, the idea prevails that the young man must be in charge of the process because only through "fighting for a wife" does a boy really become a man (Nash 1985:275).

5. In other Highland Chiapas communities, such as Chenalhó and Amatenango, the young man's family pays the brideprice. This was also the case in Zinacantán a generation ago.

6. The reaction of a young woman's parents to a marriage petition is similar in several indigenous communities in the area: petitioners are told harshly to abandon the house and to search elsewhere for a wife for their boy. The petitioners sometimes kneel for several hours at a time. Guiteras-Holmes (1961:126) notes that refusals are a way for parents to express that they are not anxious for their daughter to marry and that she will always be welcomed back.

7. Collier (1973:203) observes that young women in Zinacantán have some input in the decision to accept a suitor and may even break off an engagement if there is strong cause to do so. Also, during the period of courtship, a woman may refuse a suitor's gifts in order to persuade him to stop courting her.

8. In Chenalhó, women often respond violently when their parents accept a suitor. A woman may protest loudly and threaten to run away, but after a while, she submits to her parents' decision (Guiteras-Holmes 1961:126). See also Eber (1991:186) for the reactions and feelings of a young woman when her parents married her off.

9. The role of the father as his daughter's protector and defender in marital struggles is common in other indigenous communities in the area as well. He must always be present when his son-in-law comes to ask forgiveness. In Zinacantán, a man must heed his father-in-law's advise if he is to get his wife back (Collier 1973:189). Likewise, in Amatenango, a father will always support his daughter when presenting her case in court, and although the judges try to convince the woman to return to her husband, her father has the last word and clearly warns his son-in-law (Nash 1985:130). Nash notes (1985:108) that a father's protection may be extended to a widowed daughter-in-law by giving her shelter. A young widow, easy prey of drunken men, requires a protector.

10. In Zinacantán and Chenalhó, the all-male court has final authority to decide the fate of women. In Zinacantán, except in cases where the woman has been badly hurt, the president tries to reconcile the couple. Sometimes he threatens to make the woman's family pay for the expensive legal divorce in order to persuade them to send their daughter back to her husband (Collier 1973:189). In Chenalhó, too, a woman may be convinced to return to her husband. A widow who refuses to remarry may be entreated by the court to do so under an agreement that if the man should beat her, the authorities will be there to defend her (Guiteras-Holmes 1961:133).

11. Apparently, young people are choosing to elope in increasing numbers in several Highland Chiapas communities such as Amatenango (Nash in press) and Zinacantán (G. Collier 1989). In the latter, there are more cases of elopement than of the traditional courtship and marriage, which were almost universal two decades ago. In Chenalhó, elopements also appear to be on the rise (Eber 1991:348).

12. Parents in other communities also carefully guard their daughters to prevent elopements. Zinacanteco parents often avoid sending their daughters to school out of fear the girls may be sexually molested or may become accustomed to talking with boys, and later, when both boys and girls are older, make a deal without parental participation (Vogt

1969:193; Modiano 1974:211). Often following an elopement in Zinacantán, the young woman's brothers threaten to kill the young man (Vogt 1969:213). The woman's father appears as foolish and weak in the eyes of the community; in contrast, the man's parents give tacit approval of his actions since elopement is less expensive for them (Collier 1973:206). Eber (1991:90) reports that parents in Chenalhó also fear that their daughters will talk with boys in school and eventually decide to elope. Traditionally, following marriage, a Pedrano man, accompanied by his father-in-law, asks permission of the Holy Earth to take a wife. Their joint prayers emphasize that the groom has paid the bride's family their due; that is, he has not stolen her and therefore has a legitimate right to her (Guiteras-Holmes 1961:129).

13. Collier (1973:206) mentions that in Zinacantán the woman's father is summoned to court in many elopement cases. Because he feels so hurt, he will not accept the new marriage until the president intervenes. As a part of the reconciliation process, the man's parents and petitioners bargain for the "brideprice" to be paid by the man. This payment compensates the woman's parents for their expenses in raising her, but it is not equivalent to the brideprice gifts that are delivered in the normal process of courtship.

14. Polygyny is extremely rare in Zinacantán. Speaking of Chamulas who have more than one wife, Zinacantecos say, "they live like dogs." Zinacanteco men are not punished for having lovers, but if a wife can prove her husband is unfaithful, and she wants a divorce, she can claim some of her husband's property (Collier 1973:189). In Amatenango, adultery is also considered wrong; however, many men seem to break the rule (Nash 1985:281). Chenalhó appears to be similar to Chamula: polygyny is not frowned upon as long as the man has enough resources to support two families. A woman is considered foolish to leave a husband solely because he is having an affair with another woman, provided he continues to support her well, does not beat her, and does not bring the other woman home (Guiteras-Holmes 1961:130ff.).

15. Gifts of food are common in Chamula. In addition to money, people give cooked food or fruits to shamans and midwives to thank them for their services.

16. People in Chenalhó display a similar awareness of the differences between gifts of food and gifts of money. Although some suitors give money in addition to or instead of food, petitioners in this town strongly encourage young men to give food gifts because food "cements the bond in a way money can't" (Eber 1991:547).

Figure 2. Originally a kitchen, this structure was used as a dwelling by a newly married couple. It is typical of the homes of the poorest Chamula families. In the background is a house of cement and tile, a type common among wealthier Chamulas.

Figure 3. A woman weaves a woolen *jerkail* for her husband.

Figure 4. A young woman shrinks and felts her father's *jerkail*, pouring hot water on it and beating it repeatedly with her hands.

Figure 5. Children begin to work at a young age. A seven-year-old girl carries a heavy bundle of cabbages up a hill.

Figure 6. A nine-year-old girl contributes to the family income by producing bracelets to sell to tourists.

Figure 7. As children, brothers and sisters play together and share many tasks and adventures. Girls wear traditional Chamula clothing, but boys wear Ladino style dress.

Figure 8. A young woman sells woven belts to a tourists in San Cristóbal de las Casas.

Figure 9. Chamula women sell fruit at the market in San Cristóbal de las Casas.

Figure 10. At day's end, a family engages in lively conversation around the hearth. While the women pat out tortillas, the men await the meal.

Figure 11. While she watches over her grandchildren, an older woman earns money carding wool for a neighbor.

Figure 12. A woman teaches her son to use a hoe.

Figure 13. A woman begins a cloth doll for sale in the tourist market.

6

The Struggle for Life

The expansion of capitalism in Highland Chiapas began in the final quarter of the nineteenth century. Since that time, Chamula men have been a source of cheap labor for the farms and plantations of Chiapas. Population growth, the appropriation of indigenous lands and resources, and forced recruitment of labor have determined the nature of the community's articulation with national and international economic systems. Through the ebb and flow of Mexican and worldwide political economies of the last one hundred years, most Chamulas have had no alternative but to reproduce the patterns of unstable employment and poverty into which their great grandparents were forcibly cast. Their current economic behavior reflects this instability (J. Rus 1988; D. Rus 1990). When the economy is in decline, Chamulas are among the first to lose their jobs and to be forced to subsist on their own resources. There are no safety nets for those who are unemployed. Even in the best times, the jobs open to Chamulas are limited, temporary, and poorly remunerated. Planting milpa continues to be the idealized occupation for men, but their minuscule plots in the highlands provide, on average, less than 20 percent of a family's yearly needs. Men are forced to seek positions in the outside wage-labor market. Women's activities also go beyond the idealized role of complementing their husbands' corn production with household chores, caring for the children, and weaving family clothing. In fact, men and women explore every potential alternative in their desperate quest for an adequate livelihood. At the fringes of survival, husband and wife become authentic companions in the struggle for life. Only through untiring dedication and ingenuity are they able to maintain a viable family.[1]

In most areas of Latin American women constitute the majority of the emigrants, usually relocating in urban areas where they find work as domestics or street vendors.[2] For various reasons, Chamula does not fit this pattern. The long history of male emigration has created a pressing need for women to take over agricultural chores and other tasks that men can no longer fulfill. Although n other areas of Latin America, modern technologies and products have displaced household production and led to a surplus female labor force, this is not the case in Chamula. Artisan production enables women to make an income, however meager, while allowing them to remain in their hamlets. Finally, the conservative nature of Chamula ideology plays a powerful role in discouraging Chamula women from seeking outside employment—this contrasts with the situation of women from other indigenous communities of Highland Chiapas, who frequently look for jobs as domestics in nearby cities. Chamula mistrust of Ladinos prevents women from accepting employment or establishing any kind of long-lasting relationship with Ladinos.

As agricultural and construction workers, men have lost control over strategic work resources and processes. They sell their labor on the market at a detrimental exchange rate and leave their communities to find employment in distant places. Restrictions on female mobility and women's lack of Spanish language skills have allowed women to resist the total incorporation of Chamula into the capitalist system (Nash in press). Surplus labor is extracted from women indirectly through trade, but women are generally able to maintain control over raw materials, instruments of production, and productive processes. In comparison with men, women enjoy more autonomy from outside control. The difficulties of making a living, however, overwhelm both women and men. Women, particularly, seem exhausted by the tremendous effort of balancing home, a large number of children, highland milpas, and income-producing activities, while barely making ends meet.

The majority of Chamula men juggle several activities in addition to planting their small highland milpas. Seventy-six percent of men depend on wage labor: 51 percent of Chamula men migrate seasonally to coffee farms in the Soconusco region on the Pacific Coast; another 25 percent find temporary work as unskilled laborers in both the public and private sectors of the economy (Wasserstrom 1983a:209). The economic crisis of the 1980s was particularly difficult for Chamulas, leaving a large number of men underemployed. Even on the coffee farms, the number of jobs dwindled (Rus 1988).

Approximately 25 percent of Chamula men have taken up sharecropping or tenant farming in the Grijalva River Basin, following the example of their Zinacanteco neighbors (Wasserstrom 1983a:204-208). The latter have a long-standing relationship with Ladino landowners, and therefore the better lands are reserved for them. Zinacantecos also have more resources to cultivate larger tracts of land and thereby obtain a surplus; Chamulas are left with poorer, more rocky lands. Because they have less money to begin with, Chamulas cannot risk investing in fertilizer and workers to farm larger areas. Should they lose their crops—on account of bad weather or an invasion of the milpa by the landowner's cattle—

they will end up with a large debt and few resources for repaying it. Unlike Zinacantecos, Chamulas cannot fall back on highland milpas to meet their obligations; they either have no milpa or the milpa is too small. Thus, Chamula men prefer to work only with a son or another unpaid family member. A hectare of land produces enough maize for annual domestic consumption and a small surplus to pay for renting the land and transporting the grain back to the hamlet (Wasserstrom 1983a:208).

Men may combine tenant farming with wage labor on coffee farms or elsewhere. Some tenant farmers supplement their farming income by producing and selling liquor during the months they are in the hamlets. Other individuals combine peddling with wage labor on coffee farms. Still others combine lowland tenant farming with sales of vegetables and flowers grown on their small highland plots. Highland horticulture is more common in hamlets near San Cristóbal because the transportation of produce is easy and inexpensive. Many couples work together on a small plot of cabbages, carrots, or potatoes, which they sell at the market (Wasserstrom 1983a:203). Making a living from horticulture, however, requires a larger landholding than most Chamulas possess as well as constant disbursements for fertilizer, irrigation, and hired workers. Finally, some men earn a living as potters, charcoal producers, carpenters, or in the practice of other crafts.

SOCIAL STRATIFICATION IN CHAMULA

Although the economy of Chamula hinges mainly on its position in the larger national and international systems, the Chamula population cannot be defined as an egalitarian group of peasants exploited uniformly by the dominant society. People may invest in prestige, rather than capital, through the system of *compadrazgo* (see note 8) or through religious and civil cargos. These mechanisms, however, do nothing to obliterate the large income differences that exist among Chamulas; furthermore, the wealthy also invest in capital, thereby increasing the gap between themselves and their poorer neighbors. As has been shown in other indigenous communities, increasing stratification has a critical effect on gender relations.[3] As wives and mothers, women from different economic strata basically perform the same tasks using similar tools and technologies; there are some important differences among them, however, which I discuss in more detail below.[4]

The ability of some Chamulas to accumulate more wealth than the majority appears always to have been a function of establishing alliances with powerful Ladinos. At the end of the last century, some Chamula men helped the *habilitadores* to procure field hands for the coffee farms, fueling the legend that these Chamula men enriched themselves by selling their neighbors' souls (see chapter 2). But the creation of a consolidated group of wealthier Chamulas did not really begin until the early 1940s, when state administrators established an alliance with a group of young Chamula scribes. These individuals became the ruling elite and remain so today (see chapter 7). By manipulating these alliances so that they benefitted personally from programs designed to help the community, the scribes, their families, and their close political allies were able to amass fortunes, which they invested in the purchase of lands and trucks, and in the provision of high interest loans. Today, these people also hold a monopoly on the sales of liquor and soft drinks (Wasserstrom 1983a:201). These wealthy Chamulas are in a position to buy the labor of other Chamulas, replicating the relations of production that exist between Ladinos and Indians.[5] Even so, wage labor within Chamula is not extensive. Occasionally, the poorest women engage in wage labor within the community, but most men work for Ladino landowners. Wealthy Chamulas extract surplus value from the population they govern mainly through the monopoly they hold on essential goods and through the labor of civil and religious officials, which assures the smooth operation of the system.

The income differences between these wealthy Chamulas and their neighbors is dramatic. The majority of Chamula families live in extreme poverty. At the time of his research, from 1970 to 1974, Wasserstrom (1983a:209) found that more than 50 percent of the men were earning about $240.00 annually, barely enough to survive. How were they able to manage? Wasserstrom (1983a:211) finds the answer to this question in sheep husbandry; most Chamula families own a flock of sheep, an important source of income for the household. Some women spin and weave for pay, and yet others produce clothing and wool to sell in the local markets. Additionally, sheep provide nonmonetary income in the form of clothes and blankets for the entire family. Were these goods not produced by the women, they would have to be purchased. All of these activities represent a major contribution by women to the domestic economy. Sheep and the products derived from them account for about 30 to 40 percent of the income of the poorest families (Wasserstrom 1983a:214). Wasserstrom fails to mention, however, that women also make cash contributions to the family income—contributions that are indispensable in the struggle for survival at this level of poverty. Every Chamula woman I met, without exception, had an income-producing activity, even if irregular and yielding a low return. These activities included selling chickens and eggs; carding, spinning, and/or weaving for neighbors; retailing wool; selling potatoes or seasonal fruits in the Chamula or San Cristóbal markets; selling corn gruel in Chamula; wage labor in the hamlet during weeding or harvest time; selling firewood in other indigenous towns; and embroidering blouses, weaving belts and bracelets, and making cloth dolls to sell to tourists in San Cristóbal.

At the other extreme, a handful of rich horticulturalists, truck owners, and liquor distillers had annual incomes of over $800.00 and some individuals earned more than $10,000.00 (Wasserstrom 1983a:209). My data show that women from this class also participate in income-producing activities because their husbands' contributions to the household are usually limited to the provision of corn, beans, and other basic necessities. Men keep their money to spend on items of personal consumption (e.g., liquor or cigarettes) or to invest in their businesses. With her own money, a woman may buy other household necessities such as soap, pots, and water jugs, or luxury foods such as meat, bread, or sweets. She can pay for curing ceremonies for herself and her children or purchase clothing for the family. Although she contributes to the family's budget, her income is less vital than that of her impoverished female neighbor. Furthermore, the leverage of women from the wealthy class vis-à-vis their husbands is minimal. Even though women's work has not become a commodity that can be purchased in the market, men in this class can easily acquire another wife should the first one decide to leave. Many of the wealthiest Chamula men have more than one wife, and though their wives may be unhappy with this arrangement, there is little the women can do to change it. It is important to note that the idea of a wife's idleness as a sign of her husband's wealth and position does not exist in this community.[6] Instead, a man may prove his economic success by his ability to provide two or more wives and their children with the basic staple foods.

Between the poorest and wealthiest groups is a third group comprised of tenant farmers, peddlers, and small horticulturalists. This group accounts for about 30 percent of the Chamula population. The men in this group earn from $400.00 to $800.00 per year, a modest livelihood (Wasserstrom 1983a:209). I found that although women from this group usually can count on their husbands to supply enough corn to feed the family, they still must struggle to obtain a monetary income. In contrast to women of the poorest group, these women have enough money to invest in raw materials (e.g., thread for embroidery and cotton cloth) and thus get a better return for their work. In the unstable economic situation of Chamula, sickness, death, a bad crop, or other family crises—not unusual under conditions of malnourishment and general poverty—pose a constant threat to survival. Even in this middle group, therefore, women's cash contribution to the household economy is perceived as sine qua non.

Chamula women of all levels of the socioeconomic hierarchy devote their energies to supporting their households.[7] In contrast to the wives of wealthy men, however, women in the middle and lower groups have more leverage to assert their needs or affect their husbands' decisions. In their husbands' absence, the women of these two groups face a great number of responsibilities and a long work day. Families in these groups usually have little or no savings, so the support of the household falls entirely on the women when their husbands are away.

Even though the local economy has become highly monetized, capitalism has not fully penetrated the Chamula economy, and Chamulas meet many of their needs through reciprocity and various redistribution channels. Neighbors, compadres[8] and relatives help each other with loans, building projects, ceremonial obligations, emergencies, and they also serve as marriage petitioners for each other's sons. While the man is away, his wife maintains these relationships, and these ties constitute her support system during his absence.

The specific niche Chamulas occupy within the capitalist system provides the majority of them with little freedom or opportunity to move ahead into other positions or to accumulate wealth for investment. In Chamula, as in so many other industrializing Third World societies, capital benefits from a symbiotic relationship with the traditional subsistence economy it enforces; the unpaid work of women guarantees the reproduction of the labor force. But, paradoxically, this symbiosis limits the penetration of industrial production and consumer goods into Chamula, and thus prevents the full assimilation of Chamula into the dominant system.[9] This situation fosters the strong interdependency between husband and wife that is usual in subsistence-based economies.[10]

Several studies support Boserup's (1970) early findings that a society's absorption into the larger process of industrialization results in the deterioration of relatively egalitarian gender relations and the status of women.[11] Capitalism uses existing gender hierarchies to place women in subordinate positions, which exacerbates inequalities (Benería and Sen 1986; Arizpe and Aranda 1986). Because it rests on an ideological system with a strong male bias, capitalism supports men's access to new technologies, methods, education, and capital—resources that enable men to take advantage of modernization.[12] In the ever-widening gender gap that evolves out of this situation, women are consistently the losers. They remain tied to traditional technologies and activities, which are often defined as backward and low in prestige and which interfere in women's ability to obtain an adequate income.[13]

The above scenario may represent the future of Chamula if it becomes fully integrated into the modern world; for the time being, however, Chamula remains on the periphery of modernization. As unstable laborers, most Chamula men do not have access to the fruits of modernization. Furthermore, their work outside of the community causes both personal insecurity and conflict with their ethnic identity. At present, women's use of traditional technology is not devalued. On the contrary, it is appreciated as a symbol of ethnicity, and the goods women produce are in demand from one of the most highly remunerative sectors of the economy— tourism.

The potential for a gender gap still exists, however, because the range of options for women is narrow. Should the tourist trade wane or the goods women produce saturate the market, women will have to look for another source of income. The gender and ethnic bias characteristic of Mexican society, women's monolingualism in Tzotzil, and women's ignorance of the ways of Ladino society reduce opportunities for Chamula women. Apart from the tourist trade, the only source of income for indigenous women of this region is domestic service in Ladino households. Compared with women, Chamula men have a better knowledge of the Spanish language and more familiarity with Ladino culture; therefore, some of them are able to find better remunerated employment.

THE CASE OF TZAJAL VITZ

Wasserstrom's statistical survey of Chamula included 10 hamlets, which were selected on the basis of their differences in access to main roads and their relative distance from San Cristóbal. Size was also an important variable; relatively small hamlets (50 to 60 families) were compared with larger hamlets (about 250 families). Wasserstrom (1983a:211-212) found that the critical economic variable was access to San Cristóbal. Proximity to the city stimulated the growth of horticulture because products could be taken to the market daily without high transportation costs. Proximity to the market also contributed to more drastic internal stratification. In the hamlets nearest San Cristóbal, a group of wealthier men were gradually appropriating the lands of their poorer neighbors so that they could plant increasingly larger tracts with vegetables. Dispossessed men were incorporated into the mass of unstable wage workers. More distant hamlets, where the majority of men worked in tenant farming in the lowlands or in wage labor, showed more homogeneity.

Tzajal Vitz is relatively distant from the city. Its population is mid-size, about 150 families. Compared with the average amount of cultivated land per family in Chamula township (0.41 hectares), the average for families of Tzajal Vitz is about one-half (0.20 hectares); in Tzajal Vitz highland plots supply only 3.4 percent of a family's corn requirements. Therefore, a large number of men (69 percent) work for wages either seasonally or permanently.

How do we know that the economic life of women in Tzajal Vitz is not radically different from that of women in other hamlets, particularly hamlets with more wealth? First, the lives of women from wealthier families in Tzajal Vitz are not radically different from those of poorer women in the hamlet; they are all involved in the usual female tasks, and they all have income-producing activities. Second, the comparisons I make with the hamlet of Nichimtik, which is smaller, closer to San Cristóbal, and has a different configuration of the labor force, demonstrate similar patterns in women's lives.

Like women in Tzajal Vitz, women in Nichimtik search tirelessly for income generating activities, in addition to engaging in their traditional occupations. Although many of the men in this hamlet earn a higher income than most men in Tzajal Vitz, large families and illness create an ever pressing demand for money in both communities. While the men work in San Cristóbal as day laborers, their wives frequently plant the cornfield and vegetable gardens. The women walk into the city two or three times a week to sell their produce. Also, many married women and girls from Nichimtik earn money selling woven belts, bracelets, and cloth dolls to tourists in San Cristóbal. Although men's labor in Nichimtik may be structured differently from that of men in Tzajal Vitz, and the women may be involved in different income activities, women always work to complement their husbands' income.

In the 1970s, an average of 47 percent of Tzajal Vitz men tenant farmed in the lowlands, much higher than the average for Chamula as a whole (25 percent). In my 1984 survey of Tzajal Vitz, however, only about 28 percent of men appear as tenant farmers (see table 2). Several men mentioned their crops had failed, and consequently they had decided to relinquish tenant farming and had taken up wage labor. Men and women experiment with different alternatives, changing back and forth from one type of job to another. Manvel, for example, had been a tenant farmer for 10 years, but after acquiring a large debt, he returned to highland farming and wage labor for about six years. In 1986 he again tried planting two hectares in the Grijalva Basin, this time assisted only by his son. Other economic activities of men in Tzajal Vitz include making and selling charcoal or candles, sewing women's blouses on machines, curing, working for wages in the hamlet, tending beehives, engaging in small-scale horticulture, selling popsicles in the distant city of Villahermosa, and raising a few cows. There are two men who plant large tracts of land exclusively with vegetables and a few who plant milpas and vegetables.

My survey of Tzajal Vitz researched the married women. Like their husbands, these women undertake a variety of activities. Thirty-five percent regularly embroider blouses to sell in San Cristóbal.[14] About six percent are representatives of Sna Jolobil, the regional cooperative of weavers. These cooperative representatives act as intermediaries, receiving items woven and embroidered by women in the hamlet and taking them to the cooperative store.[15] Two married women from Tzajal Vitz have direct contacts with the owners of export businesses. In a piecework system, these women get raw materials and instructions directly from the owners of these businesses in San Cristóbal; back in the hamlet, they distribute the work among as many as 10 or 12 women, reserving some for themselves.[16] Through this process, many women in Tzajal Vitz have learned to produce garments geared to Mexican and American tastes.

Many teenage girls and young unmarried women seek to establish their own links with Ladino shops in San Cristóbal because they realize they can make a great deal more money per garment by bypassing the middlewoman; shopkeepers, however, pay very little. These girls travel to the city to buy their own materials to make blouses, which they cut, sew by hand, and embroider. When they have completed a few items, a group of three or four girls returns to the city to sell them.

Among the married women there are four or five midwives and about the same number of curers (*ilol*); these specialists also sell embroidered garments (in

Table 2

ECONOMIC ACTIVITIES OF WIVES AND HUSBANDS IN TZAJAL VITZ

(Number of individuals. Percentages in parentheses.)

ECONOMIC ACTIVITY OF WIFE	ECONOMIC ACTIVITY OF HUSBAND									TOTAL WOMEN PER ACTIVITY
	WAGE LABOR	TENANT FARMING PLUS WAGE LABOR	MILPA IN TZAJAL VITZ PLUS WAGE LABOR	MILPA IN TZAJAL VITZ PLUS SMALL HORTI-CULTURE	HORTI-CULTURE	CURING (ILOL)	CRAFTS	PEDDLING	SALARIED LABOR	
TRADITIONAL (SHEEP, CLOTHES, AND UNSTABLE SOURCE OF INCOME)	10 (12.2)	17 (20.7)	4 (4.9)	7 (8.5)	–	–	–	–	–	38 (46.3)
SELLING OF WEAVING AND/OR EMBROIDERY	14 (17.0)	5 (6.1)	3 (3.7)	5 (6.1)	–	–	3 (3.7)	1 (1.2)	2 (2.4)	33 (40.2)
WORKING WITH HUSBAND	1 (1.2)	1 (1.2)	2 (2.4)	–	2 (2.4)	1 (1.2)	–	–	–	7 (8.4)
SELLING OF FIREWOOD	1 (1.2)	–	1 (1.2)	–	–	–	–	–	–	2 (2.4)
CURING (ILOL)	–	–	2 (2.4)	–	–	–	–	–	–	2 (2.4)
TOTAL MEN PER ACTIVITY	26 (31.6)	23 (28.0)	12 (14.6)	12 (14.6)	2 (2.4)	1 (1.2)	3 (3.7)	1 (1.2)	2 (2.4)	82

SOURCE: FIELD DATA

table 2 they are classified as embroiderers, not curers, because their income from the former activity is higher). One woman, together with her divorced daughter and granddaughter, survives by making and selling pottery. Women with husbands who plant vegetables (a labor intensive task) usually work in the fields alongside their spouses. Still other women in Tzajal Vitz accompany their husbands to Zinacantán or Chamula Center to sell firewood.

It is difficult to assess the relative income of men and women because Chamulas avoid disclosing these matters for fear of arousing envy. Even if the wage per day or the cost of a blouse is known, it is not easy to generalize; men's wage labor is irregular, and women sell different numbers of garments each month. Therefore, the information below must be considered approximate.

Some men work on the coffee farms for the peak of the coffee harvest, a total of 15 weeks. In 1984, they earned about 21,600 pesos ($173.00) for the whole season. For some men, coffee farm earnings are all the cash income they make in a year. Other men, as Wasserstrom (1983a:209) notes, hold additional jobs; but the cash obtained from these jobs is no more than one-fifth of their coffee harvest earnings. Altogether, the annual cash income of one of these men in 1984 was approximately 26,250 pesos ($210.00). Men who do not plant lowland milpas or work on farms, but work at other unstable jobs, make even less. Their situation is so precarious that they will take the lowest paid jobs; for example, working for other Indians in the lowlands, where a part of their wage is paid in maize.

The few horticulturalists in Tzajal Vitz are among the wealthiest men in the hamlet. About 15 percent of the married men plant relatively large milpas in the highlands and go to the farms for a few weeks every year. Two men in Tzajal Vitz earn government salaries; one works as a truck driver for a state agency, and the other works at a museum in San Cristóbal. These two men make a great deal more money than their neighbors, since their income is both higher (about 150,000 pesos or $1200.00 a year) and more stable. Interestingly, these two men, the wealthy horticulturalists, and a rich candle manufacturer all have two wives. A few other wealthy men in the hamlet have only one wife.

In comparison, in 1984 women who independently embroidered and sold blouses claimed to net about 2000 pesos ($16.00) a month, but some months they sold more than others. A conservative estimate of a woman's income from this work would be about 14,375 pesos ($115.00) a year. Women who sell their embroidery through an intermediary make a great deal less, probably between 7500 pesos ($60.00) and 11,250 pesos ($90.00) a year. On the other hand, the women who not only embroider but also distribute material and thread to other workers make a great deal more; a conservative estimate would be around 57,500 pesos ($460.00) a year, but at least one powerful woman in the village made close to 250,000 pesos ($2,000.00).

Women who work for a wage in Tzajal Vitz, harvesting corn and beans, for example, usually earn one-half to two-thirds of what a man would earn on the same job. Spinning and weaving for neighbors also brings in considerably less money than selling woven goods outside the hamlet, especially to tourists (fig. 11). Women who sell eggs or occasionally take produce to market also make much less. An estimate of earnings for these activities is about 6250 pesos ($50.00) a year.

In 1984 the price of maize, the staple food of Chamula, was 1450 pesos ($11.50) for one *fanega* (138 kg); about ten *fanegas* will feed a family of six for a year. A family needs 14,500 pesos ($115.00) just to cover the cost of corn. If a family owns only a tiny plot in the highlands, they will also need to buy beans, potatoes, and squash. Chile and salt are also indispensable items that must be bought. In addition, a family needs money to pay for curing ceremonies, for a midwife to deliver babies, and for clothing. Liquor and soft drinks are considered basic needs. Occasional needs include meat and chicken, fruits, and other items such as soap, pots, and thread.

In general, even when the husband plants enough corn in the lowlands to feed his family, and the wife produces most of the clothing and blankets for the family, the combined income of husband and wife is barely sufficient to meet the family's needs. The couple are compelled to borrow money at the high rate of five percent a month that prevails in the community. Many women and men live hopelessly indebted.

DIVISION OF LABOR BY GENDER IN TZAJAL VITZ

Tenant Farming or Sharecropping

A large number of families from Tzajal Vitz plant milpa in the hot country. According to my data, in the majority of these cases women stay in the hot country for two or three months twice a year (during planting, from April to June or July, and again at harvest time in late November and December). The men may stay longer, making occasional visits to the hamlet. Approximately one-fifth of the families who plant in the hot country live there most of the year. They return to their homes in the highlands for two or three months each year to visit relatives, to commemorate the souls of their ancestors on All Souls Day (*k'in santo*), and for the Festival of Games or Carnival (*k'in tajimoltik*) in February. In a few cases men go to the hot country by themselves, returning every 20 days to get provisions of toasted tortillas. When working in the hot country, these men cook their beans and prepare their coffee themselves.

The division of labor between husband and wife in the hot country follows the pattern of the highlands. The men bring in the food, and the women fetch water and firewood, cook, care for the children, and spin and weave wool that they bring with them from the highlands. Usually women participate in the weeding and harvesting of the milpa. If they do not have young children, they also help with the sowing.

Women cannot sell woven and embroidered garments in the hot country because the shops that buy these goods are in San Cristóbal; hence, it is more difficult for them to earn money there. The situation is particularly inconvenient for women who live in the hot country and return to the highlands for only a few weeks or months each year. Sheep cannot tolerate the climate of the hot country; if women want to weave, they must purchase wool. These families, however, need very little wool since women and men wear clothing of lighter material and only don traditional Chamula clothes upon their return to the highlands.

Women who spend equal time in the highlands and the hot country frequently leave their sheep with a female relative. When they return to the highlands, they obtain embroidery work from the cooperative representatives. Their earnings are limited to the period of time they spend in the highlands. Less than one-third of the wives of men who plant milpa in the hot country have a regular cash income. In contrast, the group of women whose husbands make a living mostly as wage workers remain in the highlands. As a result more than 60 percent of these women have a regular income. Because women cannot earn money in the lowlands, a couple may decide that it is better for the wife to remain in the highlands. A daughter, sometimes as young as nine, may accompany her father to prepare his food and to take care of other needs. Women in the family take turns going with a father, husband, or brother to the hot country, while the other women remain in the highlands to work and to take care of the sheep.

Women may also stay behind to tend their small stores. There are at least 19 of these stores in Tzajal Vitz, which sell sodas, candles, and a few other items. Additionally, actual or forthcoming religious cargoholders sell cane liquor to help defray the costs of their positions. If husband and wife are serving a cargo, the man must make the trip from the hot country every 20 days in order to carry on the celebration of the saint that the couple sponsors. The woman remains in the hamlet to cense and pray three times a day before the family altar, an obligation that cannot be shirked.

Many women told me that they like the hot country. They enjoy its warmth, which contrasts with the cold temperatures in their mountain hamlets. Water abounds and is much closer to their homes, so they do not need to haul it long distances. They enjoy taking baths in nearby rivers and have an easier time laundering the clothes. Also, they have access to a variety of tropical fruits and animals. Women catch crabs in the river; men hunt for armadillo, iguana, and squirrel. There are also varieties of squashes and beans that are not available in the highlands.

Thus, for the group of men and women who live primarily in the hot country, the division of labor by gender is similar to that of the highlands, except that the opportunities for women to obtain a cash income are more limited. In the hot country the production of woolen clothes diminishes in importance. Women are more dependent on their husbands' earnings. Because their husbands work close by, the women are rarely on their own. They do not experience the independence of regularly employed women in the highlands, who often must manage their households alone.

Men who tenant farm may feel more self-assured. They not only are able to plant milpa to provide for their families but also can protect and keep an eye on their wives. Generally men drink less in the hot country because there is less social pressure to drink and fewer religious ceremonies. Because they share the daily tasks and the responsibilities of rearing the children, husband and wife become dependent upon one another for the goods and services each provides.

Wage Labor

According to my data, 31.6 percent of married men from Tzajal Vitz live exclusively on a wage, and 14.6 percent more combine their highland activities with wage labor. Additionally one-half to two-thirds of the men who sharecrop in the lowlands also participate in wage labor. In total, approximately 60 percent of the married male population is involved in wage labor for at least part of the year.

Wage laborers who do not plant milpas are among the poorest Chamula men. They go back and forth from their hamlets desperately seeking work in different cities and rural areas and are the cheapest source of labor in the state. As mentioned above, 62 percent of the wives of these men have a regular income-producing activity; most of them sell woven goods or embroidered blouses.[17] The rest of the women in this group stay in the highlands to care for their children, their sheep, and their homes. When pressured by the need for money, they may spin other women's wool or sell eggs, firewood, or wool. Wasserstrom's observation that nonmonetary income from sheep corresponds to one-fourth of the total income of the poorest families applies to this group.

Two-thirds of the women whose husbands both plant milpa in Tzajal Vitz and work on the farms also earn a regular income. Where men provide the basic foodstuffs and money, women's earnings are used to buy "good food" (i.e., meat, fruits, soft drinks, coffee) and to help pay for any children's clothes that the women do not weave. Some men feel that by providing their family with corn and beans, they have fulfilled their obligations; they keep any additional income for themselves. Therefore, women must spend their own income to buy other household needs such as soap, clothes, sugar, salt, and chile.

In 1983, Vel and Xalik, a young couple from Tzajal Vitz, combined many different activities to make a living. Xalik cultivated milpa on a small piece of land, and both planted cabbages on a plot they had inherited from Xalik's father. Xalik also sought wage labor outside of the hamlet for a few weeks at a time; Vel remained in the highlands. Vel tended the sheep and helped her sisters-in-law with the cooking. While her sheep were grazing, Vel, who was expecting her first child, wove clothes for the baby. In her spare time, she embroidered blouses to make some money. The money was needed to pay the midwife, who would prepare two or three praying ceremonies to entrust Vel and her baby to the deities. For each ceremony, Vel expected to spend about 300 pesos ($2.40) to cover the midwife's fee, candles, liquor, and a chicken for the ritual.

Women's role as head of the household in their husbands' absences as well as their possession of a cash income has led them to develop a sense of independence and a feeling of indispensability to the family economy.[18] Frequently men return from the coffee farms or other low-paying, low-status jobs, having spent a portion of their earnings on alcohol. Exhausted and demoralized, men often begin to drink on their return to the hamlet and may mistreat their wives. Sometimes during a drinking spell, they go so far as to take maize from the household supply or kitchen pots, which they exchange for liquor. Frustrated with the lack of control over their lives and with their relentless poverty, they resent their wives' independent attitudes. Having consumed their wages, after only two or three weeks in the hamlet, they have no alternative but to go back to work immediately. Their wives and children are often left behind with no money. In such an emergency, women who have no savings resort to selling firewood—a fast way to earn a little money—so that they can buy at least a *caltera* (one l) of corn and beans.

Working in Tzajal Vitz

Men who make a living mainly by working in Tzajal Vitz generally own enough land to meet most of their family's needs. They often combine planting milpa with vegetable plots (horticulture). They sow enough or almost enough corn to feed their families, but they also are able to earn some cash selling vegetables. Forty-two percent of the wives of this small group of men (12 men or 15 percent of the adult male population) embroider blouses to sell (table 2). Because they live in their hamlets, these women are able to take advantage of their social networks and contacts to buy raw materials; this makes their productive activities easier.

Horticulture, a labor intensive activity, requires the combined efforts of husband and wife. In some cases investment for seed and fertilizer comes from the wife's income. The couple plant and work on the vegetable patch together. During the harvest, whoever has more time takes the produce to the market in San Cristóbal. If prices are higher or if the husband is on his way to the lowlands, he may take the produce as far as Tuxtla Gutiérrez, the capital of Chiapas. When men and women work together in horticulture, they keep their money jointly and together decide how to allocate it.

Two wealthy brothers made a living entirely on horticulture. They had the largest landholdings in Tzajal Vitz (40 *cuerdas*, or 1.4 hectares a piece). They did not plant milpa but were involved exclusively in commercial agriculture. They sold cabbages, potatoes, flowers, radishes, lettuce, and other vegetables. Their economic return was high, and they could easily buy corn with only a fraction of their profits. They both had had more than one wife at different times, and these women provided a large portion of the work required to raise the vegetables and flowers.

Townspeople severely criticized one of these brothers for the way in which he exploited his wives. During my work in Tzajal Vitz, one of his wives left because he beat her repeatedly. People said that his most offensive attribute was that he beat his wives even when sober, claiming they had not worked enough. The wife who left habitually worked all day long, every day, including Sundays. She sowed the vegetables and flowers, hauled water from a distant water hole to fill a barrel, and then used a hose to syphon water from the barrel onto the plants. One day this woman had carried a big load of firewood from the woods to her house. Feeling weary, she sat down to rest. Her husband came in and accused her of resenting her work. He hit her and rebuked her, saying, "But it is your firewood you are carrying. Nobody else will get warm from it if you don't!" He also used to beat her early in their marriage when she had difficulty learning to make the candles he sold in his store. "His wives do most of the work, as if they were his peons," people in the hamlet remarked. "He hires only a few other workers. He hardly works himself; he never carries firewood or sacks full of cabbages. Only his wives do. And when he sells his produce he keeps the money. The women toil all the time and get nothing in return."

The behavior of this man and his brother, who works in a similar way although he mistreats his wives less, is considered outrageous. People tend to excuse those men who live off their wives' work or mistreat their wives only during spells of drunkenness; nobody, however, justifies the type of conscious, planned exploitation demonstrated by these rich horticulturalists. In essence, Chamula regard wives as companions in the struggle for life, not slaves.

Of the rest of the men who work in Tzajal Vitz, there are a two curers who also have other economic activities. One produces charcoal—a laborious, time-consuming process in which the whole family takes part. The other owns a few cows, which he and his wife care for and then sell for butchering before the major festivals. They invest their profit in more animals. A nondrinker, this man also sells the liquor he receives from his patients at curing ceremonies.

Men and women who work together pool their earnings in a common fund from which they both withdraw as needed. When they each have an income, the nature of their relationship determines how they keep their money. If a man does not drink too much and shares his money with his wife, she will share her money with him. Women whose husbands drink excessively often hide their personal money, changing its hiding place from time to time so that their husbands won't find it and spend it on alcohol. In this type of relationship, the man does not share his money with his wife either. He may from time to time buy household necessities, but his wife has no direct access to his earnings.

Young women realize that their productive capacity allows them to be relatively independent. The self-assurance that derives from this independence enables a woman of marriageable age to resist the courtship of a man she does not like or of one who has a reputation for drinking. "I don't need a man to support me. I can support myself," she asserts.[19]

ECONOMY AND MARITAL RELATIONSHIPS

The Economic Partnership

If husband and wife are hard working and resourceful and if the man's drinking is under control, the couple may be able to fulfill their subsistence needs and still save some money to invest in a cargo position, to build a house, or to start a small store at home. The cooperation of both partners is indispensable. Below are some cases where the economic partnership works.

Luch and Andrés exemplify the ideal Chamula couple. They both work hard, and Andrés does not drink excessively—just a few shots at fiestas with his brothers. He has never sought another wife and does not mistreat Luch. After many years of hard work, they have been able to buy land. They did not have any land previously because Andrés's alcoholic father had sold most of his land and Luch's parents came from another hamlet. They live in Nichimtik with their five young children. Andrés works every day as a construction worker or gardener in San Cristóbal. Since her husband does not have time, Luch plows, sows, and weeds the milpa. Andrés, however, cultivates vegetables and flowers, which Luch then weeds and sells in San Cristóbal. When she finishes her work in the fields each day, Luch spins and weaves. In the late afternoon, she hurries to prepare tortillas for Andrés, who returns around five o'clock famished. Andrés and Luch keep their money jointly. They consult with one another when they want to make a major investment or buy food or other goods. Many women envy Luch and wish they had a similar relationship with their husbands.

Like most Chamula couples, Manvel and Antel have gone through many ups and downs in their marriage. Manvel drinks, and he used to beat Antel on occasion, but no longer. Once he brought another woman into the house, which produced an explosive reaction from Antel. She actually left for a while and went to live alone in a house she had inherited from her father. Notwithstanding the different crises in their marriage, their relationship has always been an economic partnership. At first, Manvel and Antel worked at distilling *pox* (cane liquor). They were extremely poor and had to walk a great distance, all the way to Ixtapa, to get the brown sugar necessary for the distillation process. They returned bearing the loads of sugar on their backs. Next they would fetch a large amount of firewood and water. Assisted by some of her children, Antel would spend long hours boiling the water and sugar mixture. When the liquor was ready, Manvel would carry it on his back to sell at the houses of people who held cargos. In time they purchased mules to carry the heavy bottles of *pox*. Distilling liquor illustrates the cooperation between husband and wife; it demands careful timing and coordination of activities. One person must attend to the long and involved operation, and the other delivers the finished product. Antel and Manvel stopped producing liquor when competition brought the price down.

At another point in the couple's marriage, Manvel rented a large tract of land in the hot country to cultivate a milpa and sell the surplus. He took six workers with him. On one occasion, Manvel and his workers joined a friend who also had six workers. Antel prepared food for the entire group because the employer is responsible for feeding his workers. Antel gives an idea of what this work involves:

> The other time when we went close to Concordia, I had to feed 12 men. My husband was still working with his friend. Oh, it was tough! I don't remember how old my second son was then. He had a good heart; he helped me to grind the corn. Then I made the tortillas. I had a newborn baby. He lay there on the floor, tossing and turning. But my son Akuxtin waited for the tortillas and the posole to be ready and took them to the fields for the men.
>
> I had to work long hours. I ground the corn for about two hours since it was a lot of corn. Then I made the tortillas. But when the men came back from work, the tortillas were not ready. My baby was crying! I didn't know what to do! I had to get firewood. I had to fetch water. Everything. I cried all the time. It wasn't that I was wasting my time. My baby was crying and the tortillas could not be finished on time. But that happened only for about one month that I was there feeding all these men.
>
> Then my husband started working by himself with only his own workers. He hunted many animals for us to eat. I was working for eight men but two other women came to help me... For 10 years I went to the hot country. We spent many months every year working there, from May to November, and then we went again in December and returned to the highlands only in February or March. (C64-63)

At the time of my research, Manvel was planting his milpa in the highlands and was harvesting enough corn, beans, squash, and turnip greens to feed his family of seven for the whole year. He supplemented his income with work on the coffee farms of the Pacific Coast. At this point he was earning much less than Antel. Manvel made about 6000 pesos ($48.00) a month on the farms, whereas Antel earned close to 5000 pesos ($40.00) for a single week's work of making clothing. With her money, Antel purchases the materials she needs for her work, food for the family, and liquor and soft drinks for the couple's store. She speculates by buying corn and selling it later, in times of scarcity, at a large profit. Manvel lends out at high interest a portion of Antel's earnings.

At this stage in her life, Antel has a great deal of power in the family. She has three unmarried daughters who do most of the housework and two daughters-in-law who live in the family's compound. She is past the age where men will bother her if she walks by herself and has the self-assurance that comes with her age, her history of cargo service, her contacts with outsiders, and her economic success.

Women Who Support Their Families

When men drink to the point that they become dysfunctional, or when they leave their wives for a new woman, or when they work far away and fail to send money home, women become the main providers for the family. Conditions are precarious enough when husband and wife pool their resources, but when only one individual, especially a woman, must take over the support of the family, the situation is extremely difficult. By and large women have no access to wage labor outside the community or to rental lands in the lowlands. Their productive activities, therefore, are restricted to those defined by their community and the world outside as appropriate female occupations.

Women who own enough land in the hamlet to plant a milpa find the task of supporting the family somewhat easier because a guaranteed corn supply frees them to pursue an income. The situation of women without land for milpa, however, is serious. Despite the difficulties they face, some women raise their children by themselves with little or no help from their husbands. This illustrates, for men and women alike, the ability of women to manage—albeit precariously—without the help and "protection" of men.

Women are self-supporting in 11 percent of the households in Tzajal Vitz. These households usually include a widow and a niece or daughter who may be single or divorced with young children. In contrast, strictly speaking, only two men live alone. A third has a small house of his own, but, still a bachelor, he eats and works with his parents. A fourth man who lives by himself suffered an accident during work as a mason and lives on a government pension. All four men depend on their mothers or sisters to assist them with food and clothing. A widowed man with young children immediately looks for another wife, for it would be impossible for him to raise his family by himself.[20] Men cook only on exceptional occasions. They do not weave and would be unable to care for their children and work at the same time.[21]Below are some examples of how women manage on their own.

Several women in Tzajal Vitz earn a livelihood almost singlehandedly because their husbands either spend their money on liquor or do not want to give their wives any money. Paxku', a woman in her fifties, raised her younger children by herself. Her husband was living in Chamula Center as a scribe and did not give her any economic support. She used to plant corn and beans in Tzajal Vitz and, upon her return from work in the fields, would card and spin wool and weave garments for Tenejapanecos and Zinacantecos. With this money she purchased necessary items for herself and her children. After many years, when her husband settled back in the hamlet, he started to make and sell candles. At this point he began to give Paxku' some money.

Matal's husband, Xun, drinks too much and constantly pursues women. He spends most of his time in the city of Villahermosa, selling tacos in the streets, and returns to the hamlet with no money. He is well known in Tzajal Vitz for his irresponsibility towards his family. People comment that he spends all his money on alcohol and in the brothels of the city. He has borrowed a great deal of money that he cannot repay. When he arrives in Tzajal Vitz, his neighbors say, people expect him to try to find work or at least to plant his wife's small plot of land. He does nothing but play ball and drink. His wife takes care of their young children and works in her milpa, carrying her baby on her back. She weaves, embroiders, and sells her work. At the time I did my study, she had had to borrow a large sum of money because her newborn baby was ill and she had no funds to pay for his treatment. To top it all off, one day when Xun had been drinking, he threatened to kill her with a machete; she took a knife from the kitchen and chased him out of the house. People in Tzajal Vitz comment that her children walk around with tattered clothes, looking sad. They say that if Matal did not work so conscientiously, the children would have starved a long time ago.

Antun goes to work on the coffee farms. When he comes back with some money, he spends it all on drink. His wife chops and sells firewood to be able to buy food and some clothing. On one occasion Antun took the money his wife had saved and spent it on liquor. Now she hides her savings. When Antun has money, he goes to a bar where he orders drinks and food, which he shares with the people at the bar, but never with his wife and children.

Women living under circumstances such as these cannot always return to their parents' home. Often the parents are deceased, very poor, or live in another hamlet; the women stay on with men who provide no economic support. Frequently, these women present formal complaints to the court in Chamula Center. The women hope that a jail term will shake up their husbands and cause them to improve their behavior. The case of Lolen from Nichimtik illustrates this situation. Lolen has four children between two and nine years of age. Her husband Andrés has two other wives and does not give her any help, except for some fertilizer each year. Lolen went to court to demand that Andrés contribute to feeding their children. Andrés was forced to give her a single payment of 5,000 pesos ($40.00) for child support.

Lolen learned from her mother how a woman independently supports her family. Lolen's mother was widowed when Lolen and her four siblings were very young. Her mother worked in the milpa and made charcoal to sell in San Cristóbal. Lolen's mother had enough land to feed the children, and from the time they were six years old, the children would help her in the milpa, using the tiny hoes she made for them (fig. 12). Once the milpa was planted and weeded, Lolen's mother would gather firewood to make charcoal. Then she and her children would go to San Cristóbal, each carrying a load of charcoal to sell door to door.

Lolen laments that she did not learn the traditional skills of a Chamula woman, namely, spinning and weaving; she was always busy working in the fields. Her mother, however, taught her to use the axe, the hoe, and the machete. Later, as an adult, she learned how to weave from friends. Now Lolen plants her own milpa, but her lands are not large enough to support her family. She still must buy about half of the maize she and her family consume. When the work of the milpa is done, she makes cloth dolls from worn-out clothes and weaves bracelets and belts to sell to tourists in San Cristóbal (fig. 13). Lolen describes her many activities as follows:

> First I break the land, and then I plant the milpa and the potatoes. I sow corn, squash and various kinds of beans. Then I plant the potatoes in April. Then, in a while, I clean the milpa. I pull the weeds out and put some soil around the potato stalks. Clean and weeded, the milpa will grow up nicely and so will the potatoes. Once I finish cleaning the milpa, I start to weave the family's clothes. I weave a skirt. I weave a blouse. I weave a belt, a woolen shawl, when I finish cleaning the milpa. Well, then, in the meantime, the milpa ripens. I harvest the crop and dig for the potatoes, too. It is then that I come to San Cristóbal to sell my woven goods, my little belts. I come around Christmas time, around New Year's, and also during Carnival time because that's the time when tourists arrive. (Lolen C44-25)

Before she began selling to tourists, Lolen used to work as a day laborer in other people's milpas in her hamlet. She prefers her current work because it enables her to weave at home and watch the children. She only goes into the city three times a week. Although her husband plants a great deal of corn in the hot country, he does not share it with her. He gives corn to his first wife and sells the rest. Andrés also has a new, third wife, who lives in Chamula Center in her parents' house. When Lolen asks Andrés to help her with the children, he accuses her of eating too much, saying that she wants to enjoy meat and soft drinks. If she ate reasonably, he contends, her work would give her enough to support herself and her children. Lolen has repeatedly told him to leave her alone, but he continues to visit her and tells her that if she should ever leave, he will hire a witch to make her sick and kill her wherever she may be.

Lolen's situation is complicated by the fact that she has no parents, brothers, or sisters to help her. Her siblings were expelled from the community because they converted to Protestantism. Lolen has considered joining them but fears she would lose her land, her only security, permanently. She could look for another husband but fears Andrés, who assures her he would kill both her and her new husband, should she find one. Besides, she worries that her children might be unhappy if she remarried. As a single woman without any type of commitment to a man, Lolen would be vulnerable; men would approach her and attempt acquire her as a second wife. Perhaps her current situation is the best alternative for her at this time. With a nominal husband to "defend" her from other men's pretensions, Lolen is able to stay in the hamlet, keep her land, and bring up her children without trouble from other men or suffering the consequences of witchcraft.

Lolen's ability to meet at least half of her maize needs from her own land is an important factor in her situation. She also plants cabbage, swiss chard, chayote, potatoes, and turnip greens. If her land were smaller, her plight would be a lot worse, and it would be necessary for her to get corn from her husband or to marry a man who would support her.

Without the cooperation of a husband or her parents, it is almost impossible for a woman with no land to support her children. For this reason, most divorced or widowed women remarry. Dominga, an older woman from Tzajal Vitz, decided to marry a widower who had petitioned for her. She had spent many difficult years raising her young children after her husband died. At the time the old man came to ask for her hand, Dominga was living with one of her daughters—a physically disabled woman in her twenties—and her six-year-old granddaughter. She decided to marry the widower, thinking that her situation would improve somewhat. Because the man was a curer, she thought he would bring home cooked chicken, other luxury foods, and perhaps some money as well. She was wrong. She soon learned that his patients gave him only small pieces of chicken wrapped in a tortilla. Worse, he spent what little money he earned on liquor and mumbled the whole night long in his bed so that nobody could sleep at night. After a while, Dominga told him to leave.

Widows and single women, accompanied by a daughter or niece, make their living in different ways. If they have no children, they can make enough to support themselves. Most of them plant at least some milpa and own a flock of sheep. Additionally, they sell woven and embroidered garments or firewood. One woman, a midwife, works occasionally for wages in Tzajal Vitz. She assists with the harvesting of corn and beans or cards and spins wool for other women. Another woman, together with her divorced daughter, produces and sells clay pots. A couple of older widows buy and resell fruit daily in the market in San Cristóbal; they also bring some of this fruit to their hamlet to sell. One of them also walks from house to house selling foodstuffs. In sum, most Chamulas live as couples, especially when there are young children; however, single women, childless widows, and a few women with children earn their own livelihoods.

A WORD ON IDEOLOGY

Although in most cases, husband and wife share the responsibility of sustaining their household, underlying ideological tenets still stress the ideal division of labor in which men are supposed to be the main providers of food for the family, and women are supposed to complement their husbands' work in the traditional way. In many of the origin narratives, Our Father enjoins the First Man to bring food home for his wife to prepare. Our Father teaches the man to make milpa. The First Woman learns to render the sacred corn into edible goods, and Our Mother teaches her to spin and weave. Chamula express these ideas in a variety of ways. A man feels embarrassed if his wife helps him tend the milpa because "he is the man" and, therefore, that is his job. By the same token, some women get angry when they must spend their own money to buy corn or beans because that is their husbands' responsibility. The dream of an old widow from Tzajal Vitz illustrates just how deeply ingrained the ideal gendered division of labor is in Chamula. This woman, who has three married sons, is entirely supported by her thirty-year-old, single daughter Veruch. Veruch plants corn, beans, and squash in the highlands and buys additional corn and other foodstuffs with the money she obtains selling blouses. But, when the old woman dreamed that her husband had come to take her with him to the land of the dead, she told him, "I am staying now. I have my sons, they feed me. My sons work their milpas. I don't have to suffer anymore. They have their corn. They have their beans" (Xunka C45-48).

Ideally, men provide for their families; in fact, women often plant milpas in the highlands and help with some of the tasks in the lowlands, too. Frequently, both partners' income goes to buy corn. Men often feel that their privileged position of authority in the household is imperiled when women farm and provide cash, and some women resent having to buy the basic foods, but in general, they acquiesce to the practical demands of providing for their families. They criticize those women who leave the entire burden of feeding the family to their husbands and those foolish men who prevent their wives from going to the city to sell their woven goods.

NOTES

1. In other Highland Chiapas communities, the economic situation does not appear as desperate as in Chamula. Chenalhó, Zinacantán and Amatenango all possess some lands at lower elevations where the agricultural yield is higher. Chenalhó lands receive water from numerous springs in the mountains; Amatenango also has some lands that are irrigated. In these two communities men are able to grow both milpa for family subsistence and a cash crop such as wheat, coffee, or bananas. In general, men are able to meet the needs of their families, and the gendered division of labor seems closer to ideal expectations; however, the national economic crisis is deteriorating the situation of these communities as well (Eber and Rosenbaum in press).

2. The literature on both national and international emigration in Latin America is quite extensive. See Crummet (1987) for an overview of this literature and its different theoretical and methodological perspectives.

3. For studies on this topic in Mesoamerica, see Bossen (1984); Ehlers (1990, 1991); Stephen (1991); and Young (1978).

4. The dread of arousing anger and envy in their neighbors and provoking witchcraft upon themselves discourages conspicuous consumption among Chamulas. Observable differences between rich and poor include the size of homes and the materials used to build them (although usually shape and spatial use are similar) the number of clothes owned, and access to various foodstuffs. Economic differences do not, generally, translate into radically distinct lifestyles as they do in other communities (e.g., Ehlers 1990).

5. Zinacantán has also seen a radical transformation of its relations of production in the past two decades. In the 1960s and 1970s, the ideal and statistical norm for most men (except for a minority from very poor households) was milpa farming. In the 1980s, nearly three-quarters of the married heads of households had become proletarians or semi-proletarians, working mostly for Ladino masters in construction jobs (as compared to earlier proletarians who worked for wealthy Zinacantecos). Furthermore, rich Zinacantecos, who used to devote their energies to large-scale sharecropping of milpa, now work as truckers and vendors, involved in long distance transportation and trade of agricultural products (Cancian 1990:69; Collier 1989:117; Wasserstrom 1983a:199).

6. Indigenous communities that are rapidly integrating into a capitalist economy frequently absorb its concomitant values and attitudes. Middle class women in San Pedro Sacatepéquez, for example, aspire to emulate wealthier women, who are not compelled to work and remain at home. In San Pedro, people view a wife's idleness as an expression of her husband's economic success; this boosts a man's prestige (Ehlers 1990; see also Bossen 1984).

7. In most other indigenous communities of the Chiapas highlands, women's income-producing activities are directly related to the consumption needs of their families. The idea that a man must provide the food and basic family necessities still holds. In Zinacantán and Chenalhó, a wife's claim that her husband does not provide adequately strikes directly at his manhood (Collier 1973:187; Guiteras-Holmes 1961:130). Nash (1985:57) finds that women from relatively wealthy families in Amatenango produce little pottery, but widows and women living alone produce a large number of pieces for sale because they need the income to hire laborers for their lands. Likewise, families with betrothal or cargo expenses increase their pottery production. In Zinacantán, a widow or

divorced woman with children must work constantly to support her household (Wali 1974:47).

8.   Chamulas invest time, energy, and resources cultivating relationships with their *compadres*, ritual co-parents and the baptismal godparents of their children. At the time of a child's birth, father and mother carefully select their baby's godparents from among their neighbors, family, and friends, (in most cases a couple, husband and wife). Through life *compadres* visit and assist each other frequently. For Chamulas, the relationship between *compadres* tends to be more important than that between the godparents and the godchild. Unlike many other Mesoamerican peoples, for whom *compadrazgo* operates for other life cycle events such as confirmation and marriage, Chamulas create this relationship exclusively around baptism. In some Mesoamerican groups (see Stephen 1991), women appear as central actors in creating *compadrazgo* networks, but in Chamula, both husband and wife participate equally in selecting, petitioning, and maintaining active networks.

9.   Young (1978) documents economic change among the Zapotec of the Sierra de Juárez, Oaxaca. The extensive penetration of capitalism in this area undermined local production, interzonal exchange, and reciprocal labor arrangements, increasing internal stratification and people's dependency on industrial goods and wages (see also Arizpe and Botey 1987; Stephen 1991).

10.   For example, see Bossen (1984); Chiñas (1983); and Eber (1991). For an historical perspective, see Burkhart (in press); Leacock (1981); and Silverblatt (1987).

11.   See Tiano (1986) for a review of the effects of industrialization on women's status in Latin America. On the penetration of capitalism and its negative effects on the gender system, see Afonja (1986); Bell (1986); and Shashahani (1986). Lim (1983) and Rosen (1982) present a more positive assessment of this phenomenon.

12.   From the outset, development projects need to address the negative consequences on the gender system that may arise as a result of development. Ehlers (1991), for example, describes a development project in a Maya town in Guatemala, a weaving cooperative initiated by women and men but later appropriated by the men. The project brought about a large disparity in the contribution of women and men to the household economy, propitiating inequalities in a community where gender relationships had been relatively egalitarian.

13.   The gender gap brought about by unequal access to resources becomes an expanding vicious circle. Men continue to accumulate capital and prestige and to further their training or education because they have a stronger base than women from the start. Unskilled, with few or no qualifications, women have a difficult time catching up. Education appears to be the critical factor that allows women to gain a footing in the new system, as both Ehlers's (1990) and Stephen's (1991) studies conclude.

14.   For an interesting description of women's work from the perspective of a Chamula woman, see Komes Peres (1990).

15.   For more information on the cooperative movement, a relatively recent development involving women in the Chiapas highlands, see Eber and Rosenbaum (in press).

16.   The income of these two women is quite high because they act as intermediaries in allocating piecework in their hamlets and earn some money for each item produced. It is interesting to note that these women were able to forge contacts with Mexican and export businesses through the intermediacy of powerful outsiders. Because they control the contacts with buyers and because supply far exceeds demand, other weavers have no alternative but to sell through them.

17. Jan Rus and Diane Rus (1986:10) present a Chamula woman's own statement of the gendered division of labor between a wage worker and his wife as well as other testimonies from Chamulas who work on the farms.

18. Stephen (1991:115) reports similar feelings of independence and self-assurance among Zapotec women from Teotitlán that resulted from their husbands' long absences to work as braceros in the United States. When the men returned home, the women challenged their authority.

19. Young women potters in Amatenango also claim they prefer to live without husbands. As the price of pottery rose in the 1980s, by virtue of its attractiveness to tourists, the value of maize agriculture fell behind. In this process, women have gained a feeling of self-assurance and independence (Nash 1985:336).

20. In Zinacantán, a widower or a man living alone is viewed with pity; he must depend on a female relative to feed him and weave his clothes (Haviland 1977:71; Vogt 1969:131). In contrast, widowed women often prefer to remain independent, making it difficult for widowers to remarry (Collier 1973:199).

21. Nash (1985:70) notes that in Amatenango (and these observations hold for most other highland communities) women can live without men because male labor is a market commodity, and women are able to hire laborers. On the other hand, women's household work is not such a commodity and cannot be purchased. Furthermore, men define their activities more rigidly than do women and will not transgress gender lines to cook, make tortillas, or weave. Women, on the contrary, may work in the milpa and take on other male activities if there is no spouse present to perform these tasks (Wali 1974:53). Men have chosen to be dependent on woman for their most basic needs, but this dependence is not devoid of anger. As Laughlin notes, "a man when drunk may have need of his wife's care, but he might resent his wife's control over him and express anger by beating her" (cited in Wali 1974:67).

7

The Quest for Prestige and Power

How does a person become a "somebody" in Chamula society? On what basis is he or she granted respect? As in many indigenous communities in Mesoamerica, Chamulas become well known, respected and, eventually, powerful by participating in the various civil and religious positions of their community's social organization. These positions are called cargos. The most important political and religious structures in Chamula are the *Ayuntamiento Constitucional* (Constitutional Town Council), the *Ayuntamiento Regional* (Regional Town Council), and the religious hierarchy.

This chapter begins with a discussion of the wider historical context of Mesoamerican cargo systems. It continues with a description of the general composition of civil and religious cargo systems in Chamula, a detailed view of the various practical and ritual roles of men and women in religious and civil cargos, and an analysis of the symbols expressed in one cargo ritual—the *alperes* (Standard Bearer). Finally, it deals briefly with the explicit ideological pronouncements about men and women that are made by public officials in the court.

HISTORICAL CONTEXT

Scholars who work in Mesoamerica have long recognized the centrality of cargo systems in indigenous societies. Recent ethnohistorical studies reveal that civil-religious hierarchies represent specific historical instances where previously distinct civil and religious cargo systems merged into a single hierarchy.[1] Individuals alternated between the cargos of each system as they climbed the ladder of prestige and power in their communities (Carrasco 1961; Nash 1958). The intertwining of these systems illustrates the inextricable links, manifested in different forms through time, between religion and politics in Mesoamerica.[2] Indigenous peoples have employed religion as an idiom to speak about power, unity, solidarity, and conflict. They have rallied around religious symbols to strengthen their claims, defend their systems from outside interference, pursue sovereignty, and express political dissidence and dissatisfaction with the status quo. Rulers have often obtained power and legitimized their status through religion.[3]

Following the Mexican Revolution, the national government set out to gain control over the affairs of indigenous communities. Opposing the right of indigenous peoples to political autonomy, officials resolved to penetrate their communities and modify the structure of local governments in order to integrate the native communities into the national political and party structures. Thus, it was decreed that every municipio in Mexico would elect civil officials to a council that would represent the community and report to the state and national governments. These new positions had to be filled with individuals who were proficient in Spanish, preferably literate, and skilled and experienced in dealing with political bureaucracies.[4] These regulations resulted in a system that circumvented the traditional routes to power, in which people had been eligible to higher leadership positions by virtue of participation in religious cargos and lower civil positions. The time frame and the processes through which indigenous communities slowly acquiesced and adopted the imposed councils varied greatly. Although, in general, local autonomy was severely restricted, native communities reacted diversely, thus affecting the long term consequences of state interference.[5]

In about 1915, Chamulas finally found themselves free of the oppressive *jefes políticos* (political bosses) who controlled the affairs of native communities in the period leading up to the revolution.[6] Native leaders retrenched and designed a political strategy aimed at protecting Chamulas from the abuse of native leaders in collusion with state authorities—a direct response to circumstances that Chamulas had suffered in the recent past. Under the new system, *principales* (community elders)[7] elected the municipal president and all municipal officers from the ranks of monolingual elders (Rus and Wasserstrom 1980). Each year the elders selected new civil officials from among the men who had held religious cargos and chose younger men to fill the vacancies in the religious hierarchy. The power of the elders continued unabated until 1936, when Lázaro Cárdenas became president of Mexico.

From the beginning, the Cárdenas government sought to mobilize the peasants and to integrate them into the official party structure, thereby obtaining peasant support for the revolutionary measures of the government. It was reasoned that the support of the peasants would give Cárdenas the necessary power to neutralize opposition to his programs. Erasto Urbina, head of the *Departamento de Protección Indígena* (Department for the Protection of Indigenous People, referred as DPI), was fluent in Tzotzil and Tzeltal. He realized immediately that in order to effect an institutional link among the reformist Cárdenas government, the newly founded *Sindicato de Trabajadores Indígenas* (Union of Indigenous Workers), and the native communities, he would have to bypass the monolingual elders that governed Chamula (and the other indigenous highland communities). Therefore, in 1938, he recruited a group of bilingual, literate young men whom he appointed as scribes to their communities' councils. Within a few years, these scribes had accrued a lot of power since they were also appointed to positions in the Union of Indigenous Workers and on the agrarian committees of their communities; they also became leaders of the local branches of the official party. In 1938 the DPI decreed that municipal presidents had to be able to speak Spanish. The elders in Chamula defied this injunction for some time but were finally forced to accept a compromise: a "traditional" president would be in charge of Chamula's internal affairs, but one of the bilingual scribes, locally defined as an aide to the president, would represent Chamula in its dealings with the outside world. Thus, from 1938 to 1940, there were two presidents in Chamula.

The scribes did not obtain their positions through the traditional track of the civil-religious hierarchy and therefore lacked legitimacy with the community. In 1942, the scribe who was elected to be president of Chamula in 1943 decided to appease the elders by promising to serve a religious cargo as soon as he finished his term as president. In an added move to please the elders and to gain their acceptance of the new leaders, the DPI allowed prospective religious cargoholders to sell liquor, a profitable and attractive enterprise that would help defray the high costs of service. The scribes further legitimized their power by organizing the community's opposition to the state government, which in 1946 imposed severe restrictions on purchasing *pox* (Rus ms). The "Pox War" lasted about four years, and by the time it ended, the scribes had won respect from the traditional elders and had become firmly entrenched in their positions of power. From the late 1930s to the present, this group of scribes and their close relatives have ruled Chamula, serving religious cargos to legitimize their authority. Moreover, through their connections with state officials, they have been able to turn many government programs to their advantage. Through the years they have become prosperous; they own trucks and stores, and monopolize the best paid government jobs.

At the time the system of scribes was initiated, the elders were able to keep a measure of power by forcing political newcomers to take on religious offices to legitimize their unorthodox arrival to power. In the 1970s, several presidents fell into disfavor with the elders for a variety reasons (e.g., chronic absenteeism, lack of competence in handling serious court cases, misuse of municipal funds, and disrespectful behavior towards prestigious religious and civil cargoholders), and one of them was forced to flee (Linn 1976; see also Earle 1990). According to J. Rus (personal communication), in the mid-1970s a new system to further subvert the authority of the elders was put in place by the *Asuntos Indígenas* (Bureau of Indian Affairs) with the cooperation of the presidents of Chamula. By law each hamlet was required to have an agent to represent the authority of the municipal president. Currently these agents, appointed by the Chamula's president, arbitrate all disputes that arise in their hamlets, referring only the most difficult cases to Chamula Center. This system effectively loosens the elders' firm grip on the adjudication of conflicts, an arena where community traditions and mores are constantly enforced. It is too soon to assess the consequences of this change, which will ultimately hinge on the types of persons selected as agents as well as the defensive reactions of the elders to this virtual coup. According to Rus (ms), these alliances between local and state officials have changed the overall commitment of native authorities; from leaders who once safeguarded their communities from outside exploitation, they have become leaders who utilize community traditions against the people.

Rus's analysis of the integration of the local political structures of Highland Chiapas into the political structures of the state and nation, with the consequent undermining of native autonomy, coincides with the findings of other authors from different areas of Mesoamerica.[8] Although the influence of the national (and international) political economy over native communities is unquestionable, the case of Chamula illustrates the complexity of the situation. Earle (1990) convincingly argues that despite the corrupt, opportunistic behavior of the municipal presidents (which Chamulas themselves recognize), the Chamula people have to some extent been able to contain the more aggressive penetration of state and religious institutions. Chamulas have countered the threat of cultural and sociopolitical disintegration by maintaining a fanatically centralized political and religious organization and by taking drastic measures to discourage dissidence (Gossen 1986b:228). The very preservation of the cargo system, as Chance (1990:39) suggests, indicates the success of Chamulas in retaining some local autonomy and community identity. In this respect, Chamula appears triumphant. Its religious cargo system displays an extraordinary vitality. Although the Constitutional Town Council imposed by the state reigns supreme, members of the Regional Town Council continue to exercise influence and to govern in close connection with the community's religious tenets. The strength of its traditions and the integration of its religious and civil institutions make Chamula a remarkable case among the indigenous communities of Chiapas and Guatemala (Earle 1990:135).

It is unlikely that such integration and resilience could have resulted exclusively from policies developed by the elite in Chamula—an elite which colludes with state authorities to manipulate, control, and exploit the general population of Chamula. By focusing solely on a political economy analysis, one might arrive at such a conclusion;[9] as anthropologists, however, it is also important to listen carefully to the voices of the indigenous men and women, agents of their own reality and history, lest their words and actions appear as illusory reflections or epiphenomena of "real" macroeconomic or political processes, or lest they appear as puppets impelled by superior forces that they do not comprehend and can do nothing about.[10] Scholars must seek a dialectical understanding of the interaction between local dynamics and meanings and the larger sociopolitical and economic processes that impinge upon them.

In words and actions, Chamulas express their commitment towards community and tradition. In reacting to the negative experiences they face daily because of their disadvantaged position in the Ladino world, they have carved out a space where they can make a bid for power in local arenas. Men and women feel they can affect, to some extent, the way in which they live their lives by establishing a network of people who respect them and who they, in turn, can influence. This network is particularly important for women: because their outside contacts are limited, and their contribution to civil cargos remains within the home, their participation in religious cargos gives them a taste of power and status. Both men and women feel empowered by the relationship they establish with their deities.

As several studies have shown, however, civil and religious cargos are not usually open to every person in the community. Since Cancian's classic study of the cargo system in Zinacantán, ethnologists have become aware that religious cargos represent a way to exchange wealth for prestige in a community (i.e., a way to buy prestige). Religious cargos, therefore, are usually open only to individuals in the high and medium strata of society.[11] In many of the societies where cargo systems have been examined, cargo service is a way to legitimize wealth differences and to display a commitment towards one's community through serving the deities that oversee the well-being of the whole group. Although the lesser cargos, such as *mayol tajimol* (policeman of the Festival of Games) or cargos serving minor saints,[12] are accessible to many Chamulas, the vast majority of the population are too poor to ever afford a cargo.[13]

Nevertheless, the structure of cargos in Chamula allows many people to obtain some prestige by assisting cargoholders with specific tasks. For example, in addition to the gifts of food and liquor that they receive for their service, Cooks, Bartenders, Corn Gruel Makers, Flower Bearers, and so forth also get tokens of respect from the cargoholders and the people present at the fiesta. Moreover, an assistant who is reliable and works efficiently may establish a professional name in the community, and prospective cargoholders will court that person to participate in their retinue. Sometimes people walk several miles to distant hamlets in order to recruit the best person for a specific job. Although the status of these helpers is not raised as much as that of the cargoholders, they still accrue respect. Years after their service, people continue to call them by their official title as members of the cargo retinue, *me' jtzayavil* (Lady or Mother Cook), *julovil* (Corn Gruel Maker), and so on.

Given the large number of religious cargo positions in Chamula, each one involving the participation of many assistants, several hundred or even thousand people participate actively in the cargo system every year.[14] As can be seen, the system motivates more than just a few, wealthy Chamulas. Moreover, the thousands who attend the celebrations, partake in the communal distribution of liquor and food, and enjoy the different activities and ritual sequences of each cargo also support the system through their presence and their enthusiasm. Although there is no prestige to be derived from this type of participation, the participants share in the general effervescence and exalted feeling of community that characterize these celebrations.

Consensus is far from general in Chamula. Evidently not everybody has a similar stake in preserving the system. Many Chamulas antagonize their leaders and consider the religious system to be manipulated by them. These people often choose to change their religion, an act which sends a strong message of political opposition. Since the late 1960s, when Protestant missionaries began to make inroads in Highland Chiapas, the central government of Chamula has expelled thousands of people who have converted to Protestant sects or to the "new" Catholicism. Many of these converts publicly defy the authorities, whom they accuse of forcing them to participate in the system against their desires and economic possibilities. I agree with Earle (1990), who stresses that religious conversion in the context of Chamula means a great deal more than just changing religions: because of the close tie between religion and politics, conversion implies sedition and an explicit rejection of the social, political, and moral bases of Chamula society. Any solution to the problem will require more than the establishment of a system that accepts religious pluralism because conversion is perceived as a threat to the stability and integration of the community itself. As Earle (1990:135) explains, the phenomenon must be evaluated in terms of the limited options of those who lack political power beyond their own community.[15]

This policy of purging dissenting individuals from the community has created a tremendous human problem. Thousands of converts from Chamula and neighboring indigenous communities live in squatter settlements around the Ladino city of San Cristóbal (chap. 8).

ASSESSING THE ROLE OF WOMEN IN CARGOS

For many decades, research on the cargo systems overlooked the presence of women as cargoholders. Women share the positions with their husbands or, in some communities, with other male kin. In many cases where they are not cargoholders themselves, women are crucial supporters whose participation in the creation of the necessary infrastructure is sine qua non to the successful undertaking of a cargo (Mathews 1985). The slight of women's participation in the cargo system is partly a result of the androcentric bias that characterized anthropology before the feminist critique. But indigenous communities themselves appeared to confirm this bias by granting recognition of the cargo position exclusively to men: men alone are inscribed and sworn in as the holders of the cargo. The failure to officially recognize women as cargoholders may be a continuation of a Spanish colonial practice in which men were considered the official representatives of their households and the only ones eligible to hold civil or religious positions (Mathews 1985:290; Stephen 1991:159).

According to several recent studies, women play crucial roles in their communities' religious systems.[16] As I show in the following pages, Chamula women apply themselves with energy and devotion to the service of a religious cargo; they describe their participation as a challenging and exciting experience. Amidst the poverty and uncertainty of their lives, women are empowered by their direct contact with the deities through dreams and through the rituals of the cargo; at the same time, they relish the prestige they obtain in the community for their service to the gods (Rosenbaum 1990). Like men, women who serve cargos wield influence in the community (Stephen 1991:161ff.). By expanding their social network, developing contacts with other civil and religious cargoholders, and becoming important members of their community, Chamula women increase their knowledge of the political world. They are able to enter discussions and hold definite opinions about what is going on and what should be done. Notwithstanding the sacrifice involved, women enthusiastically embrace cargo service because of the benefits it may bring to their marriages. The marriage relationship grows stronger because communication and cooperation between husband and wife are greatly increased in the process of fulfilling a common goal.

In his study of 23 ethnographic cases of civil religious hierarchies, Chance (1990) documents a definite trend towards the divorce of the civil and religious branches. This separation, which appears to lead eventually to the demise of both civil and religious cargos or to the diminished importance of the religious branch, has a negative effect on women's status. The new criteria for public office (literacy, fluency in Spanish, and skill in dealing with state officials and bureaucracies) transform the nature of the power and prestige structures and limit women's access to them (Mathews 1985; Stephen 1991). Stephen argues that with the decline in the celebration of *mayordomías* (the cargo positions among Zapotecs), the prestige previously obtained by Zapotec women from cargo service has been transferred to the celebration of life cycle rituals. But there has been a net loss for women in the process: women are no longer associated with the supernatural beings that represent the whole community, an association that provided a direct vehicle for authority and influence.

Although civil and religious systems operated jointly for some time in Highland Chiapas, today they are separate (Rus and Wasserstrom 1980). When national authorities imposed Constitutional Town Councils in 1917, women did not have the right to vote (Stephen 1991:176). Women in native communities still lack access to the important civil cargos. Through religious cargo service, however, women do acquire power, and they exercise it, albeit in informal ways, by expressing their opinions and by trying to influence other people's views. In places like Chamula, where the religious cargo system remains strong, women also discharge critical religious duties that complement their husbands' civil posts. Ever since Weiner's (1976) cogent analysis of Trobriand women's rituals illuminated the importance of women's power beyond the political and economic realms, anthropologists began to pay attention to the nature of women's relations to transcendental beings. Indeed, a close connection to the deities gives people a claim to power in societies where the cosmic and social orders are bound to each other. Chamulas define both civil and religious service as assisting the deities in the fight against the forces of chaos and evil in order that light, life, and order may prevail in the universe. In this context women's ritual duties should be given serious consideration.

In the following pages I discuss the experience of serving a religious or civil cargo as seen from within, especially by women. The analysis highlights the power that Chamula women have in these contexts—as compared with Ladino women and indigenous women from many other areas, who no longer have the possibility of cargo service as a means to build positions of power and prestige. I also discuss the issue of gender inequality within the cargo systems. I show that there are symbolic and structural elements in the religious cargo which symbolize male dominance, but it is the court system, a part of the civil cargo structure, that gives the depiction of women as weak and timorous its paramount expression.

OFFICIALS AND THEIR DUTIES IN CHAMULA

The Constitutional Town Council is a body of 12 officials (plus one municipal agent from each hamlet) who are literate and bilingual, as mandated by Mexican law (Linn 1976:170): The *peserente* (president) is the official spokesman for Chamula in its relationships with the outside world, the ultimate authority in civil disputes, and the main collector of taxes for fiestas and municipal projects. The *jves* (judge) assists the president at court and keeps statistics of major crimes such as murder or theft; the *jves suplente* (assistant judge) helps the judge in his tasks. The *sintiko konstitusional* (legal official) assists the judges and serves as the intermediary between Ladino law agencies and the local court in cases of serious crime, usually murder. There are six *rejirol konstitusional* (aldermen of the constitution), two for each barrio of Chamula, who assist the president and help organize the scribes (officials in the Regional Town Council). The *tesorero* (treasurer) is chosen from the scribes and keeps the accounts of taxes collected and expenditures. The *komandante de polisia* (chief of police) directs the policemen of the Regional branch and represents Chamula in legal affairs. The *sekretario* (secretary), a Ladino representing the Mexican government, interprets Mexican policies to the local officials. Finally, the *agente munisipal* (municipal agents), mandated by the Bureau of Indian Affairs since 1974, serve as representatives of the president in each hamlet (Pérez López 1987:6). Theoretically, all of these officials are elected, but in fact, they are chosen by the Chamula oligarchy and past cargoholders. Their terms usually last three years.

The Constitutional Town Council deals with state and national agencies on matters such as military service, work and pay conditions on the farms, and the construction of schools, roads, water systems, and monuments. Linn (1976:157) observes that while the Regional Town Council explicitly reinforces Chamula values and traditions, the Constitutional Town Council operates as an arena in which Chamula's ruling families struggle for power and economic benefits.

The president of the Constitutional Town Council is also president of the Regional Town Council, thus linking the two governing bodies. The Regional Town Council, or traditional civil hierarchy, comprises about 80 officials (Linn 1976:169): 16 *alkalte* (mayors), who assist the president and judge in arbitrating court cases, collect municipal taxes from hamlets, and help choose the successors in civil and religious cargos; 12 *mayol kavilto* (aldermen), who also assist in court hearings and in choosing civil and religious cargoholders; 12 *kominarol* (governors), whose duties involve buying food for Chamula prisoners in San Cristóbal prisons and overseeing public works; six *alkalte sintiko* (mayoral trustees), who help take the census, collect market and hamlet taxes, and take care of the repairs needed in public areas; 10 *mayol* (policemen), who capture wrongdoers, take messages to the hamlets, work on municipal projects and police fiestas, prevent intrusions by tourists and other outsiders, and guard the church against thieves; and 18 *eskirivano* (scribes), whose duties include assisting the governors, the mayoral trustees, and the policemen and keeping all written records. One of the most important responsibilities of the scribes is the supervision of presidential elections. The scribes are apprentices of the political processes of Chamula and often move on to the Constitutional Town Council.

The traditional hierarchy of the Regional Town Council probably resembles the old system of government among indigenous peoples in the area before the intervention of national and state controls in local affairs (Pozas 1959:136). The main function of these officials is to uphold the traditional values and mores of Chamula society. They are involved in all conflicts that arise in the hamlets and cannot be resolved by the disputants. Litigation over land, problems between husband and wife or adult children and their parents, divorce, conflicts related to drunkenness, cases of malicious gossip, accusations of witchcraft, and minor crimes are brought to Chamula Center and aired before the president and his assistants. The Constitutional Town Council, however, handles cases of murder and other serious crimes like rape, turning them over to state authorities for trial and punishment.

In the past, most of the positions on the Regional Town Council were held by monolingual individuals since bilingualism was not a requirement for participation. During their one-year term, the designated cargoholders leave their hamlets to live in Chamula Center. They are selected by a group of respected community elders and by the current members of the Regional Town Council and act as representatives of their respective barrios.[17] Over the years, the group carefully selects men from all the outlying hamlets in order to achieve equal representation within each barrio. (Gossen 1974:14).

The civil officials of the Regional Town Council carry silver-tipped batons to signal that religion sanctions their authority; in their prayers, Chamulas say that these officials govern "beneath the hands and feet of San Juan." The silver-tipped baton represents both the baton of San Juan, Chamula's patron saint, and the saint himself (Linn 1976:153). Not surprisingly, this group of civil cargoholders also serve important religious functions such as swearing in the new religious cargoholders, blessing the ritual liquor for the fiestas, and participating in the baton washing ritual before every major fiesta.

The president, a member of both civil councils, is the only member of the Constitutional Town Council with religious or ritual functions. His religious duties include presiding over baton washing at all the fiestas, leading prayers and lighting candles for major fiestas, and participating in rainmaking and water hole ceremonies (Linn 1976:170). As representatives of the president, some municipal agents, but not all, also govern under the patronage of San Juan. All other members of the Constitutional Town Council govern exclusively by virtue of Ladino law.

The religious hierarchy is a body of officials (there were 61 in 1968 (Gossen 1974:13)) who sponsor public and private celebrations in honor of the saints. By praying, dancing, singing, offering fresh flowers on the altar of a given saint every 20 days, and hosting a major celebration on the saint's day, these religious cargoholders exalt the deities and seek their blessings on behalf of all the Chamula people. Chamulas dramatize the importance of this religious service to the community through several narratives in which the destructions of earlier worlds are attributed to the failure of ancient peoples to celebrate the saints as they are celebrated today. Today the deities are "fed" and kept happy by the religious cargoholders and therefore would not consider destroying the modern world.

Both civil and religious cargoholders are ranked. Prestige is granted to them according to the responsibilities of their office and their financial expenditures. The most important religious positions are *martoma* (Steward), *alperes* (Standard Bearer), *nichim* (Flower), and *paxon* (Passion). There are eight different Steward positions each year (the most prominent ones are *jtotik*, *San Juan*, *oxib vinik*, and *martoma santo*) and 17 Standard Bearer positions (the most prestigious ones are *San Juan*, *San Machyo*, *San Pedro* and *Santevasyan*). Steward and Standard Bearer positions are ranked according to the importance of the saint to whom they are devoted. Expenditures are also tied to the relative importance of the saint. Flower and Passion honor the sun and moon deities and are the most important and prestigious religious cargos. The Passion cargo, in particular, requires an enormous expenditure. There are six Flower cargos and six Passion cargos, two from each barrio. The Steward and Standard Bearer serve one-year terms; the Flower and Passion serve for two years.[18]

Civil cargoholders do not spend as much money as their religious counterparts; however, since their presence at Chamula Center is required at all times, they cannot leave for the farms to earn money to help cover their expenses. Their small salary (in 1984, 1500 pesos monthly ($12.00)) does not compensate for their disbursements. If they cannot count on a son or close relative to help them plant their milpa, they may have to borrow money to buy food and to pay for their other expenditures. Religious officers, on the other hand, are not required to live in Chamula Center; they are able to go to the hot country and even to the farm, as long as they return to their hamlet every 20 days to celebrate the saint on their home altar.

There are other similarities between religious and civil cargo positions (Linn 1976:163-8). All cargoholders, civil and religious, exercise the prerogative of selling cane liquor before and during their term to help defray the costs of cargo obligations. Both types of cargoholders are seen as rendering a service to the gods and the community. It is expected that this service will bring supernatural rewards to the cargoholders, their families, and the community. Both civil and religious cargos should be undertaken wholeheartedly and sincerely lest misfortune fall upon the cargoholder or even the community. In both types of service, cargoholders fear the anger, envy, and hostility they may attract while involved in public life.

Nevertheless, there is an important difference between the religious and civil systems. Religious cargos are largely voluntary, with waiting lists of up to 25 years for the most prestigious positions; civil appointments, on the other hand, are mandatory, regardless of the financial hardship that an appointee may incur. Initially, most people receive an appointment to civil office with dismay. The only means of avoiding civil cargo service is to flee Chamula for a few years—a shameful, undesirable option. A great deal of tension is generated within the family of an individual who refuses a cargo because the officials invariably attempt to fill the position with a close relative of the original appointee. Eventually, most people recover from their initial shock and their desire to reject the position. They bow to the authority of the governing body in the belief that ultimately their sacrifice will bear fruit—good health, plentiful crops, wealth, and respect for them and their families—because by serving an office, they fulfill their obligations to San Juan.

The importance of women in the cargo system varies greatly between the two branches of the civil system and between the civil system and the religious cargos. It is no coincidence that women have no role in the Constitutional Town Council. The exclusion of women is evidence of the strong, androcentric bent that is characteristic of Mexican society, in general, and the Mexican political system, in particular. With regard to the input and participation of women, the contrast between the Constitutional Town Council, imposed by Mexican law, and the more traditional Regional Town Council and religious system could not be more drastic. The indigenous institutions have been less affected by recent intrusions and provide women with more opportunities to engage in service to their community in ways that are considered worthwhile and rewarding.

Although women are barred from posts in the Regional Town Council, their fulfillment of ritual responsibilities has important consequences both to the success of the cargo and to the welfare of the cargoholder's family. By praying and burning incense three times a day to her husband's symbol of power, the baton, a woman procures the blessings of the deities to counteract the potential dangers inherent in her husband's work (e.g., problems with Ladino authorities, conflicts with other Chamulas, sickness, failure of crops, and other misfortunes that may result from envy and witchcraft).

Interaction with the deities through the role of religious cargoholders brings to the fore the complementarity of husband and wife; the possibilities of cooperation and increased communication between them are fully realized. Women have a voice from the very beginning of the process, including the decision to take a cargo. They actively participate in the cargo by saving money, weaving the special ceremonial clothes for themselves and their husbands, and discussing and recruiting potential helpers. Although some aspects of the men's ritual activities are more visible and dramatic, women are also involved in ritual performances either with their husbands or separately with their female retinue.

One may ask why women are prevented from formally creating or carrying out community policies side by side with men, in the same way that they work together with men in the religious system. More ethnohistorical research is needed on the extent of women's participation in decision-making processes in native communities before the arrival of the Spanish.[19] At the present time, women's absence from the group of community elders, together with the rulings of the court and its use of language demeaning to women (discussed below), underscores women's powerlessness, lack of independence, and need for "protection." In such a climate, how could women's decision-making authority be taken seriously?

HELPING THE DEITIES CARRY THEIR BURDEN

Although the ritual of the religious cargo system is only one aspect of the religious experience in Chamula, it is an overwhelmingly important one, judging by the thousands of people who flock to Chamula Center on the days when religious cargoholders celebrate the fiestas of their saints. Even though the economic situation of most Chamulas is quite precarious, people will "... actively seek the privilege to spend their last peso and borrow perhaps thousands more to sponsor the religious celebrations with food and drink which gladden the saints" (Linn 1976:1).

Gossen (1974:40) argues that the primacy of the male principle is evident in ritual life because women have no official cargo position, and whatever rituals women participate in "do not really count" in the cargo system. This holds true for the formal aspects of the process, in which only the man is sworn in by the civil authorities. He sits at the foot of the cross that represents his barrio while the authorities make the sign of the cross on his forehead, nose, mouth, and heart with the silver-tipped baton (Linn 1976:332):

> Later, when they exchange glasses of cane liquor inside the armory, they pray for the religious cargoholder to execute his office with dignity, using his head and eyes to learn all he must do, his nose to guide him to keep the flowers and incense fresh and never place foul odors before the saint, his mouth to say the prayers, and his heart to serve in willing enthusiasm. The cargoholder's wife does not receive the authorization from the baton, but she sits to one side apart from the man, and is included in the drinks and the prayer sequences. A cargoholder is always accompanied by his wife when receiving the oath of office... (Linn 1976:333)

Even when women remain "officially" out of the cargo, it is clear that the cargo also belongs to them. Like men, women are addressed by a respectful title such as *me' martoma* (Mother or Lady Steward). Other gestures of respect, for example, bowing and releasing the bow, are made to both husband and wife cargoholders; people salute both in drinking and use a polite tone of voice to address both. But most importantly, the way women talk about the cargo leaves no doubt that they experience it as belonging to them as well as to their husbands, and they view their ritual activities to be of prime importance.

How do men and women decide to serve a cargo? Usually, but not always, the man suggests the idea to his wife and solicits her opinion. In many cases the woman initially opposes the service for fear of going broke and takes the opportunity to scold her husband for drinking too much or not working hard enough:

> "Would you like us to have a cargo? I want to ask for a cargo," he said.
> "Well, how do you think you will be able to discharge the duties of a cargo if you continue to behave like this? You are drunk all the time," I said. (Mikul C52c-29)

After discussion, they eventually reach an agreement. If the wife is not willing to cooperate, the man will have to forget the idea; he will never be able to take on a cargo without his wife's full support.

Once a positive decision is made, both husband and wife must devote all their efforts to saving sufficient money to pay for most of their cargo expenditures. They agree to limit their daily expenses and to cut down on luxury foods and liquor. Cargoholders sell liquor to help fund their obligations. The wife attends the customers while her husband is out working. Her job is difficult since it entails supervising the drinkers and trying to prevent fights among those that are drunk. Both husband and wife worry about their financial ability to fulfill the cargo obligations. They fear incurring a large debt or being forced to abandon the cargo; abandonment of a cargo results in tremendous shame, criticism, and even imprisonment.

Paxku' paid almost all the expenses of the first cargo she and her husband served (*mayol tajimol*, one of the less expensive cargos). At the time, her husband was very poor, and she bought the corn and beans for the ritual; he only gave a small amount of money. For their second cargo, Passion (the most expensive and prestigious), they both contributed about the same amount of money. Her husband's finances had improved, and he bought the corn and beans. She bought the "food" for Our Father, the incense. Every 20 days, she went to San Cristóbal to buy 10 to 15 pounds of incense.

The economic contribution of the wife is essential to the success of the cargo.[20] In addition to sharing the expenses, women weave the special clothing that they and their husbands wear when they go to Chamula Center for one of the major celebrations. The man's black jacket is very large and difficult to weave. If the woman is too busy to make it, she will order it from another weaver, which makes it very costly.

Women who I interviewed saw their cargos as coming directly from Our Father, Our Mother, San Juan, or one of the saints. The cargo was conferred upon them in their dreams,[21] sometimes many years before the couple actually decided to serve:

> Well, many years ago, when I still hadn't married my husband,
> I had the same dream three times, and I think it meant that I was
> given a cargo.

> "Are you here?" the woman asked.
> "Yes, I'm here," I replied. Then a man came.
> "Are you here, niece?" he asked.[22]
> "Yes, I'm here uncle," I said.
> "I came to visit you," he said.
> "Come sit down uncle. Come in," I told him. They both sat down.

"What do you say?" I asked him.

"Nothing, niece, I have come to visit you. I have come to talk to you," he said. He brought a vessel for the incense. It was new, quite big.

"I will give you this. Please take it. You will support Our Father," he said. "This is for you to support him with."

"Oh, but I don't know how to!" I said.

"You will learn, the Monkeys (see note 32) will show you," he said. "Please take it; don't be rebellious," he insisted.

Then they came another time and brought a few pine needles with them.

"This is what you will take care of," he said. The man gave it to me, the woman gave it to me...(Maruch C29-57)

Our Father and Our Mother came to Maruch's house bringing all the clothing she was to use during her cargo. Maruch said that when she and her husband were initiated in their cargo of Flower, everything was as she had seen it in her dreams. All of the women I interviewed who have held cargo positions described dreams similar to Maruch's, in which the cargo is handed over to them by the deities. Antel said that she had always wished to be a Steward for Saint Rose, the patroness of weaving in Chamula; she was very excited about this possibility and dreamed that she was dancing while she held Our Mother. Her desire was so strong that she had the same dream several times:

Many times I have seen Our Mother Saint Rose in my dreams, and also Our Mother the Virgin of Rosary.

"Don't you want to hold me in your arms?" asked the woman.

It was a beautiful, big woman with clothes like mine. Well, I tried to carry her in my arms, but I couldn't stand up with her. If I had been able, I would have become a Steward for Saint Rose. (Antel C63c-42)

A little more than a year before entering their cargo, the man and his wife begin to consider who they will recruit to serve in the cargo retinue. At this point they begin to sell liquor and to honor the saint of the cargo every 20 days.[23] For these celebrations, called *k'ex nichim* or Flower Changing, the retinue meets at the house of the cargoholder to dance, sing, and pray to the deity. The cargoholders offer food and liquor to everybody as a token of gratitude for their assistance. The success of a cargo and the happiness of the saint depend to a large extent on the reliability and trustworthiness of the retinue.

Every cargo has several helpers, and there are a great number of them in the major cargos of Flower and Passion. All cargos minimally must have an Advisor (*yajvotik*), a Flower Bearer (*jkuch nichim*), a Bartender (*javil*), a Corn Gruel Maker (*julovil*), a Cook (*jtzayavil*) an Incense Bearer (*jtzan pom*), a Cannoneer (*jantunyero*), and a group of musicians (*mastaro*). Like the cargo positions, these helpers are ranked in terms of prestige, according to the responsibilities of their jobs. The Advisor is by far the most important job since the performance of the cargoholder and his wife depend directly on the teachings of the Advisor and his wife. The other members of the retinue are usually people who are too poor to be able to hold a cargo by themselves. By cooperating with a cargoholder, they fulfill a religious obligation and become well known in the community for carrying out a specific aspect of ritual (Linn 1976:127).

Some of the helper positions (e.g., the Bartender, the Corn Gruel Maker, and the Cook) are carried out jointly by husband and wife, and they receive their tokens of regard together (Linn 1976:134). The Flower Bearer, the musicians, and the Cannoneer, who are always men, and the Incense Bearer, who may be either a man or a woman, do not ritually obligate the spouses, although the latter may also go to the house of the cargoholder to help prepare food or to distribute liquor. Like the cargoholders, the helpers and their wives are addressed for life with the title of their job: Lady (or Mother) Incense Bearer, Bartender and Lady (or Mother) Bartender, and so on. The use of life-long titles suggests that although less prestigious than the position of cargoholder, participation in the retinue also carries prestige.

Husband and wife carefully select their helpers after a great deal of thought and discussion. Once the candidates have been chosen, the couple begins to recruit them, sometimes walking long distances to their homes and always bringing gifts of liquor to beg for their assistance. Husband and wife go together on these recruiting expeditions. Helpers are often chosen on the basis of their reputation for previous responsible service in a particular position (Linn 1976:127). Members of the cargoholders' families may be recruited for less important positions, but their recruitment also involves a long process of prayer and gift giving that may last a few hours.

For their cargo of *mayol tajimol* (Policeman of the Festival of Games), Antel and Manvel went from house to house to recruit a Flower Bearer, a Corn Gruel Maker, a Cook, four Monkeys, a Harp Player, and a Bartender. In each house, a different prayer is uttered by the cargoholders to convince the prospective helpers to join in the service of the saint. The prayers emphasize the importance of each helper to the success of the cargo and the fact that the helper will be working for Our Father, Our Mother, or one of the saints. The following was part of a prayer used to recruit a husband and wife to serve as Corn Gruel Makers:

"Well then, please,
do us the great favor,
uncle, aunt,

are you going to help us,
for the distribution [of corn gruel]
for his sacred heart [the corn gruel]

of the Lord of Heaven,
of the Lord of Glory,

his sunbeam,
his shadow,

will be spread,
will be distributed,

at the doorstep of his house,
at the doorstep of the place of his wealth,

at his hands,
at his feet,

in the big feast,
in the big celebration,

of the Lord of Heaven,
of the Lord of Glory,

his body,
his flesh,

will be distributed,
will be spread,

with his guitar,
with his rattle,

in the meeting of his children,
in the meeting of his descendants.

Will you do us the favor?

Will you help us then
uncle, aunt?"
we told the would-be Corn Gruel Makers. (Antel C24)

In addition to the official assistants, many of the couple's neighbors go to the woods to collect firewood for cooking the large quantities of food that will be distributed during the festival. Antel described the fiesta vividly, savoring in every word her pride and happiness:

Well I was just sitting down at my home before going to Chamula Center.

"Lady *mayol tajimol*, Lady *mayol tajimol*," they asked me, "what do you want to eat? Do you want corn gruel?"
"No, I will drink cane liquor," I replied.

Then we came to Chamula Center. From the hamlet, the Monkeys started to dance. They came down dancing, dancing. The Monkeys went down dancing all the way on the road. Oh, it was so beautiful! Then we arrived in town. People came to grind the dough for the corn gruel. The basket for the dough was huge! Then, when they began cooking the corn gruel, the Monkeys started singing and dancing again...When the corn gruel was ready, we all stood up to dance... (Antel C24)

Indeed, although women worry at first that they will not be able to raise the necessary money and corn for the celebration, often crying in fear, they all seem to enjoy their cargos thoroughly. They feel gratified when making the three daily prayers to Our Father and Our Mother at morning, noon, and dusk—alone or with their husbands—lighting the candles and burning incense. They enjoy the Changing of Flowers, singing and dancing with their helpers.

The women voice the delight they feel when participating in the major fiestas with their husbands and helpers. Dressed in their elegant ritual attire, all the participants attend church in Chamula Center. There they take part in different rituals such as changing the saint's clothes, burning incense and praying to the saint, taking the saint out of the Church for a procession, and giving out or receiving ritual food and drink. The hundreds or thousands of people in attendance, according to the relative importance of the fiesta, give recognition to the cargoholders and acknowledge their willingness to serve the saints and the community. The cargoholders become more than just another face in the crowd. They are on their way to becoming prestigious members of the community.

Women talk about their fiestas with nostalgia, remembering the beauty of their clothes—the special glass bead necklaces, the rosary necklaces, and the colored ribbons in the woolen shirts. They reminisce about the joy they felt as they danced, sang, and carried the saints around the church atrium. All the women who have held cargos recall feeling sad when their service was over.[24] They miss "talking" with and "feeding" Our Father each day and having a house full of people every 20 days. They long to be the center of attention once again for the fiestas and the Changing of Flowers ceremony:

> When we finished our cargo, when we unloaded Our Father, we remained empty. I felt depressed without it. I did not have Our Father to "support" everyday, anymore. My heart was full of sorrow. I saw how the other women were rejoicing in their cargos. I went to watch the Steward. I went to watch the Flower. I went to watch the Passion. They seemed so happy in their fiestas.
>
> "But why? Why can't I do what they do?" I said to myself. "I want to enjoy it, too. Her house looks so nice," I thought to myself. "Her blouse is so pretty. Her clothes are so good. Why can't I also do it?"
>
> Well we had unloaded our cargo just 20 days before, and oh God, it already hurt not to be able to talk to Our Father!
> "Should we ask for another cargo or are you tired of serving Our Father?" my husband said. "Should we request another one?"
> "Let's go," I said. "I want it badly".
>
> So we went again and requested another cargo, and it was given to us. We got drunk. I was so delighted that we had acquired our work! My heart was happy. (Maruch C29-54)

Husband and wife learn the long, complex prayers and songs for their cargo from a ritual advisor, the most important member of their retinue; they also must learn the different ritual activities for the fiestas and the Changing of Flowers. The Advisor counsels them on practical matters as well, such as the amount to spend for flowers, liquor, and food on each ritual occasion.

Like their husbands, women suffer through the anxiety of carrying out the cargo successfully and of going into debt to pay for the expenses. But, also like their husbands, they experience the intense satisfaction of serving the deities, and the supernatural and social rewards that accompany service. Chamulas recognize that the cargo involves continued cooperation and communication between husband and wife. They see the cargo as a means to solidify the marital relationship and to obtain supernatural help in solving their problems. Notwithstanding their shared commitment and responsibility, the system still favors men by granting them official recognition of office and reserving the most salient ritual performances for them.

GENDER SYMBOLS IN CARGO RITUAL

This section deals mainly with the ritual of the Standard Bearer. Although I attended the ritual of the incoming Standard Bearer for the Virgin of Guadalupe, I have drawn on Linn's (1976:760ff.) careful descriptions to complement my observations.[25]

Chamula ritual activity is tremendously rich, long, and elaborate, and the rituals vary greatly according to the cargo position. Steward, Standard Bearer, Flower, and Passion cargos have different functions. Their ritual activities vary, as do the numbers and roles of the members of their retinues, the amount and type of ritual food and drink offered, and the days when they perform their rituals, prayers, music, and songs. Moreover, there are important differences among the Stewards and among the Standard Bearers, according to the saint being served. Rituals also vary with regard to where they are performed. Some rituals take place in the cargoholders' house in the hamlet; others in the cargoholders' ceremonial house in Chamula Center; still others are performed within and outside of the Church. The following description considers only a very small segment of ritual life in Chamula.

The major responsibilities of the Standard Bearer are to take care of the flags of the different saints. There are 17 Standard Bearers in Chamula, each one serving a major or a minor saint for a year. The flags, flagstaffs, and the detachable crosses on the tips of the staffs are just as holy as the saints themselves (Linn 1976:83). The cross and the flag are kept in a red bandanna and carried with utmost respect to the flower-decorated home altar of the Standard Bearer, where incense is burned to them three times a day.

All Standard Bearers unfurl their colorful banners at the major fiestas as part of the saints' procession at noon. Unlike the other cargoholders, the Standard Bearers assume and relinquish their cargos on the day of the saint whose flag they bear. In this way, the celebration of the saint is incorporated into the complex rituals of entering and leaving office (Linn 1976:84).

At the time they enter their cargo, and again when they hand it over to a successor, the Standard Bearers, like all religious officials, must rent or borrow a house in Chamula Center. People gather in the incoming Standard Bearer's house for an entire week to help prepare for the *k'ex alperes*, the Change of Standard Bearers. The cargoholders and their retinue are assisted by many others who procure firewood and prepare and distribute food to the crowd (including ritual food for all onlookers). When they leave office on the day of the fiesta, Standard Bearers also serve food to their helpers and ritual food to onlookers. But the ritual of the outgoing Standard Bearer is further complicated by the construction of a high platform on oak poles, raised four or five meters off the ground. This platform, called *moch* (basket), is decorated with flowers, and there the flag is raised to bring it closer to the sun (Linn 1976:84). A representative of the Standard Bearer, always a man, sits on the tower. Gossen (1974:36) interprets this arrangement to symbolize the heights that the outgoing official has achieved in his year of service to the community by helping the Sun to maintain order.

The incoming and outgoing Standard Bearers, their wives, and the most important members of their retinue wear special ceremonial clothes. The clothes of outgoing male Standard Bearers—deerskin trousers under a black tunic—are different from those of incoming ones—a bright red coat with matching, knee-length trousers. Female Standard Bearers wear brown woolen shirts with colored ribbons on the front of the bodice, glass bead necklaces, and new, black woolen skirts similar to their everyday skirts, but finer. In general, there are fewer differences in the clothing worn by women in different cargo positions than in those worn by men.

Chamula women are ubiquitous in the ritual of the religious cargo system. Unlike cargo wives in neighboring Zinacantán, who dedicate most of their time to supervising food preparation, the wife of a cargoholder in Chamula has solely ritual obligations. She is not supposed to be involved in food preparation but should devote her full attention to dancing, praying, singing, offering and receiving liquor, and holding and carrying holy objects. In the rituals for changing Standard Bearers in Zinacantán, the wives of the cargoholders watch their husbands dance, parade, and exchange flags. In Chamula, Standard Bearers and their wives share the tasks of praying, dancing, and feasting; the flag cannot be passed to the incoming official until husband and wife together cense the staff (Linn 1976:73). Chamula women complement their husbands' cargo rituals: they are ritually bathed, they partake of the ritual meal, they pray and burn incense at the home altar, and they pray outside their house before the courtyard cross, or inside the Church.[26]

Ritual activity is usually a privileged locus for making important cultural tenets explicit. Rituals underline the dominating themes of Chamula social order and cosmology. Thus, although their input and participation in the cargo are essential, women are absent from some of the most visible and central ritual roles. In several ritual sequences, women literally observe from the sidelines. For example, in the ritual of the incoming Standard Bearer that I observed, only men handle the saint's flag and cross-shaped tip. The Standard Bearer, his Advisor, his Flower Bearer and his Jockey go to the Church to retrieve and replace the flag several times during the four days of the fiesta. The Flower Bearer places the banner on the staff and brings it out of the Church. He hands it to the Standard Bearer, who carries it to the Cabildo (the government building) and points it at the four cardinal directions. Then, the Standard Bearer, carrying the flag, and the Jockey mount their horses and return to the cargo house (Linn 1976:765). While the men are in the Church dealing with the ritual objects, the women remain outside marching at the rear of the group.

Women are also conspicuously absent in one of the most impressive and colorful events in the Standard Bearer ritual—the horseback ride on the fourth day of the fiesta and the procession that follows. The Jockey, mounted on his horse, begins the event with a ride through the marketplace in front of the Church. A trumpet announces his entrance. At the Cabildo the rest of the men, including the incoming and outgoing cargoholders, observe the ride. When the Jockey is done, an all-male procession of about 10 members steps out, attracting a large number of onlookers. The outgoing Standard Bearer, on horseback, carries the flag. He is accompanied by the mounted Jockey, followed on foot by two Incense Bearers, the incoming Standard Bearer with his helpers, and some of the retinue of the outgoing Standard Bearer. The procession marches three times around the marketplace in a counterclockwise direction. They stop at each of the crosses which mark the corners of the marketplace, before the Church, and at the center of the west side of the marketplace. At each stop, the helpers remove the hats of the two Standard Bearers, who then pray while the other men cense the crosses.

During this activity, the women sit on a ledge on the western side of the marketplace and watch. The day I observed this ritual, two drunken women were lying on the ground in the marketplace. When they saw the procession coming, they stood up and walked in front of the men for some distance until, finally, they were removed. The wives of the cargoholders and their helpers commented indignantly on the shameless behavior of these women "who were ruining the Standard Bearer's horseback ride."

Ritual duties are not distributed equally between men and women.[27] Especially in the central places where most onlookers gather (outside the Church, in the marketplace, and at the Cabildo), women seem to have less of a presence. Women's and men's ritual duties appear more balanced in the context of the cargo house. Therefore, it appears that gender complementarity and inequality coexist within the institution of the religious cargo.

RELIGIOUS CARGOS AND THE MARITAL RELATIONSHIP

Cargoholders enjoy various rewards that result from their service and which act as powerful motivators to participate in the religious system. Men and women enjoy stepping out temporarily from their mundane roles as parents, spouses, and workers, to become helpers of the Sun, the Moon, and the saints. But an additional motivating force acts as powerfully as any of the above: holding a religious cargo seems to improve and strengthen a marriage.

Antel pointed out that holding a cargo has the same effect as the formerly practiced *nupunel*, or church wedding (chap. 5, n. 2):

> If we have not had a *nupunel*,
> if we have never had a cargo,
> it is a male goat whom we will receive as our husband.[28]
>
> The male goat comes to meet us when we arrive,
> when our soul leaves our body three days after we die.
>
> "Heh, heh, heh, heh, heh," says the disgusting goat.
>
> It is so big! Its beard is so long!
> The goat hugs us since it is our husband.
>
> We do not join a man anymore.
> We join a male goat.
>
> Instead, those who have had cargos,
> and those who have gone through a *nupunel*,
> experience a different fate.
>
> If the man dies first, he comes to wait for us.
> If the woman dies first, there she goes to meet him,
> when he finally dies.
>
> There we will talk just as we did when we were here on earth.
> (Antel C35-69)

Like the *nupunel*, cargo service guarantees that in the afterlife the souls of husband and wife will rejoin, and it prevents their souls from being transformed into animals after death.

Chamula men and women realize that serving a cargo has a profound impact on the relationship between husband and wife, and they express this variously.[29] In many instances Chamula men take on the responsibility of a cargo to try to amend their wrongs, especially excessive drinking, wife beating, or womanizing. For example, when Antel's husband became involved with her younger sister, he beat Antel. Antel took both of them to court, and they were sent to jail in Chamula.

After a few days, when Manvel was released, he decided to request a cargo and to try to "erase his crime." Antel was uncertain whether she should go along with this plan, but the officials in Chamula persuaded her. "Take on your cargo," they told her. "Put yourselves in the hands of Our Father." Tumin's husband was also going to take up a cargo:

> I talked to my aunt, the former Lady Flower.
>
> "Look," I said, "Marian has already found another wife," I said. "So I'm leaving."
> "Don't go," she said. "Talk to Our Father, take the cargo with your husband. Talk forcefully to Our Father so that he sets it firmly in your heart. Wait and see, maybe it works," she said. (Tumin C31-47)

Also, women who hold a cargo and have difficulties with their husbands get supernatural help from Our Father and Our Mother. They are helping to carry the burden of the deities and so expect the deities to reciprocate by aiding them. Thus, many women narrate how Our Father appeared in their dreams after they had fervently prayed and talked to him about their problems:

> When my husband asked for his cargo, he had another woman. I wanted to leave the house. So, Our Father talked to me in my dreams.
>
> "Don't go," he said. "It's better if she leaves [the other woman]. She is not the one who will support me, and I don't want to support her either. Please don't leave," he said. "I have thought about it, please don't go. Strengthen your heart, endure the beatings. Look at my face," said Our Father.
>
> Oh, the face of the poor man! It was covered with blood. When my husband hit me, Our Father felt the blows too.
>
> "All right," I said, "I will not go now," although I really wanted to leave.
>
> Well, the other woman was still there that night, but the next evening she had left. When I came back from the fields, she wasn't there anymore. She had taken her clothes with her. Our Father had chased her out. He did not want to be fed by her. (Antel 63c-25)

Holding a religious cargo does not, of course, guarantee that the marital relationship will improve. I was told of several couples who had serious conflicts at
the time they were holding their cargo. However, the entire process entailed in
serving a cargo, in addition to the supernatural blessings and the social rewards of
increased status, stimulate a strong cooperative bond. Communication increases
greatly as responsibilities, anxieties, and thrilling moments are shared. Together
the couple meet with other religious cargoholders and their retinues, and together
they attend the fiestas in Chamula Center. They have many new experiences to
talk about. The beneficial effects of a cargo on the marital relationship are also
extended, up to a point, to the couples that constitute the retinue.

Husband and wife cargoholders share a deep commitment to the goal of com-
pleting the cargo. Both fear they may be unable to serve after they have been
sworn in, or they may fail to execute their obligations successfully for lack of
resources. Their worst fear is the supernatural punishment that will befall upon
them should they fail. In this punishment, their spirits are condemned to serve the
cargo after death, working eternally with no possibility of liberation. Thus, husband and wife dedicate themselves with intensity to complete their responsibilities successfully.

In a society where the activities of men and women are usually segregated
and where social gatherings are characterized by separate men's and women's
groups, religious cargos bring them together in the pursuit of the most cherished
communal values and strengthen their ties to one another. Even though the symbolism of male primacy emerges recurrently, Chamulas are reminded that the close
cooperation of husband and wife is critical to the survival of the cosmic order and
the society that depends upon it.

WOMEN AND CIVIL CARGOS

The civil cargo system's main function is to uphold and underscore Chamula mores,
especially through the arbitration of civil disputes. Women do not have a voice in
the adjudication process or in the other political affairs of the community that
occupy their husbands. They play their role as religious counterparts to the civil
offices at their home altars.[30] As far as public rituals go, women are present only
during cargo changes and baton washings (Linn 1976:896).

Women consider their role of taking care of San Juan's baton a crucial one
since it ensures the saint's blessings. As with religious cargos, women dream that
San Juan calls them to serve:

> When the time of the nominations of civil authorities came, we
> were not in our hamlet. We had left for Chiapa de Corzo to

harvest our corn. Then some men arrived there looking for us.

"You must go back to Chamula. You were appointed to a cargo," they said to us. When they left I told my husband,

"Let's not return. Let's stay here." We didn't want another cargo, for we had no money. We had no corn.
"I'm not going, forget it," I said.

Oh, but Our Father comes to look for you. He comes to get you. He appeared in my dreams.

"Let's go, hurry up!" he said. "Don't waste any more time. Let's go. We will accompany one another," the man said in my dreams. My husband had the same dream.

"Let's go then," we said, and we came back to serve our cargo.
(Antel C25-31)

In their daily prayers to San Juan, women fervently ask him to protect them, to allow them to carry their cargo through successfully, and to not let them experience jail or the wrath of Ladino authorities. In their prayers at mid-year and when the authorities for the new year are being elected, women pray that their replacement be found soon because the time to end their cargo is near. This indicates that women consider the cargo to belong to them as well as to their husbands and feel that they share the perils to which their husbands are exposed because of their political roles and their interaction with Ladino officials.

As in the religious cargo system, women at first fear they may fail to fulfill their obligations for lack of money. But once in the cargo, they enjoy the deference they receive from both civil and religious officials and from the general public. They like living in Chamula Center because they meet new people and establish contacts with the wives of other important officials. Their lives are exciting since a great deal more goes on in the Center than in their hamlets: disputes are brought to court, festivals are underway, religious officials enter and leave their cargos, and so forth. They feel sad when the year is over. As one woman put it, "'We weep when we come; and we weep again when we leave'" (Pozas 1959:44).

When civil officials take their cargos, their wives are present. The importance of the wife's ritual role is stressed in the address the outgoing official makes during the swearing in of his successor. He stresses that the new official will worship San Juan with his wife and his children. Indeed, Antel argued that it was impossible for a single man or a widower to take up a civil cargo, "Who would feed San Juan's baton? Who would pray to it?"

Also, in the ritual of baton washing, the presence of women and their contribution of cane liquor are indispensable for the celebration of the ritual. Upon assuming their cargos, mayors, aldermen, and their wives must contribute cane liquor to be used for three festivals, those of San Sebastián, San Juan, and the Festival of Games. Mayors contribute one liter of liquor, aldermen, half a liter, and their wives give a quarter liter each. The rank of the officials is symbolically expressed in the amount of liquor presented. Their wives' contributions are not ranked according to the prestige of the husband's office, but in terms of their own position vis-à-vis the men.

The scribes give the batons a second washing in cane liquor, laurel, and flowers. Next the officials, in hierarchical order, drink shots of this liquor, and then their wives do the same. The scribes hand each cargoholder his baton to be kissed. Again in order, each male official kisses his baton. When their husbands have finished, the batons are kissed by the women (Pozas 1959:47). Thus, women are symbolically integrated into the civil cargo system as assistants in the ritual activities that complement their husbands' political responsibilities.

The ritual role granted women in the civil cargo system exemplifies one aspect of the Chamula view of women. A woman serves her community and is able to attain a position of prestige under her husband's aegis and by complementing his political activities with her ritual duties at home. The civil cargo system clearly demarcates men's and women's places. A man's responsibilities pertain to the whole community and its relationships with the outside world. Civil officials keep the Chamula world together. The locus of the cargo system is the heart of Chamula Center, namely, the Cabildo, the marketplace, and the church atrium.

Within the ideology of the civil cargo system, women do not belong in public, potentially dangerous places. This is expressed metaphorically by Antel, who says that Our Father San Juan attended the Festival of Games elegantly dressed as one of the Monkeys who maintain order during the celebration, while Our Mother remains at home:

> Our Father walks around with his Monkey hat, with a group of Monkeys. He walks sturdily; we don't know that it's him. He looks like any Chamula man celebrating the fiesta. Our Mother, instead, is hidden, since it is Crazy February.[31] She is in another place; she is locked inside her house. She doesn't want to go out; she is scared of the Monkeys.[32] (Antel C64-5)

The political world belongs to men. Women entreat the deities, who ultimately control everything, from the privacy of their homes.

GENDER IDEOLOGY AND WOMEN IN THE CHAMULA COURT

In this section I examine a few aspects of the gender ideology of civil cargos, particularly the way in which the court deals with women, both implicitly and explicitly. A detailed study of the courts would yield a great deal of material on gender, but here I barely touch the surface.

Because the administration of justice takes place out-of-doors, everyone is able to witness it. The court's pronouncements, therefore, set distinct precedents for acceptable and unacceptable behavior and the consequences of transgression; they carry the weight of authority. The most important Regional Town Council members, the community elders, flaunt their power in a very concrete, visual way. They walk in a group, elegantly dressed in special attire, with the batons of power under their arms.

In the civil hierarchy, the primacy of men is indicated not only in the complete absence of women in public decision making but also in the way in which problems between men and women are handled. It is also expressed through the language employed by the authorities to discuss men who act cowardly and refuse to fulfill their responsibilities. The court has been an important author in the characterization of women as weak, timorous, and in need of male protection. The all-male composition of the court reinforces the ideas that women need the protection of men, and men are always the problem solvers. Because women are generally regarded as easy victims, men must defend them against the abuses of other men.

Women can and do take cases to court.[33] They are encouraged, however, to pursue a case with the backing of a man (i.e., husband, father, brother, uncle, or son) so that their arguments are more forcefully presented and carry more weight. For example, in a case in Tzajal Vitz, a girl's reputation was at stake. The girl and her mother, a respected woman who had held many cargos, made a trip to Chamula Center to ask the president how best to present the case in court. The president advised the woman to wait until her husband returned from the farm where he was working because the father could state his daughter's position in the best way. Indeed, the president said, the culprits would be thrilled if the girl's mother presented the accusations by herself.

The court usually sentences a man who mistreats his wife to a short term in jail and states explicitly that wives should be respected, well-treated, and appreciated. Court rulings, however, confirm the dependence of women on men and, in a way, make it easy for men to persist in irresponsible behavior. For example, when an unmarried girl is pregnant, the father of the baby is forced to pay for the expenses of the midwife and to give a one-time child support payment. In a permanent separation, the man must provide a one-time child support payment for each child. Many women comment that this payment is not enough to cover the child's food for a few months, let alone the expenses of clothes, curing ceremonies, and so forth. Because Chamulas are very poor, where many children are involved, most men are unable to make even this one disbursement without great hardship; however, usually the man borrows the money. Once he has paid the child support, the man looks for another wife.

The woman who is left with several children has a hard time supporting them and has no alternative but to remarry, whether or not she so desires. Thus, court practice in cases of separation leaves women in very difficult situations. In a way, this practice acts as a mechanism to guarantee that these women remarry and to ensure that all women remain "protected" and "cared for" by men.

The view of women as helpless, incapable of confronting aggressors, and always choosing flight over confrontation is further strengthened by the authorities' incessant use of female insults to define men who act in ways considered unworthy of males:

> They sent the policeman to get Akuxtin to question him. But they couldn't find him or anyone else in his house. Apparently he had fled.

> "Well, then," said the president. "So the cunt has left for good," he said. "So the ass has left for good. So the little girl has left for good."

> He said that in front of all the people who were there listening at the Cabildo.

> "Well, the cunt left for good, then" he reiterated. "It will not come back anymore." (Loxa C33-27)

With this powerful language the highest authority in Chamula shamed the absent man with the certainty that his friends would find him and deliver the message to him. To deny the charges that he behaved like a woman, the man had to return immediately to face the accusations against him in court. The practice of shaming a man by calling him a woman, asserting that he has shown a woman's vulnerability by defining him in reference to female genitals, is not an occasional incident at the court. There, in front of a large audience, these male justices construct the image of women in this fashion and lend constant credence to their creation. Their statements blatantly contradict the reality of women who work side by side with their husbands in the struggle for survival and for prestige and power.

NOTES

1. For detailed ethnohistoric studies of the cargo systems, see Chance (1990); Chance and Taylor (1985); Wasserstrom (1983b); and Rus and Wasserstrom (1980).

2. See Bricker (1981); Cancian (1965, 1990); Earle (1990); Rus (in press); and Wasserstrom (1980).

3. For example, Chance (1990); Earle (1990); Rus (ms, in press); Stephen (1991); and Wasserstrom (1983b).

4. See Mathews (1985); Rus (ms); Stephen (1991); and Stephen and Dow (1990).

5. See Chance (1990) for a general analysis, and Rus (ms, in press) for details on similarities and differences among these processes in Zinacantán, Chamula, and San Pedro Chenalhó.

6. The analysis in the following paragraphs draws substantially from Jan Rus (ms, in press).

7. The *principales* were elders who had moved through the ranks of religious and civil positions in the community. Today this group includes the members of the Regional Town Council as well as prestigious religious and civil officials (usually those who have served several cargos). They wield a great deal of power.

8. See Greenberg (1990); Mathews (1985); and Stephen (1991). See also Cancian (1990) for an analysis of the effects of the larger political and economic systems on religious cargos in Zinacantán.

9. Wasserstrom (1983a:178), for example, speculates that the state authorities who imposed the new leadership on indigenous communities also directed the leaders to serve as religious cargoholders. In this way, the authorities used local religious institutions to serve their own purposes; by enforcing public order in the highlands, they ensured the availability of cheap labor for commercial agriculture, which was expanding in Chiapas. He suggests this happened in many highland communities, including Chamula, Chenalhó, Cancuc, Mitontic, and Tenejapa.

10. Gossen (1986b) advances a similar argument in his analysis of *k'in tajimoltik* (The Festival of Games). He demonstrates the political and historical awareness of Chamulas as expressed in this rich, ritual festival. Chamulas clearly analyze their disadvantaged position vis-à-vis the dominant society and conclude the ritual by confirming a commitment to their own traditions and way of life.

11. Mathews's (1985:292) study of the correlation between family resources and religious cargo service clearly illustrates this point.

12. Cargos are usually named for particular saints, and therefore I refer to saints when describing the cargos. There is not, however, a clear distinction between "Catholic" and "native" aspects of Chamula deities, rather these aspects are interwoven into a complex cosmology.

13. In the 1970s, the expenses of a lesser cargo were between 2000 and 3000 pesos ($160.00 to $240.00, at an exchange rate of 12.50 pesos to the dollar), whereas the most important ones were between 20,000 to 50,000 pesos ($1600.00 to $4400.00) varying with the generosity of the cargoholders (Linn 1976:58). In view of their low income, even minor positions were and continue to be out of reach for most Chamulas.

14. Gossen (1986b:231) estimates that there are more than 2000 official roles in the celebration of *k'in tajimoltik,* the largest festival in Chamula.

15. In my conversations with indigenous leaders of the Liga Maya, an organization that aims to revitalize Maya culture by going back to its prehispanic sources, they compare the potential consequences of the aggressive proselytism by Protestant fundamentalists in Guatemala to those of the Spanish invasion and the evangelization programs of the Catholic Church over the last 500 years. They consider the former to be as devastating to Maya culture as the latter.

16. For example, Chiñas (1983); Eber (1991); Linn (1976); Mathews (1985); and Stephen (1991).

17. There are three barrios in Chamula: San Juan, San Pedro, and San Sebastián. The barrio is the next organizational level below the municipio and structures both the religious and political systems. Cargoholders are chosen as representatives of their barrios (Gossen 1974:8).

18. Linn (1976:89) mentions that the Flowers from the San Sebastián barrio serve only one year because the people from this barrio are considered to be poorer than those of other barrios. She does not report a similar consideration for the Passions.

19. Silverblatt's (1987) cogent analysis on the subject in Inca and colonial Peru is an example of the type of studies needed in order to evaluate prehispanic gender systems in Mesoamerica. See also Burkhart's (in press) illuminating work on the Mexica.

20. The wife's economic contributions are important in other Highland Chiapas communities as well. In Amatenango, all cargos are financed partly by the female relatives of both the cargoholder and his wife; these women join to produce pottery for this purpose (Nash 1985:212). In Zinacantán, a man relies on the members of his family, especially his wife, his relatives, and his *compadres*, to help him farm larger milpas and to lend him money (Vogt 1969:264). The same is true for the Zapotecs (Mathews 1985; Stephen 1991).

21. Women in Chenalhó also receive their cargos in dreams (Eber 1991:151ff.).

22. The rules of respectful interaction require that young men and women address older men and women (those of their parents' generation or older) as uncle or aunt; they, in turn, are addressed as nephew or niece.

23. These ritual gatherings every 20 days correspond to the ancient solar calendar of the Maya, which had 18 months of 20 days each and five "lost days" at the end.

24. Pedranas also mourn the loss of their cargos, their direct connection to something bigger than themselves (Eber 1971:172).

25. Eber (1991:140ff.) provides a detailed description of the ritual of the Standard Bearer for Saint Peter in San Pedro Chenalhó—beginning with the recruitment of the retinue and including the congregation of helpers to prepare for the fiesta and the major ritual sequences of the outgoing Standard Bearer.

26. In San Pedro Chenalhó, women also fulfill ritual duties. Wife and husband cargoholders have personal assistants, who stand by their side and help them to dress, and ritual assistants, who relieve them from the tasks of preparing and distributing the special foods. In this way, both husband and wife can be devoted entirely to ritual activity (Guiteras-Holmes 1961:99). In contrast, the situation in Amatenango del Valle is more like that of Zinacantán. Women's role is important, but it follows the basic division of labor. Women gather to cook inside the house, and men sit on the benches outside and pray. In the ritual for the incoming Standard Bearer, a Woman Speaker serves as the Advisor to the cargoholder's wife and instructs the wife in dressing her husband. Then all the women who are inside, including the cargoholder's wife, are called out to dance. This dance appears to

be the only ritual participation of women in the cargo ceremony. Amatecos say the dance symbolizes the women's help in financing the cargo (Nash 1985:216).

27. According to Gossen (1974), a multitude of ritual symbols underscore the primacy of men. For example, in most rituals men stand or sit on benches, while their wives sit on the ground: this expresses the primacy of up, symbolizing the rising sun, which is closely associated with men. Likewise, men usually position themselves towards the east, the most prestigious position because it associated with the rising sun, while women stand or dance to the rear or west.

28. The goat seems to symbolize an ill-tempered man. The trait that Chamula women emphasize when they talk about the goat is its beard, especially its exaggerated length. Women say that bearded men are ill-tempered and, therefore, they are afraid of them.

29. A similar conception exists in Chenalhó, where husband and wife share a cargo to such an extent that their souls are thought to be bound together in the service. If the man or woman dies while serving a cargo, the spouse must hold a special ceremony to release the soul of the deceased from the cargo (Guiteras-Holmes 1961:76).

30. Chenalhó resembles Chamula in conferring ritual duties on wives of civil officials. A women censes and worships her husband's staff every Wednesday during the year he holds the cargo. At the same time, the idea that power in the public arena is to be wielded exclusively by men is clearly demonstrated in the way the woman is required to handle the staff. She may touch it only when it is wrapped in an embroidered napkin, for the symbol of the power of men is taboo to her touch (Guiteras-Holmes 1961:85). In Zinacantán and Amatenango, women have no role whatsoever in the civil cargo system.

31. Chamulas sometimes give the name Crazy February to the Festival of Games (*k'in tajimoltik*) because the ritual involves turning the whole social system "on its head" by restaging precultural times when cosmic and social order had not yet emerged (Gossen 1986b:229).

32. The Monkeys are members of the retinue of some of the cargoholders and perform especially for the Festival of Games. These characters wear a conical hat made of monkey skin and represent the evil monkeys of antiquity and the chaotic precultural stage of Chamula society (see Gossen 1986b:234). There are two groups of Monkeys during this Festival: The members of one group are recruited as ritual assistants for the Passion, Flower, and other cargos. Their role is to keep order and to punish people who interfere with the celebration. The members of the other group are independent; any man can dress as a Monkey. These Monkeys are usually drunk. They torment the women by whipping them with dry bull penises. Evidently, Our Father goes around with the first group of Monkeys, the keepers of order, while Our Mother is fearful of the independent Monkeys.

33. Robert Laughlin (personal communication) notes the significance of Chamula women's access to the court. They are in a much better situation than women in many other groups (for example, Ladino women in San Cristóbal) because even though the court is under male control, they at least have a vehicle from which they can make an appeal. They are able to air publicly any grievances they may have against their husbands or any other person.

8

The Dynamics of Gender Interaction

K'OP RIOX: RELIGIOUS CONVERSION AND GENDER

In my original fieldwork, I did not directly address the issue of religious conversion and its effects on gender.[1] A comprehensive study of this movement would require its own volume; however, the magnitude of the problems generated by the spread of the "new religions," compels some discussion of the issue here. The conversion of thousands of Chamulas to *k'op riox*,[2] that is, various Protestant denominations as well as the Catholic Action or Catechist movements, has generated an explosive situation in the region. Beginning in the 1970s, the elites in Chamula have confronted religious change by expelling the converts from Chamula territory.[3] Over a period of 20 years, about 15,000 men, women and children have been forced to leave their lands and homes in the highlands. The majority of these exiles have founded *colonias* or squatter settlements which form a "misery belt" around San Cristóbal de las Casas. Converts have organized with the assistance of lawyers and politicians from San Cristóbal and Mexico City. Their main goal is to pressure Chamula leaders to stop the expulsions and to allow the converts to return to their homes.[4] The Mexican Constitution, they argue, guarantees freedom of religion, and the government of Chamula has no right to demand that religious dissenters leave the community. Furthermore, converts allege, they have not committed any crime to justify their being treated as criminals.

Although off and on the various parties engage in talks to try to find a solution, recently the conflict has escalated. In April, 1992 a direct confrontation took place between traditionalists and converts. The problem began in Chamula Center when a new group of converts were jailed for a few days prior to being expelled. Infuriated by these new abuses, evangelical Chamulas from La Hormiga (one of the convert settlements), kidnapped and abused the judge, an important official of the Chamula government. The traditionalists responded by calling on the men of every hamlet to congregate and go in trucks to La Hormiga, where they planned to liberate their dignitary. The confrontation in La Hormiga began with each party throwing stones and degenerated into a fight with machetes and guns. The fight lasted several hours and left eight people dead and about fifty injured.[5] The immediate consequence of this struggle has been a further polarization of the two groups, which makes a truce unlikely for the time being. Most of the population from La Hormiga went into hiding at the INI (*Instituto Nacional Indigenista*), and the traditionalists refrained from entering San Cristóbal for a few days.

Various Protestant denominations and Catholic groups based on liberation theology have attracted large numbers of converts among all segments of the population throughout Latin America.[6] In few places, however, has conflict between traditionalists and converts erupted as it has in Chamula. In other Highland Chiapas communities, such as Chenalhó, entire hamlets have converted to one or both religions. Although the process has generated tension everywhere, people in these communities actively seek to resolve their differences and to live together in a relatively peaceful atmosphere.[7] Other highland communities, such as Zinacantán and Amatenango, follow Chamula's example and expel converts from their territory.

Stavenhagen contends that "this is a conflict about power, where the actors are identified by their religion. Clearly, [conversion] pulls the rug out from under traditional community controls and power" (Darling 1992). Converts and their advocates construe the situation as one in which the political bosses in Chamula seek to eliminate any dissidence that would challenge their political and economic power. Chamula leaders and their close allies keep a tight grip on the population so that they can continue to make money through sales of cane liquor and soft drinks and through their money-lending businesses. Tradition, the converts assert, serves no purpose if it only brings oppression and poverty to the population. Requests that state and national authorities intervene to solve the problem and punish the political bosses for violating Mexican laws have not been heeded. Converts interpret this silence as collusion between the state and Chamula authorities, who guarantee the electoral success of the Partido Revolucionario Institucional (Institutional Revolutionary Party), the ruling national political party commonly known as PRI (Nash and Sullivan 1992:15).

Traditionalist Chamulas argue that the converts insult and ridicule their beliefs. They fear that the unity of Chamula will be lost if only some people follow the traditions of the ancestors. Indeed, conflict first erupted openly when newly converted Chamulas refused to give *cooperación*, a monetary contribution to buy firecrackers and other basic items for the celebration of the saints.[8] For centuries community solidarity has been vested in public rituals. Traditionalists perceive the converts' rejection of public fiestas, cargos, and ritual offerings of liquor, incense, and candles as a threat to community solidarity and to the survival of Chamulas as a distinct people.

Prior to the expulsions, traditionalists say, converts were actively involved in proselytism in their hamlets. The converts exhorted their relatives and neighbors to give up liquor, cargos, and celebrations because these were inspired by the devil. "God is only one, and he just wants our prayers," they said. "Don't pray to those images in the Church because they are but pieces of wood, like mannequins, and wood rots and gets infected with fungus."[9] According to traditionalists, the converts asserted that *jtotik* and *jme'tik* have nothing to do with God but are merely sources of light, like a light bulb or a flashlight. Finally, they attempted to persuade their potential recruits that if they had money to waste on candles and *pox*, the food of the saints, they ought to spend it on clothes or food for themselves instead. Traditionalists contend that Evangelical and Catholic converts are not willing to spend money to further communal pursuits but only to foster their individual well-being.[10] It seems clear that although the elders have a personal stake in maintaining the system, a large number of other Chamulas also want to perpetuate the ancient tradition of their forefathers; it is a way of life they value highly.

Why do Chamulas convert? Most of the converts I spoke with recounted stories of poverty and hopelessness. They described lives of despair from which they saw no escape and cited deprivation, alcohol abuse, womanizing, tensions between husband and wife, physical abuse, or the death of one or more children as motivating factors in their decision to convert. For most, conversion brings the hope of changing their fate, finding new directions for their lives, and improving their situation.[11] Individuals feel empowered, for their well-being rests on their direct relationship to God through prayer. They need not depend on intermediaries such as the *ilol* (curer/shaman),[12] who intervene between individuals and the deities, or on practices such as cargo service or ritual offerings. If through conversion they stop drinking permanently (which sometimes happens), and they save the money that would have been spent on *pox*, curing rituals, and celebrations, family members may, indeed, experience an improvement in living conditions.

Life in San Cristóbal poses many problems for converts. The city offers no infrastructure whatsoever for the newcomers. The immigrants buy small plots of land and build humble, one-room houses crammed close together. In the new setting there is no land to keep domestic animals, to pasture sheep, or to plant small milpas. Water, corn, wool, wood, all the necessities of Chamula life that are relatively easy to obtain in the hamlets, must be purchased in the city. Jobs in the city have become scarce, and the labor market cannot accommodate the increasing population of immigrants. Women weave, braid, or sew small, inexpensive items to sell to tourists. They walk around town to hawk their goods or sit in the Santo Domingo market where, allegedly, only converts are allowed to sell.

Ladinos complain constantly about the presence of Chamula converts in the city but make no effort to alleviate their difficult conditions. On a visit I made in 1990, one high-ranking official in San Cristóbal explained that the local government refused to provide services or to assist the converts because it did not want to encourage continued immigration to the city. If the government were to help the immigrants, he said, the flow of indigenous men and women into the city would be endless.

Prejudice against Chamulas runs high among Ladinos. Of all the indigenous groups in the area, Chamulas seem to be the most disliked, feared, and distrusted. Those who have settled among Ladinos must deal with discrimination and mistreatment.[13] As Nash and Sullivan (1992:15) remark, education appears to be the key for immigrants to take advantage of this new environment and to gain access to better jobs. Otherwise, these converts will have given up their traditions without gaining new opportunities.

From my interviews with converts, it appears that women often initiate the change in religion. A friend may relay information on the new religion at some critical point in a woman's life, when she has a very sick child or when problems with her husband have reached a peak, and she has nowhere to turn. She then tries to convince her husband to convert. Frequently, women say, men are afraid to make such a drastic change and send their wives to attend religious services to see what they are all about. Only after the woman has made up her mind to join will her husband follow. Sometimes women make the decision to convert and go to San Cristóbal on their own, leaving their husbands behind until they should decide to join, too. But if a man has no intention of leaving the hamlet or abstaining from alcohol, he may prevent his wife from converting and leaving. This is the story of Xtumin, who converted 12 years ago:

> I knew this woman from another hamlet who had converted, and I went to visit her in San Cristóbal. I told her I wanted to learn the word of God because I was always sick. My husband worked only at the coffee farm and coming back he would get drunk. That's how all our money was lost! There were lots of problems when he returned from the farm. That's why I was always feeling ill. When he drank, he started hitting me. He threw his shoe at me one time and cracked my head open! That's how the money would disappear. I had to look for a curer. I confided with this woman about my situation.
>
> "I cry," I said. "My heart hurts on account of our poverty!"
>
> She showed me where the temple was and urged me to come on Sunday to the service. I came and liked it very much. I spoke to

my husband upon his return.

"Since you yell at me so much and hit me so much, I went to
learn the word of God," I said. He answered angrily,
"Go, go find other husbands, go find a good husband."
"Look, you're getting angry again. Look how your money is
quickly used up. We have to look for the curer and our money
is finished. We have nothing left," I told him.

But he wouldn't go with me. It wasn't until he became ill while
working in the farm that everything changed. They gave him all
kinds of medicine, but to no avail.

"Look," the foreman said, "you should learn the word of God.
You should enter the new religion, nothing else will cure you,"
he told my husband.

When he returned home sick that time, he asked me where I had
been learning, he wanted to learn too. I felt so happy! Not until
he encountered sickness was he willing to convert..." (C3).

What are the effects of religious conversion on the gender system? Throughout this book, I have discussed the multiple ideas and symbolic associations that
underlie the dynamics of male/female interaction. Constraints and pressures from
the various regional and local social systems affect gender interaction and related
practices. It is hard to assess, therefore, the direction which gender relationships
will take in the new environment. With regard to economic life in the urban settlements, women and men continue to work hard to make ends meet. In many cases
women are the major cash contributors to the family since they can sell their crafts
to tourists. Their husbands' jobs are usually irregular and poorly remunerated
(McVey-Dow 1986:130). Will the old ideology and practices gradually give way,
perhaps, to "modern" ideas and behaviors akin to those held by nonindigenous
people in the region? Will Chamulas appropriate and reshape the new ideas into
still another synthesis of Maya ideology?

Having lost their ties to the Sun, the milpa, and the Earth in the urban environment, how will the converts choose to construct their identity? The majority of
men no longer wear the traditional *chuj* and *jerkail* (McVey-Dow 1986:136), and
although most women still wear the black skirt, some have begun to wear Ladino
clothes because they are less expensive. Women continue to speak Tzotzil, but
young women are attending school in increasing numbers, learning Spanish rapidly and expanding their contact with the non-Tzotzil world.[14] How will they define gender identity? Some converts mention that a newborn baby no longer

receives the tools that define him or her as farmer or weaver. Only older women converts weave traditional clothes. Younger women prefer to weave simpler items for tourists and are not interested in learning to spin or to weave with more complicated techniques (McVey-Dow 1986:146). There is no *jak'ol* or formal petition for the bride; the young man, with or without his parents, goes to the young woman's home and converses directly with her parents to ask for her hand.

What will take the place of shared responsibilities between husband and wife cargoholders? In the new situation, what other mechanism will enhance the relationship between husband and wife? Some converts argue that genuine conversions by husband and wife lead to harmonious interaction and a peaceful married life. Others mention that men still drink or look for lovers even following conversion. What characters will replace the powerful *me' ik'*, *pak'inte'*, *yajval banumil* and his daughter (all of whom, converts say, are nothing but the devil's deceptions)? Where will the power of women derive from in symbol and practice? What will be the basis for men's power? As extended families are broken apart by conversion, what support networks will emerge in the urban settlements? The transformation of traditional gender conceptions and practices that results when people are uprooted and forced to relocate in an alien environment is an important issue for future study. The plight of the Chamula converts epitomizes the quest for a better life undertaken by many ethnic groups who have been marginalized by the dominant society.

CONCLUSIONS

In this study I show that gender meanings and differentiations penetrate virtually every aspect of social life. I pursue links among the economic, political, and ideological systems in order to investigate how people realize structures through their practices, and how they manipulate and even transcend ideological statements and structural constraints when they are faced with compelling demands or perceive an opportunity. My goal has been to study male and female interaction in its cultural specificity, to make one more cultural case and gender system available to the human record. I hope my analysis will allow comparisons to be made with other Mesoamerican systems as well as facilitate generalizations at the level of processes of transformation and change.

I have attempted to show that the dynamics of the gender system in Chamula respond to local ideology and social arrangements, which, in turn, interact dynamically with historical developments and sociopolitical and economic forces of the national society that impinge on Chamula. Through this analysis, Chamula emerges as a community at a critical juncture: impelled by strong forces towards social change, yet anxious to defend their community from outside intrusion,

Chamulas see themselves in a struggle to preserve the traditions bestowed them by their forebears. Perhaps this critical condition exacerbates conflictive connections, inducing the different social systems to generate myriad diverse and contradictory gender meanings and practices. The complexity of gender interaction in Chamula substantiates the importance of a multifaceted perspective to understand gender—a perspective that challenges previous feminist attempts to locate single variables as causal explanations of gender hierarchies.

The brief comparative information from other communities of Highland Chiapas makes possible a cautious extention of the basic conceptualizations and social arrangements found in Chamula to the situations of other indigenous women in the surrounding area. The economic and political circumstances of these communities, however, are not identical to those of Chamula; more studies of women and gender in several of these communities will enable the development of a regional picture.

I have not dealt here with the issue of origins, although I have tried to delineate the historical transformations of the gender system that led to the contemporary situation (i.e., the effects of and responses to the encroachment of capitalism and concomitant forces of social change such as religious conversion). In this study, I attempt to transcend the circularity of the dichotomies feminists have employed in the past to explain gender hierarchy. These scholars asserted the universality of male/female inequality, even while acknowledging that the cultural content of the dichotomies varied. In their analyses, symbol and practice remained disconnected. Throughout this work, I stress the dynamic interaction between symbol and practice in different areas of the social system in order to uncover the complex, multifaceted nature of the gender system.

What are the sources of female power in Chamula? The symbolic association of women with the Earth and its fruits as well as with the regeneration of the group gives them a place of central importance in Chamula ideology. Many of these associations have prehispanic roots. In their daily lives, women act out these symbolic roles as they provide for their families, take charge of milpa production in the highlands, and complement their husbands' contributions to the family income through their own cash-generating activities. Like the daughter of the *yajval banumil*, Chamula wives represent the wealth and well-being of the family. The value of women to the family is expressed in the marriage petition process, which requires great effort and expenditure from the young man seeking a wife. Furthermore, as wives, women are thought to have a determining influence on their husbands' success by steering them away from liquor, working with them to raise a family, and joining with them in the pursuit of a religious cargo.

The role of women as mothers is also deeply appreciated in this culture, which places a high value on children. In my interpretation of Chamula history, I stress the focal significance of motherhood at times when the physical survival of the group was at stake, and this focus seems to linger on. Perhaps the value modern

Chamulas place on children, aside from their very real economic contribution, arises from the perception that the community is continuously besieged, in spite of a relatively numerous population.

In the struggle between autonomy and increasing integration into and dependence on the outer world, Chamula women enact—in symbol and practice—the more traditional aspects of their society. For most Chamula men, the issues of ethnicity and personal identity are rife with anxiety. The power women derive as the primary vehicles of tradition exacerbates men's conflicts over their own identity as Chamulas. Still, the view of women as more authentic representatives of their community than men finds expression in the recurrence of women as central figures in quests to revitalize Chamula society. Moreover, in the religious cargo system, women complement their husbands' roles with remarkable parity (although rituals tend to give a symbolic edge to men); and, in the civil government system, women hold important religious responsibilities that are necessary for the successful completion of their husbands' civil obligations. Women's importance results from a combination of their symbolic endowment as the regenerative power of the Earth and the social group, their role as exemplars of traditional culture, and their position as central actors in the community's structures of prestige and power. Women's power appears solidly grounded in Chamula ideological configuration, in the structure of the family, and in both the political and economic systems.

Nevertheless, other symbolic constructs contradict the aforementioned associations of women as well as women's fundamental roles in production and social reproduction by emphasizing female weakness and vulnerability. Women's sexuality determines their vulnerability, for in both oral tradition and social life, demons and men are able to overpower and rape women or trick them into sexual intercourse; therefore, Chamulas assert, women need protection. They should not engage in conversation with men or select their own mate; they must accede to the father's control of the marriage process if they are to avoid serious trouble. Thus, even though the difficult economic situation encourages autonomy, ingenuity, and initiative in women, their efforts are hampered by fears something will happen to them or that their independent actions will arouse the anger of a husband or father. Women, however, are controlled and protected not only because they are vulnerable but also because they are powerful (like the *pak'inte'* and *me' ik'*), and this power is deemed dangerous. The threats of rape, vicious gossip, and domestic violence act as powerful deterrents on women's freedom of mobility and independence.

Patrilineage groups, which have lost their material bases but remain firmly rooted in ideology (as evidenced in the *jak'ol*), appear to strengthen the authority of husband over wife and limit women's access to their own support group. As Nash (1985:320) observes, the repetitive behavior of rituals projects the past into the future, creating the illusion that everything is the same. Even in the face of the clear disintegration of patrilineages and tendencies toward nuclear families and bilaterality, the marriage ritual recreates a situation from a past when patrilineage groups were stronger.

I argue throughout this study that the articulation of Chamula at the lower levels of the Mexican socioeconomic system debilitates and impoverishes Chamulas, causing strain between the genders. Historically, women's independence and assertiveness have been furthered by their husbands' seasonal emigrations. For men, however, this very emigration and the underlying situation that provokes it lead to feelings of frustration and powerlessness. Unable to meet the needs of their families, as they are enjoined to do in Chamula ideology, men are forced to be absent from their homes for several months a year. Their absence undermines their ability to "protect" their wives, and their lack of adequate lands undermines their command of their children's labor. Chamula men have experienced a drastic erosion of their power in the last decades. Furthermore, the insecurity created by frequent immersion in a society that scorns indigenous people, together with an attraction to Ladino goods, compounds men's sense of inadequacy. Drinking prevails when men return to their highland homes with their small earnings from a season on the farms. Often men resent their wives' new independence and attempt to control them. Wife beating in this context is not unusual. In many cases, it appears that men's control over women, through the various mechanisms I have described, intensifies in order to compensate for male feelings of powerlessness.

Both men and women express a general feeling of malaise because of relentless poverty and the lack of opportunities to change their situation. Interaction between husbands and wives turns conflictive, and their family's survival is constantly jeopardized. Women scold their husbands for spending money on drink when the children have barely enough to eat. They worry that their husbands may bring other women into the house. Men, too, suffer, as manifested by the autodestructive behavior of drinking. Many men say they would like to stop drinking. In several cases, I was told, men feel genuinely guilty and even cry when their wives relate to them what they said or did while drunk. Serving a religious cargo provides an escape from the drinking habit and relieves marital tension for many Chamulas. For some, though, religious conversion becomes the most apt metaphor for radical change.

Many feminist studies discuss the negative effects of capitalism and national society on ethnic enclaves. At present, Chamula women benefit from the expanding tourist market, but men continue to depend largely on unstable, low-paying jobs. Both men and women find rigid limits to their economic options. The potential exists, however, for a vast inequality to evolve between male and female opportunities because the male bias of the larger society may reinforce the bias already present in Chamula society. Most women are illiterate and monolingual and, therefore, have little access to jobs in the larger system. Men, in contrast, tend to be literate and conversant in Spanish. If men had access to more and better jobs, their resources would increase tremendously, and women would inevitably lag behind; this has already occurred in some Chamula families where the men hold well-paying jobs. Paradoxically, although their monolinguism and minimal contact with the outside world empower women as symbols of Chamula traditionalism, these same traits could be the seeds of overwhelming gender inequalities.

Internal stratification in Chamula proceeds at a rapid pace. The increasing intervention of Ladino authorities in the native government over the last 50 years has intensified this process of stratification, which continues to advance through ever strengthening ties between powerful Chamulas and outsiders. Internal stratification affects women in different ways. Poor and middle-income women must exert themselves to make ends meet. But because their income is indispensable to the household, they have more leverage vis-à-vis their husbands than do wealthier women whose income is less critical for family survival.

The influence of the Mexican political system has severely limited women's access to political positions in the community. The Constitutional Town Councils, forced on municipios by national law, condone male prominence in the community through the insistence that positions be filled by literate, bilingual individuals with experience in dealing with Ladino authorities. Women have no presence on Chamula's Constitutional Town Council. Their conspicuous absence from public decision making reinforces the view that men are in charge of public life.

The strongest statement of men's preeminence and women's vulnerability, however, is put forth by the all-male court. Ostensibly defending women, this pivotal public body actively seeks to reproduce the gender hierarchy. It decides women's fates, often against their wishes, and it discourages women's independence through its rulings. It uses references to female genitals as a means to insult men. It reiterates the views that men and their institutions (e.g., the court) should protect women and that women should submit to their husbands, fathers, or brothers. I concur, therefore, with Edholm, Harris and Young:

> ...women's exclusion from certain forms of representation is yet another means by which they are controlled, by which their invisibility is created. Women do not naturally disappear; their disappearance is socially created and constantly reaffirmed... Keeping women out of public roles is in fact a positive and time-consuming aspect of social organization. (1977:126)

Indeed, wresting power from the hands of women at the beginning of time did not permanently establish the unquestioned sovereignty of men that many Chamula narratives would have one believe. On the contrary, under the present social circumstances, making women keep their heads bowed requires continual effort.

NOTES

1. In a visit to Chamula in 1990, I had the opportunity to talk with and interview several converts, especially women. At that time I also discussed the issues with traditionalist Chamulas to obtain their views on the subject.

2. *K'op riox* (the word of God) is the Tzotzil name for the new religions. For the basic differences in ideas and practices between Protestant and Catholic groups, see Eber (1991:362-395).

3. See Gossen (1989b) for a historical background of the movement.

4. Chamulas who have been expelled have organized into political groups that present their demands to local, state, and national authorities. One of these groups, CRIACH (Consejo de Representantes Indígenas de los Altos de Chiapas), edited a monthly newsletter called *Indio* during 1985 and 1986. In this newsletter, CRIACH aired its grievances over the authorities' lack of determination to find a prompt solution to the converts' situation.

5. The information on this incident comes from a letter that Xalik Kusman wrote to Jan Rus and from Darling (1992). Kusman's letter details the participation of women in this incident. When traditionalist Chamula men arrived in La Hormiga, women started to hurl stones and limestone at them. (Powdered lime is added to the water in which corn is boiled and is readily at hand). The women's intent was to blind the men with the lime, but the men were not injured. Instead, they collected the lime in plastic bags and threw it back at the women. When a new, large group of men arrived, the women became terribly afraid and, under a onslaught of stones, lime, and gunshots, ran for their lives to the woods atop the mountain where La Hormiga is located. Kusman explicitly and jokingly compares this incident with the battle of 1867, Cuscat's rebellion, in which women lifted their skirts in front of the enemy lines to "cool" the Ladino guns and thus defeat them. Once again, women were not passive spectators. On the contrary, they attacked their aggressors and tried to defend their community; only this time, says Kusman, they employed a different strategy from that of the last century.

6. This phenomenon and its significance and consequences for social change have received widespread attention by scholars working in the region (e.g., Annis 1987; Goldin 1992; Goldin and Metz 1991; Martin 1990; Stoll 1990; for the Chiapas area, see Eber 1991; and Gossen 1989b).

7. See, for example, Eber's (1991) examination of the coexistence of traditionalists, Catholics, and Protestants in San Pedro Chenalhó.

8. See Gossen (1989b:224). Eber (1991:364) recounts similar problems with *cooperación* in Chenalhó.

9. This quote comes from an interview with a traditionalist woman.

10. This tendency towards individualism (disclosed already in Weber's study of the Protestant Ethic at the end of last century), which propels traditional communities into the modern world, has been noted by scholars studying the effects of conversion in Mesoamerica (for example, Annis 1987; Eber 1991; Goldin 1992; and Goldin and Metz 1991).

11. Some traditionalist Chamulas comment that many people seem to convert to the new religions merely to justify practices or personal philosophies that are contrary to traditional patterns. They cite as examples people who want to accumulate capital, people who

have been in school for several years and would like to "modernize," or people who have always avoided drink and are taunted by their fellow Chamulas.

12.   Avoidance of the expense of an *ilol* is one of the most often cited reasons for religious conversion. Many people feel that *ilol* treatments are not effective in curing illnesses, and they resent the considerable expense in candles, *pox*, chickens (the sacrificial offering), and fees. Many say that these curers only get drunk on the pox and eat well from the chicken offerings, while their patients often die. Evangelical converts believe that only God cures, and therefore they need not spend any money on treatments. They also may be reluctant to see doctors or buy medicines. Because of poverty and dire living conditions, sickness is ever present in Chamula. One can easily understand how a formula to fight sickness that involved no expenditure would be an extraordinarily attractive proposition.

13.   See, for example, accusations by converts against Ladinos in the article "Bu chabat? Shibat ta Jovel" (1986).

14.   In her survey of schools, McVey-Dow (1986:139) found that in San Juan Chamula 27 percent of the total school enrollment was female, compared to 47 percent of the school enrollment in Nueva Esperanza, a convert colony.

Appendix

This short collection of stories was selected from a large corpus I gathered in 1983-84. They are included here to illustrate the type of narratives on which I base the analysis of gender in Chamula oral tradition (chap. 5). The stories were narrated by Chamula women in Tzotzil; in my English translation, I have rendered the narratives as literally as I could in order to convey a sense of the flow of the Tzotzil language. The format follows the emphases and pauses of the narrators, and, where applicable, brings out the couplet structure frequently employed by Tzotzil storytellers.

TEXT 1

When Our Mother came,
when Jesus was about to be born,
when she had her child in her womb,
Our Mother suffered much.

They hit her.
They scolded her.
She suffered so much!
The people did not want her.

Our Mother had her husband,
but she had not had sexual intercourse
with him as yet.

The child was already there.
He had only been given to them.
The child was there.
But they had not had sexual intercourse.

And the child grew.
He grew.
Our Mother's womb was already very big.

When she started with her pains she left.
She fled to the mountain, Our Mother.

She had a horse, or a donkey.
She rode on it, Our Mother.

But she had labor pains already.
And she went very far on her horse.

She left because they wanted to kill her son.
Some bad people did not want her child.

Because already in his mother's womb,
the child had his light.
He had his radiance inside the womb.
That is why they did not want him.

But she did not let them kill her son, Our Mother.
She went far away to give birth.

She left.
She already had a husband when her child was born,
Saint Joseph.

They left.
They went together.

But the earth became dark
when Our Mother's son had not yet been born.

When Our Mother's son was born,
the earth was lit.
When Jesus was born.

Our Father, Jesus, grew up very rapidly.
That's what people say.

They tormented him.
They hurt him.
They wanted to kill him.

He had to flee, Our Father.
When he was still on earth.

They went to look for him.
They finally caught him.

They beat him.
They put thorns in his head.
With thorns they killed him.

They did not want him.
They did not want him to light the earth.

But it is much better that Our Father came.
It is much better that Jesus came.
The earth is light.

We can walk well.
We can work well.

He fixed the land for us.
The bad people did not want him.

But they did not really kill him.
He went up to the sky.
He went up to the sky with Our Mother.
(Tumin C39)

TEXT 2

They say there was another *jtotik* [Our Father] before,
at the time Jesus was walking on the earth.
The demons came to kill him, the other *jtotik*.
He told them, "do not hurt me.
Do not kill me.
You can kill my sheep, instead."

Jesus came walking along.
"Why are your sheep like this?
Why have they been hurt and killed this way
by the animals?"
This is what Jesus asked the other *jtotik*.

"Well, they had to die,
because the demons had come to kill me!"
he answered.

"I will never let them kill my sheep.
I will see them.
I will take care of them," Jesus said.

Well, he was talking about us.
He took care of his sheep then.
The wild animals came but he defended us.

"If you will, kill me.
I feel sorry for my sheep.
I don't want anything to happen to them," he said.

"How come you can do this?
You are very strong.
Who knows where you come from!

You have defended your sheep.
You have taken care of your sheep.

Who are you?
Where do you come from?
Could it be that we cannot hurt you?"
they [the demons] inquired.

Then they pulled him by the hair.
They put spines in his forehead.
They pulled his ears.
They undressed him.
The people eaters tormented him.

"If Jesus would not have existed,
we would have perished a long time ago."
That's what people say.

They [the demons] killed him.
He allowed them to kill him,
so that they would not touch his sheep.

But on the third day, he came to life again.
"Well, then, you came back to life, son," his mother said.
"Yes, I came back to life.
I defended my sheep.
I allowed them to kill me,
because I felt sorry for my sheep," he said.

This was a long time ago,
when Our Father was walking on earth.
It was then,
when he was still arranging the earth.

He prepared the earth.
He defended his children,
his descendants.

Then he went up to the sky.
Our Mother went to the sky too,
to accompany her son.

But he suffered so much!
Our Mother did not have problems.

She only felt sorry for her son.
But her poor son!
He was the one who suffered for us.
That is why they say that Our Father paid for us.
(Tumin C59-7)

TEXT 3

Well, Our Father has compassion for his children,
if they do not have anyone.

He wants us to be married,
to be joined.
He wants us to have a spouse.

"Oh, it is so sad to be alone!" he said.
"I suffer being alone.
Well, it's better that I find a companion," he said.

So he took out one of his ribs.
They come from his rib, the women, let's say.
From Our Father's rib.

Thus he took out one of his ribs,
and it remained as his wife.

That's why we are the rib of Our Father.
Because the rib became his wife.

Thus he went to pick a fruit,
I don't know whether it was an orange or a lemon.

He had already taken out his rib.
There he found the woman, then.
There he found his companion,
when he went to steal the orange.

"What is that?" the woman said.
Well, Our Father took the fruit.

It was thus that his wife was created.
It was thus that his children were born.
It was thus that we multiplied.
When Our Father was on earth a long time ago.
(Tumin C59-7)

TEXT 4

Our Lord made only one man.
One man came as a seed to the earth.

There still was no woman.
But she came out from the rib of the first man.

It happened that his rib came out and became a woman.
They were two then.
A woman.
A man.

Thus it was that Our Lord put him here.
A man came, who looked like Our Lord.
He created a man.

But the woman came out from his rib.
From a rib like this one came the woman.

Then, when the woman was born,
when she came out of the man's rib,
Our Mother gave the woman her wisdom.

Well, then, since there were two of them,
they had their children.

It was thus that people on earth reproduced.
They learned to work.
They learned what they had to do.

Everything was given to them
by Our Father and Our Mother.
(Veruch C62-10)

TEXT 5

When Our Father was born, a long time ago,
only one man was born.

He was not complete.
His body was rigid like this.
Our poor Father!

He did not have a companion.
There were still no women, no children.
He was alone, Our Lord.

He was rigid and stiff like a stick.
He had no joints.

Then Judas came.
He came and broke his bones, here and there,
and formed his joints.

"Well, can you tolerate being alone?" said Judas.
"Can you make it?" he asked him.

"Well, yes, I can.
But anyway where would I find a companion?
I don't know where to look for one,"
said Our Father.

"Would you like to accompany me?" asked Judas.
"No, I don't, I don't," the demon answered.

"Well now, say it clearly.
Tell me if you really want a companion,"
the demon insisted.

"Eeee, yes I think I do, if there were one.
But where should I find one?" Our Father wondered.

"Well then, close your eyes," the demon instructed.
And he took out one of the ribs from Our Father.

When he took out the rib, he broke it in two.
When he looked, a woman was already standing there.

"Do you want to accompany her?" the demon invited.
"Oh, where did you bring her from?"
our First Father inquired.
He did not realize that the woman
had sprung from his rib.

"Do you want to be with her?" the demon asked.
"Yes, yes, if you give her to me,"
replied our First Father.

"Well, then, be with her," said the demon.
"But how is it that I should accompany her?"
our First Father inquired.
"Because I don't know how."

"Oh, you don't know?
Well, this is the way you are going to join with her,"
said the demon.

And he showed him how to have sexual intercourse.
Thus it was for all people that they should multiply.

Everywhere.
That is how we all do it.

It was the demon who taught him.
"This is how you will do it," he said.

Well, he showed him then.
Well, Our Father saw it, and he learned.

That is how people increased.
If it had not been like that,
there would be no people.
We would not be alive.
(Antel C64-6)

TEXT 6

It is only the drunkards who find her,
when they are walking at night.
They find the *pak'inte'*.

"Come here," she says. "Come here!
The road is this way, come!" she cries.

"Come this way, I am your wife," she says.
And the men go with her.

They do what she says.
They can't see her.
They get to the place where she was standing,
but she is not there anymore.

Suddenly they realize
they are already at the edge of a precipice.

They get there, but at night.
She comes at night.
She looks just like a Chamula woman.
Pak'inte' wears a skirt, a blouse,
a folded cloth on her head.

So they say.
I haven't seen her.

"There she is, the *pak'inte'*," they say.
"With the mist she comes.
From a precipice comes the *pak'inte'*."

There she lives,
since she is the owner of the earth.

She comes out of the precipice.
Then she deceives the drunkards.

"Come here, come here.
Here I am," she says.

"I am your wife," she says.
But it is not true.

But then the men realize
that they are at the edge of the precipice.
It is not until they remember
what to do [that they will be able to return].

They turn their clothes inside out.
They turn their pants inside out.
They turn their shirt inside out.
They turn their white tunic inside out.
It is not until they do this that she lets them go.

But if they don't turn their clothes inside out,
if they wear their clothes normally,
she will then take them inside the earth.

They will have sexual intercourse.
She is always looking for a husband, the *pak'inte'*.

She deceives men and takes them to the precipice.
She only looks for drunken men.
(Tumin C58c-2)

TEXT 7

Pak'inte' finds a man in the road.
Since the man is drunk,
she finds him lying in the road.

"Let's go," she says.
"Come, let's go."

"Come, come and sober up," she repeats.
The man obeys.
He goes with her.

"All right," he says,
since it is probably a pretty girl
who is deceiving him.

Well, he lies down.
He lies down in the precipice.
He has sexual intercourse with the *pak'inte'*.

It is not until then
that he realizes how cold she is.
She is very cold when he sleeps with her.
He can't sleep with her.

It is not until then that he returns to his senses.
He doesn't know anymore how to go back.
He doesn't even know how he got there.

Until he turns his clothes inside out.
He turns his pants inside out.
He turns his shirt inside out.
He turns everything he is wearing inside out.
Only then will he remember [the location of] his house.

But if he doesn't turn his clothes inside out,
he will not remember.
He will stay forever with the *pak'inte'*.

There he will have his children with the *pak'inte'*.
The *pak'inte'* is so crazy!

"Pull out the lice from my hair,"
she orders sometimes
when she deceives the young men.
She has many fleas, they say.

"Pull out the lice from my hair," she tells them.
But she has these horrible poisonous caterpillars
in her hair.
Those are her lice!

"I have many lice, pull them out," she insists
as she scratches her head.
There they are walking on her head,
about five centimeters long.

But they sting so badly!
Our hands will get swollen.
The *pak'inte'* is so mean!

She looks only for men.
[She wants] Only men, they say.

She wants a husband.
She leads him to her cave, they say.

She looks entirely like a Chamula woman.
She is a pretty woman.

"Come, you must sober up.
But why do you drink so much?
Why do you lose your head?
Come, sober up," she says.

She takes him.
Even if he does not want to go,
she takes him forcefully.

Then, when he sobers up,
when he comes back to his senses,
he will return.

The man thinks she is really a woman
and he sleeps with her.
But then he realizes...
It is the *pak'inte'*!

He feels so cold when he lies down with her,
since she is the disgusting owner of the precipice.
That is where she lives.

This is when they feel they cannot sleep with her.
She is very cold.
(Antel C35a-36)

TEXT 8

Pak'inte' takes the people away.
"Come, this is our house," she says.

She opens up the way as if it were a good road.
But it is not so.
She makes us envision things.

She is a woman.
Her hair is very thick.
She does not have good [real] hair, they say.

She looks for men.
She takes away men with deception.

"Let's go, I am your wife.
You will join me," she says.

Well, the man is drunk.
He is lying there in the path.
Then she drags him.
She takes him away.

He does not realize,
until he comes back to his senses,
that he is inside a cave.
It is not his house.
It is a cave.

Well, they say the head of the *pak'inte'* is not good.
It has an opening in the middle.

One day a man realized
he had been taken inside the earth.
He was inside the precipice.

In the hole, he could only see some sunlight
when he looked up.

"How did I get here?" he inquired.
"I brought you
because I wanted to get together with you,"
the woman said.

"Well, then, you brought me here,
but now you have to let me out," he told her.
"No, I will not let you out," said the woman,
"because I want to join you."

"Well, then, let's see the lice in your hair,"
said the man.
The man started to pull them out.

Well, the man had some money with him.
He had a coin.

He took the coin and stuck it into her head,
in the place where it is open.

In a moment the woman became a pile of bones.
In a moment she was nothing but bones.

Who knows what [secret] the money has in it.
It was thus that the man was saved, they say.

The *pak'inte'* is horrible, people say.
She is disgusting.

She lives in the woods.
When there is mist she comes out.

Sometimes the men will die.
They will not be able to stand it.

She deceives people.
She also deceives the women.

When there is mist she comes out.
She comes our way.

We cannot walk well because of the mist.
Sometimes when women lose their sheep,
they start calling them.

"Here are your sheep,
Here are your sheep," the *pak'inte'* cries.

It is not a woman who responds,
it is the *pak'inte'*.
She draws the women into the woods.

She looks like one of us.
She deceives us,
and sometimes we get lost in the woods.

It is not until we come back to our senses
that we are able to come out from the woods.
Who knows how she makes us get lost.

She is horrible, people say.
(Lolen C54d-1)

TEXT 9

Pak'inte' comes out when the clouds are very thick
and it gets dark.

It is then that you will hear her cries.
"Uuuuuh, uuuuuh," she says
from the other side of the hill, it seems.

"Be quiet, be quiet," the girls
who are taking care of their sheep say to one another.
We get scared.

Then we start walking back home.
She walks behind us.

"Uuuuuh," she says.
Her voice sounds like a man's.
Her voice sounds like a drunkard's.

She lives close by to the place where I come from.
There she lives in the mountain.
There she lives in the woods.
In the precipice.

She looks like a woman.
She takes away the men, the drunken men.

She goes to fetch water.
She goes to fetch water with her little gourd.

Then, "Get up!" she tells them.
"Get up!" she commands.

She lifts the drunkard's head.
"Get up," she tells them.
"Sit!" she tells them.

"What are you doing there lying face up?" she asks.
"Let's go home," she says.

Then she sticks them into a crevice of the cliff.
She sticks them into a row of maguey plants.

"Do you want to drink water?" she inquires.
She goes to get water.
She pours water over the man's head.

She takes the men with her,
because she is looking for a husband, they say.
She wants to have sexual intercourse, they say.
And the drunkards want that too.

But if you go to her house, you become rich.
I don't know what it is that she gives you,
if it is a little gourd or what.
But you become rich.

Sometimes she gets us lost in the maguey.
Sometimes she gets us lost in the woods.

Sometimes the men go crazy
and don't know how to get back home.
Sometimes they can't find their way
until Our Father [the sun] comes out.

A long time ago she used to take them to her house.
And there she fed them.

"Eat!" she told them.
And then they slept together.

That happened to a man a long time ago.
"Get up!" the man said.
"But what is the matter?" *pak'inte'* asked.

I don't know what happened,
if the man pushed *pak'inte'* against the floor,
or if she did this.
One of them got on top of the other.

I do not know how it was,
if her little gourd was there.
But he was able to seize the little gourd.

Oh, but the man became so rich!
The gourd was very green.
It had money, they say.
(Maruch C56-29)

TEXT 10

There is a man here in the hamlet of Tzajal Vitz
who found the *pak'inte'*.
He found her on the path
after he had been drinking cane liquor
at the house of the Standard Bearer.

He was walking on the road.
The *pak'inte'* was also coming,
and he bumped into her.

"Where are you going?" she asked him.
"I am going home," he answered.

"Oh, you are going home,
but I have come to meet you on the road," she said.
"If you want, let's go to my house," she invited.

"But I don't know who you are," he said.
"You don't know who I am?
Can't you see it's me?" she replied.

"Well, then, take me.
Where is your house?" he asked her.

She took the man.
She pulled him by the hand.

Then she let go of his hand.
"Come here, come here, my house is right here,"
she said, walking in front of him.

He went.
When he realized,
he was already inside the precipice.

Her house is the precipice itself.
Oh, the man felt so scared
when he realized this was not his house.

He realized that he had not been able to walk well
when he was going towards the precipice.

The land there was no good.
There was no path.
It was not possible to walk.

It was nothing but cliffs.
Nothing but scrub grass.
Nothing but thorns.

"Come, my house is here.
Take this path," she instructed him.
But it was a lie, there was no such path.

He realized she was in the precipice.
The *pak'inte'* deceives the people.

Oh, the man wanted to go back [home].
But he didn't know how to get out of there.
He had lost his head.
He did not know anymore where his house was.

But they did not sleep together.
She was looking for a husband, the *pak'inte'*.

But the man did not go all the way to her house.
If he would have arrived there,
then she would have made him her husband.

But he did not get there.
He realized in time.

When he wanted to return, he did not know how to.
But then he remembered.

He took his pants off and turned them inside out.
The front side to the back and inside out,
and he put them on again.

He took off his shirt and put it back on inside out.
He took off his white tunic and turned it inside out.

After doing this, he remembered the way.
When he turned everything inside out, he remembered.
And he went back home.

The *pak'inte'* doesn't bother the women,
since they don't walk at night.
It is only the men who walk at night.

The drunken men go crazy.
She deceives them and takes them with her.
She harasses them.

But women don't walk at night.
Well, the women who drink walk at night.
They go out at night, let's say,
but they are not deceived by the *pak'inte'*.

It is the men of flesh and bones who rape these women.
They are seized by drunken men.
(Veruch C61-3)

TEXT 11

There is a "Mother of the Wind," people say.
Her head is huge, they say.

She dances constantly
and causes a frigid wind with dust.

I don't know how she does it.
It is that her hair is very strong.

I have only heard people say,
"It's the disgusting, messy-haired wind!"

Her head is this big, they say.
She dances a lot and thus brings about cold winds.
But I haven't seen her.

It is a woman, I think,
who lives inside the earth.

Oh, the strong wind comes constantly.
We cannot sit and rest because of it,
for it is extremely cold.

We cannot walk on account of it.
It is caused by the dancing *me' ik'*, so they say.
"Mother of the Wind" they call her.

Her hair is very messy, they say.
And she has a huge head.
(Tumin C31)

TEXT 12

My grandfather told me the story.
When a very strong wind comes,
sometimes it breaks the cornstalks.

"Hule, hule, hau, hau, don't come to steal.
Don't steal the milpa!
Catch the thief, damn it!"
that is what my grandfather used to yell.

And it worked, said my grandfather.
In the olden times.

"The strong wind comes from the precipice,"
he told me.
"The woman has a very big head.
Her head is this size," he said.

"There it comes [the wind].
There, in the sky, its mother is flying,"
he used to say.

"She flies in the sky.
She flies together with the wind.

She flies.
She walks in the sky,
but she destroys the milpa," he said.

"Does she want to eat us?" I asked.
"No," he replied.

"It is only that when she finds a man
she deceives him.

"Because she wants a husband," he explained.
"The 'Mother of the Wind' wants a husband."

When the wind calms down,
it is because it has become tired.
"Oh, ay, ay!" she moans.

There she is moaning.
When she finds a big tree she is caught in it.
And it is thus that she gets tired.

She gets tired then.
Because when you hear
that the strong wind has quieted down,
that there is no more wind,
it is because its mother has become tired.

She is exhausted.
She lies there on the ground.
"Who is it? Who is it?
Who is lying on the ground out there?" people wonder.

"Where did you see her?" they ask.
"Out there," someone answers.

"Oh, maybe it's the horrible old woman,
who became very tired," my grandfather said.

"The mother of the strong wind
is a woman," they say.

She looks just like a woman.
"It is that she became really tired,
the disgusting old woman."

"Oh, then she must be the one I saw
lying on the ground," people say.

Well, she tires from wandering around
everywhere on earth.
She steals along her way.
She steals maize.
She steals trees.

Sometimes she topples the trees.
Sometimes she topples very big trees.
It is there where you find her lying on the ground.

"She looks just like a person,
like a woman," they say.

She looks just like a Chamula woman.
This is what my grandfather and grandmother
used to tell me.
(Antel C35a)

TEXT 13

Well, *me' ik'* is another figure.
She also comes from the cave [like the *pak'inte'*].

The "Mother of the Wind" brings strong winds.
She looks like a woman, people say.
She deceives the people thus,
because she looks like a woman when you see her.

She is a little like an *anjel*.
She flies rapidly, they say.
She walks on a horse, they say.

They look like Germans, they say.
Like a woman and a man riding a horse.
But they are the originators of the wind.

The "Mother of the Wind,"
Could it be that she is not like an *anjel*?
I think she is.

She tries to carry us away.
Have you heard about the whirlwind?

The 'Mother of the Wind,' the whirlwind,
comes from the hill.
(Lolen C55-35/37)

TEXT 14

The "Mother of the Wind" is the *pak'inte'*.
The *pak'inte'* is a woman.
Her disgusting head is enormous, they say.

But when she has passed by a certain place,
when the strong wind has gone by,
her body is wounded.

She is gaunt.
Her body is covered with bruises.

She gets hurt with the stones along her way.
She gets hurt with the trees along her way.

Then, when she is finished,
when she has done everything she could,
when she is tired,
she becomes hungry and thirsty.

She is like a serpent,
and she belongs to the *anjel.*
She is the "Mother of the Wind," let's say.

That is what originates the strong winds, then.
She blows with so much force!

It is *me' ik'.*
She strikes with her own body, they say.

"*Pak'inte'*," they call her.
"*Me' ik'*," they call her.
(Dominga C49-61/64)

TEXT 15

The "Mother of the Wind" comes from a cave.
It comes from a mountain.

In the caves, in the mountains it lives thus.
But it comes out only as a punishment to people.

Then the corn will not grow.
Then the beans will not grow.

It is that Our Lord sends us a punishment.
It is Our Lord who sends out the wind.
It is Our Lord who tells it to come.

Well, there is a "Mother of the Wind, they say.
Its head is very big.
It is the "Mother of the Wind," then.

I have heard that sometimes
it looks like a young boy.
But it is a very strong wind that blows people away.

It comes from the mountain.
It is sent by Our Father.

The wind is moving her long hair here,
among the *nance* trees,
among the grasses.
It is moving her hair then.

Then, when the wind stops,
it is maybe because the "Mother of the Wind"
has gone back into her cave.

She is already inside it, then.
Then the earth is quiet.
Everything is all right.

It is the "Mother of the Wind," they say.
I have never seen it,
but I have heard people say,
"The disgusting 'Mother of the Wind' is coming."

Then she comes to break the cornstalks,
to break the beanstalks.
Everything we have planted.

But she comes from a cave, from a mountain.
From big mountains or cliffs,
that is where she comes from.
(Maruch C56)

TEXT 16

In my hamlet there are two women
whose hair is a lot longer
than that of the rest of the women.
There is one who lives close to my house.
There is one who lives a little farther.

The other women have shorter hair.
But these two have very long hair.

It seems that they are bad women
because they have no husband.

One of them had a husband before,
but now she doesn't anymore.
They divorced.
Well, now she doesn't have a husband.
Her hair is longer.

These women, it seems,
are like the "Mothers of the Wind."

When there is a very strong wind,
it is because they have thrashed about their hair.
Their hair is so long!
That is what people say.

When these women shake their head,
they fling their hair,
and they unleash the winds.

That's why they are bad women.
They don't have children.
They don't want children.
Or maybe they just don't want to have a husband.

There are men who talk to these women
[about marrying them].
But the women don't want to marry.

They want to be all by themselves.
They know how to do everything.
They can fell trees too.
They get their firewood and sell it,
so they can buy their food.

They don't plant their cornfields far away
[like men often do].
They plant their corn at home.

They have a cornfield.
They have everything.
And they have money because they sell firewood.

They sell their firewood in San Cristóbal.
And then, when it is finished,
they fell another tree.
They have an axe to cut down the trees.

These women are like men.
They are a little bad, you see.

Well, people don't want to talk to them.
When people see that they have no intention to marry
and that their hair is so long,
they don't want anything to do with these women.

When there is a strong wind,
it knocks down the cornstalks.
When the wind comes through,
you would think it's a person.

It destroys only some people's cornfields,
and not others.
It seems that it knows
who the owners of the plots of land are.

On one plot the corn is all knocked down.
On the other one,
even when the corn may be in a more fragile stage,
nothing happens.

Thus it is that these women
want to ruin only some people's cornfields.
They do not destroy all of them.

There are also other "Mothers of the Wind."
They are very, very blond men.

In the same way,
when there is too much wind,
we say it's a person.

When the wind has waned,
when morning comes,
they are very tired.
They are there, lying on the ground bruised,
because they have been through trees and everything.
The women with very long hair,
and the blond men too.

Well, the strong winds come at night.
When there is strong wind at daytime,
they say that it is the blond man.
He only does it at daytime.

When it happens at night,
it is always caused by the women.
(Xun C6-5)

TEXT 17

A man was walking in the woods.
He was walking there when he found this woman.

Well, when he saw the woman,
"do you want to live with me?" he asked her.
"Well, all right," she answered,
"if you don't look for other women."
"O.K.," replied the man.

"Well, I know you have a wife.
I know you have children.

But from now on you will only talk to them.
Give them money.
Give them what you want.
But do not lie with your wife anymore,"
the woman instructed him.

"Don't have sexual intercourse with her anymore."
So the woman told him.
"All right," he agreed.

Well, while he did not sleep with his former wife,
while he did not have sexual intercourse with her,
the woman he had found in the woods stayed with him.

She was not a real woman,
the one he had found.
He was living with an *anjel*.

One day when the man returned home,
"You have come," the woman greeted him.
"Yes," he said.

"Well, I have seen that you had sex with your wife,"
said the woman.
"No," said the man, "I have not."

"Well then, I will go,
because I don't like this," she said,
the woman he had found in the woods.

"Please don't go.
You are not going," he told her.
He held her and hugged her and tried to convince her.

"Well, then, if you don't let me go..." she said.
And right there she became a serpent.

She became a huge serpent,
when her husband still wanted to have sex with her.
She left dragging herself on the ground.

The man missed her a great deal.
But what could he do?
She had already turned into a serpent.

He had boasted so much of having such a wife,
but there was nothing he could do anymore.
She was an Earth Lord.
(Lolen C55-10)

TEXT 18

There are many people who have found it.
They say that in the hamlet of Bapot,
they have found a very big clay pot.

Two big clay pots,
but they did not have to dig very deeply.

They said they had also seen a serpent.
"I saw it," a man said. "It was this long!"

But you see it either on a Thursday or a Friday.
Sometimes on a Tuesday.

Who knows where it comes from.
Perhaps from a big mountain.

Well, people don't have to dig too much.
Close to the surface they usually find it.

It depends on the person's luck,
if the person is lucky.

But who knows if we have to pay the Earth Lord for it.
Who knows if we don't.

Sometimes you will find a little statue of a saint,
or sometimes a hand grinder
like the ones we grind our corn with.

It is green like a maize field,
very green and beautiful.
The little saint.
The little stone hand grinder.

Then we will become rich.
Our cornfields will grow easily.
Our beans will grow easily.
Whatever we may plant...
since it is its "little mother"
[the one who originates wealth].

If we find the serpent, we will have piles of money.
If we get scared, it turns back into a serpent.
If we don't get scared, it climbs on our shoulders.

It licks us.
It smells us,
if we are not scared of it.

If we are not scared,
it gives us who knows how much money.
It won't bite us because we are not afraid.

Then the serpent transforms itself.
It turns into a little stone, this size.
But the little stone is so green!

Then we wrap it in a handkerchief,
and hide it under our clothes,
and take it home.

When we get home,
in front of the courtyard cross,
we feed the serpent.
We cense the serpent.

We look for a box to keep it in.
And the serpent returns every month to it.
Every month.
You will hear the sound the serpent makes.
"Chahahaha, chahahahaha," it goes.
It shakes off its "children" [money] every month,
and leaves them there.

At dawn you find the money there.
It leaves a lot of money.

People have found these objects in many places,
not too deeply inside the ground.

Sometimes they find a little pot.
Sometimes they find a little porcelain jar.
Or a gourd.

Then people become wealthy.
Their corn and their beans grow easily.
Whatever they plant will grow well.
(Maruch C56-48/55)

References Cited

Adams, Richard E.W.
  1977 *Prehistoric Mesoamerica*. Little, Brown and Company, Boston.
Afonja, Simi
  1986 Changing Modes of Production and the Sexual Division of Labor among the Yoruba. In *Women's Work*, edited by Eleanor Leacock and Helen Safa, pp. 122-135. Bergin and Garvey, South Hadley, Massachusetts.
Annis, Sheldon
  1987 *God and Production in a Guatemalan Town*. University of Texas Press, Austin.
Ardener, Edwin
  1975 Belief and the Problem of Women. In *Perceiving Women*, edited by Shirley Ardener, pp. 1-17. Malaby Press, London.
Ardener, Shirley
  1975 Sexual Insult and Female Militancy. In *Perceiving Women*, edited by Shirley Ardener, pp. 27-54. Malaby Press, London.
Arizpe, Lourdes and Josefina Aranda
  1986 Women Workers in the Strawberry Agribusiness in Mexico. In *Women's Work*, edited by Eleanor Leacock and Helen Safa, pp. 174-193. Bergin and Garvey, South Hadley, Massachusetts.
Arizpe, Lourdes and Carlota Botey
  1987 Mexican Agricultural Development Policy and Its Impact on Rural Women. In *Rural Women and State Policy*, edited by Carmen Diana Deere and Magdalena León, pp. 67-83. Westview Press, Boulder.
Bell, Diane
  1983 *Daughters of the Dreaming*. McPhee Gribble Publishers and George Allen and Unwin, Melbourne.
  1986 Central Australian Aboriginal Women's Love Rituals. In *Women's Work*, edited by Eleanor Leacock and Helen Safa, pp. 75-95. Bergin and Garvey, South Hadley, Massachusetts.

Benería, Lourdes and Gita Sen
   1986   Accumulation, Reproduction and Women's Role in Economic Development: Boserup Revisited. In *Women's Work*, edited by Eleanor Leacock and Helen Safa, pp. 141-157. Bergin and Garvey, South Hadley, Massachusetts.

Blaffer, Sarah
   1972   *The Black-Man of Zinacantán*. University of Texas Press, Austin.

Bloch, Maurice
   1987   Descent and Sources of Contradiction in Representations of Women and Kinship. In *Gender and Kinship: Essays Toward a Unified Analysis*, edited by Jane Collier and Sylvia Junko Yanagisako, pp. 324-337. Stanford University Press, Stanford.

Boserup, Esther
   1970   *Woman's Role in Economic Development*. Allen and Unwin, London.

Bossen, Laurel
   1983   Sexual Stratification in Mesoamerica. In *Heritage of Conquest: Thirty Years Later*, edited by Carl Kendall, John Hawkins, and Laurel Bossen, pp. 35-72. University of New Mexico Press, Albuquerque.

   1984   *The Redivision of Labor*. State University of New York Press, Albany.

Bourque, Susan and Kay Warren
   1981   *Women of the Andes: Patriarchy and Social Change in Two Peruvian Towns*. University of Michigan Press, Ann Arbor.

Brandes, Stanley
   1981   Like Wounded Stags: Male Sexual Ideology in an Andalusian Town. In *Sexual Meanings: The Cultural Construction of Gender and Sexuality*, edited by Sherry Ortner and Harriet Whitehead, pp. 216-239. Cambridge University Press, New York.

Bricker, Victoria
   1973   *Ritual Humor in Highland Chiapas*. University of Texas Press, Austin.

   1981   *The Indian Christ, the Indian King: The Historical Substrate of Maya Myth and Ritual*. University of Texas Press, Austin.

Brumfiel, Elizabeth
   1991   Weaving and Cooking: Women's Production in Aztec Mexico. In *Engendering Archaeology: Women and Prehistory*, edited by Joan M. Gero and Margaret W. Conkey, pp. 224-251. Basil Blackwell, Oxford.

Burkhart, Louise
   In Press   Las Mujeres Mexicas en el Frente del Hogar: Trabajo Doméstico y Religión en el México Azteca. *Mesoamérica* 23 (1992).

Bu chabat? Shibat ta Jovel.
   1986   *Indio* 7:1. CRIACH (Consejo de Representantes Indígenas de los Altos de Chiapas).

Calnek, Edward E.
   1988   *Highland Chiapas Before the Spanish Conquest*. Papers of the New World Archaeological Foundation No. 55. Brigham Young University, Provo.

Cancian, Francesca
1975   *What are Norms?* Cambridge University Press, New York.

Cancian, Frank
1965   *Economics and Prestige in a Maya Community: The Religious Cargo System in Zinacantán.* Stanford University Press, Stanford.

1990   The Zinacantán Cargo Waiting Lists as a Reflection of Social, Political and Economic Changes, 1952 to 1987. In *Class, Politics, and Popular Religion in Mexico and Central America*, edited by Lynn Stephen and James Dow, pp. 63-76. Society for Latin American Anthropology Publication Series Vol. 10, American Anthropological Association, Washington, D.C.

Carmack, Robert M.
1981   *The Quiché Mayas of Utatlán: The Evolution of a Highland Guatemala Kingdom.* University of Oklahoma Press, Norman.

1983   El Popol Vuh como Etnografía del Quiché. In *Nuevas Perspectivas sobre el Popol Vuh*, edited by Robert Carmack and Francisco Morales Santos, pp. 43-60. Piedra Santa, Guatemala.

Carrasco, Pedro
1961   The Civil-Religious Hierarchy in Mesoamerican Communities: Prehispanic Background and Colonial Development. *American Anthropologist* 63:483-497.

Chance, John K.
1990   Changes in Twentieth Century Mesoamerican Cargo Systems. In *Class, Politics and Popular Religion in Mexico and Central America*, edited by Lynn Stephen and James Dow, pp. 27-42. Society for Latin American Anthropology Publication Series Vol. 10. American Anthropological Association, Washington, D.C.

Chance, John K. and William B. Taylor
1985   Cofradías and Cargos: An Historical Perspective on the Mesoamerican Civil-Religious Hierarchy. *American Ethnologist* 12:1-26.

Chiñas, Beverly
1983   *The Isthmus Zapotecs: Women's Role in Cultural Context.* Waveland Press, Prospect Heights.

Chodorow, Nancy
1974   Family Structure and Feminine Personality. In *Woman, Culture and Society*, edited by Michelle Rosaldo and Louise Lamphere, pp. 43-64. Stanford University Press, Stanford.

1978   *The Reproduction of Mothering: Psychoanalysis and the Sociology of Gender.* University of California Press, Berkeley.

Collier, George
1976   *Planos de Interacción del Mundo Tzotzil.* Instituto Nacional Indigenista, Mexico City.

1989   Changing Inequality in Zinacantán: The Generations of 1918 and 1942. In *Ethnographic Encounters in Southern Mesoamerica: Essays in Honor of Evon Z.*

Vogt, Jr., edited by Victoria R. Bricker and Gary H. Gossen, pp. 111-123. Institute for Mesoamerican Studies, State University of New York at Albany, Albany.

Collier, Jane

1968   Courtship and Marriage in Zinacantán, Chiapas, Mexico. *Middle American Research Institute Publication* 25: 139-201.

1973   *Law and Social Change in Zinacantán.* Stanford University Press, Stanford.

1974   Women in Politics. In *Women, Culture and Society*, edited by Michelle Rosaldo and Louise Lamphere, pp. 89-96. Stanford University Press, Stanford.

Collier, Jane and Michelle Rosaldo

1981   Politics and Gender in Simple Societies. In *Sexual Meanings: The Cultural Construction of Gender and Sexuality*, edited by Sherry Ortner and Harriet Whitehead, pp. 275-329. Cambridge University Press, New York.

Comaroff, John

1987   *Sui Generis*: Feminism, Kinship Theory, and Structural "Domains". In *Gender and Kinship: Essays toward a Unified Analysis*, edited by Jane Collier and Sylvia Junko Yanagisako, pp. 53-85. Stanford University Press, Stanford.

Crummett, María de los Angeles

1987   Rural Women and Migration in Latin America. In *Rural Women and State Policy*, edited by Carmen Diana Deere and Magdalena León, pp. 239-260. Westview, Boulder.

Darling, Juanita

1992   Ancient Modern Beliefs: Clash in Hills of Chiapas. *Los Angeles Times* 7 May:A32.

Dolgin, Janet, David Kemnitzer, and David Schneider

1977   As People Express Their Lives So They Are. In *Symbolic Anthropology*, edited by Janet Dolgin, David Kemnitzer, and David Schneider, pp. 3-44. Columbia University Press, New York.

Earle, Duncan

1990   Appropriating the Enemy: Highland Maya Religious Organization and Community Survival. In *Class, Politics, and Popular Religion in Mexico and Central America*, edited by Lynn Stephen and James Dow, pp. 115-142. Society for Latin American Anthropology Publication Series Vol. 10. American Anthropological Association, Washington, D.C.

Eber, Christine

1991   *Before God's Flowering Face: Women and Drinking in a Tzotzil-Maya Community.* Ph.D. dissertation, Dept. of Anthropology, State University of New York at Buffalo.

Eber, Christine and Brenda Rosenbaum

In Press   That We May Serve Beneath Your Hands and Feet: Women Weavers in Highland Chiapas, Mexico. In *Artisan Production in the World System*, edited by June Nash. State University of New York Press, Albany.

Edholm, Felicity, Olivia Harris and Kate Young
  1977   Conceptualizing Women. *Critique of Anthropology* 3(9- 10):101-130.
Ehlers, Tracy
  1990   *Silent Looms: Women and Production in a Guatemalan Town.* Westview Press, Boulder.
  1991   Debunking Marianismo: Economic Vulnerability and Survival Strategies among Guatemalan Wives. *Ethnology* 30:1-16.
Elmendorf, Mary
  1976   *Nine Mayan Women. A Village Faces Change.* Schenkman Publishing, Cambridge.
Engels, Friedrich
  1972   *The Origin of the Family, Private Property and the State.* International, New York.
  1978   Letter to Joseph Bloch. In *The Marx-Engels Reader*, edited by Robert Tucker, pp. 760-765. W.W. Norton, New York.
Favre, Henri
  1984   *Cambio y Continuidad entre los Mayas de México.* 2nd. ed. Instituto Nacional Indigenista, Mexico City.
Garibay K., Angel María
  1958   *Veinte Himnos Sacros de los Nahuas.* Universidad Nacional Autónoma de México, Mexico City.
Garza Caligaris, Anna María and Juana Ruiz Ortíz
  In Press   Madres Solteras Indígenas. *Mesoamérica* 23 (1992).
Geertz, Clifford
  1973   *The Interpretation of Cultures.* Basic Books, New York.
Gilligan, Carol
  1982   *In a Different Voice.* Harvard University Press, Cambridge.
Godelier, Maurice
  1977   *Perspectives in Marxist Anthropology.* Cambridge University Press, Cambridge.
Goldin, Liliana
  1992   Work and Ideology in the Maya Highlands of Guatemala: Economic Beliefs in the Context of Occupational Change. *Economic Development and Cultural Change* 41:103-124.
Goldin, Liliana and Brent Metz
  1991   An Expression of Cultural Change: Invisible Converts to Protestantism among Highland Guatemala Mayas. *Ethnology* 30(4):325-338.
Goldin, Liliana and Brenda Rosenbaum
  In Press   Culture and History: Subregional Variation among the Maya. In *Comparative Studies in Society and History* (1993).
Gómez Quiles, José
  ms   *Perspectiva del Desarrollo Ovino: Estudio del Proceso Textil.* Parte 1. Centro de Investigaciones Ecológicas del Sureste, San Cristóbal de las Casas.

Goodale, Jane
1971 *Tiwi Wives.* University of Washington Press, Seattle.
Gossen, Gary H.
1974 *Chamulas in the World of the Sun.* Harvard University Press, Cambridge.
1984 Una Diáspora Maya Moderna: Desplazamiento y Persistencia Cultural de San Juan Chamula, Chiapas. *Mesoamérica* 5:253-276.
1986a Mesoamerican Ideas as a Foundation for Regional Synthesis. In *Symbol and Meaning beyond the Closed Community: Essays in Mesoamerican Ideas,* edited by Gary H. Gossen, pp. 1-8. Institute for Mesoamerican Studies, State University of New York at Albany, Albany.
1986b The Chamula Festival of Games: Native Macroanalysis and Social Commentary in a Maya Carnival. In *Symbol and Meaning beyond the Closed Community: Essays in Mesoamerican Ideas,* edited by Gary H. Gossen, pp. 227-254. Institute for Mesoamerican Studies, State University of New York at Albany, Albany.
1986c Estilo Poético y Visión del Cosmos entre los Chamulas de Chiapas, México. In *Mito y Ritual en América,* edited by Manuel Gutiérrez Estévez, pp. 111-124. Editorial Alhambra, Madrid.
1989a El Tiempo Cíclico en San Juan Chamula: ¿Mistificación o Mitología Viva? *Mesoamérica* 18:441-460.
1989b Life, Death and Apotheosis of a Chamula Protestant Leader: Biography as Social History. In *Ethnographic Encounters in Southern Mesoamerica,* edited by Gary H. Gossen and Victoria R. Bricker, pp. 217-229. Institute for Mesoamerican Studies, State University of New York at Albany, Albany.
Gossen, Gary H. and Richard Leventhal
1993 The Topography of Ancient Maya Religious Pluralism: A Dialogue with the Present. In *Lowland Maya Civilization in the Eighth Century A.D.,* edited by J.A. Sabloff and J.S. Henderson, pp. 185-218. Dumbarton Oaks, Washington, D.C.
Greenberg, James
1990 Sanctity and Resistance in Closed Corporate Indigenous Communities: Coffee Money, Violence, and Ritual Organization in Chatino Communities in Oaxaca. In *Class, Politics and Popular Religion in Mexico and Central America,* edited by Lynn Stephen and James Dow, pp. 95-114. Society for Latin American Anthropology Publication Series Vol. 10. American Anthropological Association, Washington, D.C.
Guiteras-Holmes, Calixta
1961 *Perils of the Soul.* The Free Press, New York.
Haviland, John
1977 *Gossip, Reputation and Knowledge in Zinacantán.* The University of Chicago Press, Chicago.
Harding, Susan
1975 Women and Words in a Spanish Village. In *Toward an Anthropology of Women,* edited by Rayna Reiter, pp. 283-308. Monthly Review Press, New York.

Hunt, Eva
1977   *The Transformation of the Hummingbird*. Cornell University Press, Ithaca.
Kellogg, Susan
1991   Hegemony out of Conquest: The First Two Centuries of Spanish Rule in Central Mexico. Paper presented at the 47th International Congress of Americanists, New Orleans.
Kelly-Gadol, Joan
1987   The Social Relation of the Sexes: Methodological Implications of Women's History. In *Feminism and Methodology: Social Sciences Issues*, edited by Susan Harding, pp. 15-18. Indiana University Press, Bloomington.
Komes Peres, Maruch
1990   *Ta jlok'ta chobtik ta k'u'il*. Collected and translated by Diane Rus and Xalik Guzmán. Instituto de Asesoría Antropológica para la Región Maya, A.C., San Cristóbal de las Casas.
Kuhn, Annette
1978   Structure of Patriarchy and Capital in the Family. In *Feminism and Materialism: Women and Modes of Production*, edited by Annette Kuhn and AnnMarie Wolpe, pp. 42-67. Routledge and Kegan Paul, London.
Lacy, Sara
1976   *Antel*. Bachelor thesis, Dept. of Anthropology, Harvard University.
Lamphere, Louise
1974   Strategies, Cooperation and Conflict Among Women in Domestic Groups. In *Woman, Culture and Society*, edited by Michelle Rosaldo and Louise Lamphere, pp. 97-112. Stanford University Press, Stanford.
Landa, Frey Diego
1959   *Relación de las Cosas de Yucatán*. 8th ed. Editorial Porrúa, Mexico City.
Laughlin, Robert
1975   *The Great Tzotzil Dictionary of San Lorenzo Zinacantán*. Smithsonian Institution, Washington, D.C.

1977   *Of Cabbages and Kings*. Smithsonian Institution Press, Washington, D.C.
Leacock, Eleanor
1981   *Myths of Male Dominance*. Monthly Review Press, New York.
Leacock, Eleanor and June Nash
1982   Ideologies of Sex: Archetypes and Stereotypes. In *Annals of the New York Academy of Sciences* 285:618-45.
Lim, Linda
1983   Capitalism, Imperialism, and Patriarchy: The Dilemma of Third World Women Workers in Multinational Factories. In *Women, Men, and the International Division of Labor*, edited by June Nash and Kelly Fernández, pp. 70-91. State University of New York Press, Albany.

Linn, Priscilla R.

1976　*The Religious Office Holders in Chamula: a Study of Gods, Ritual and Sacrifice.* Ph.D. dissertation, Dept. of Anthropology and Geography. Oxford University.

MacLeod, Murdo

1973　*Spanish Central America: A Socioeconomic History, 1520-1720.* University of California Press, Berkeley.

Maher, Vanessa

1987　Sewing the Seams of Society: Dress Makers and Seamstresses in Turin between the Wars. In *Gender and Kinship: Essays toward a Unified Analysis*, edited by Jane Collier and Sylvia Junko Yanagisako, pp. 132-159. Stanford University Press, Stanford.

Martin, David

1990　*Tongues of Fire: The Explosion of Protestantism in Latin America.* Basil Blackwell, Oxford.

Mathews, Holly H.

1985　'We are Mayordomo': a Reinterpretation of Women's Roles in the Mexican Cargo System. *American Ethnologist* 17:285-301.

McVey-Dow, Vicki

1986　*Indian Women and Textile Production: Adaptation to a New Environment in Chiapas, Mexico.* Ph.D. dissertation. Dept. of Geography, University of Colorado.

Miles, Susan

1965　Summary of Pre-Conquest Ethnology of the Guatemalan-Chiapas Highlands and Pacific Slopes. In *Archaeology of Southern Mesoamerica, Part 1*, edited by Gordon R. Willey, pp. 276-287. Handbook of Middle American Indians, vol. 2, Robert Wauchope, general editor. University of Texas Press, Austin.

Modiano, Nancy

1974　*La Educación Indígena en los Altos de Chiapas.* Instituto Nacional Indigenista, Mexico City.

Morris, Walter F.

1988　*Living Maya.* Harry H. Abrams, New York.

Mukhopadhyay, Carol and Patricia Higgins

1988　Anthropological Studies of Women's Status Revisited 1977-1987. *Annual Review of Anthropology* 17:461-495.

Murphy, Robert

1971　*The Dialectics of Social Life.* Columbia University Press, New York.

Murphy, Yolanda and Robert Murphy

1974　*Women of the Forest.* Columbia University Press, New York.

Nadelson, Leslee

1981　Pigs, Women and the Men's House in Amazonia: An Analysis of Six Mundurucu Myths. In *Sexual Meanings: The Cultural Construction of Gender and Sexuality*, edited by Sherry Ortner and Harriet Whitehead, pp. 240-272. Cambridge University Press, New York.

Nash, June

1978   The Aztecs and the Ideology of Male Dominance. *Signs:* 4:349-362.

1980   Aztec Women: The Transition from Status to Class in Empire and Colony. In *Women and Colonization: Anthropological Perspectives*, edited by Mona Etienne and Eleanor Leacock, pp. 134-148. Bergin and Garvey, South Hadley, Massachusetts.

1985   *In the Eyes of the Ancestors*. Waveland Press, Prospect Heights.

1989   Gender Studies in Latin America. In *Gender and Anthropology*, edited by Sandra Morgen, pp. 228-245. American Anthropological Association, Washington, D.C.

In Press   Household Production and the World Crisis. In *Artisans in the World Market*, edited by June Nash. State University of New York Press, Albany.

Nash, June and Kathleen Sullivan

1992   Returns to Porfirismo. In *Cultural Survival Quarterly* 16(2):13-16.

Nash, Manning

1958   Political Relations in Guatemala. *Social and Economic Studies* 7:65-75.

Okely, Judith

1975   Gypsy Women: Models in Conflict. In *Perceiving Women*, edited by Shirley Ardener, pp. 55-86. Malaby Press, London.

O'Laughlin, Bridget

1975   Marxist Approaches in Anthropology. *Annual Review of Anthropology* 4:341-370.

Ortner, Sherry

1974   Is Female to Male as Nature is to Culture? In *Woman, Culture and Society*, edited by Michelle Rosaldo and Louise Lamphere, pp.67-88. Stanford University Press, Stanford.

1981   Gender and Sexuality in Hierarchical Societies: The Case of Polynesia and Some Comparative Implications. In *Sexual Meanings: The Cultural Construction of Gender and Sexuality*, edited by Sherry Ortner and Harriet Whitehead, pp. 359-409. Cambridge University Press, New York.

Ortner, Sherry and Harriet Whitehead

1981   Introduction: Accounting for Sexual Meanings. In *Sexual Meanings: The Cultural Construction of Gender and Sexuality*, edited by Sherry Ortner and Harriet Whitehead, pp. 1-28. Cambridge University Press, New York.

Otzoy, Irma

In Press   Identidad y Traje Maya Indígena. *Mesoamérica* 23 (1992).

Pacheco Cruz, Santiago

1947   *Usos, Costumbres, Religión y Supersticiones de los Mayas*. Triay, Mérida.

Paz, Octavio

1959   *El Laberinto de la Soledad*. Fondo de Cultura Económica, Mexico City.

Pérez López, Enrique

1987 *Chamula*. Dirección de Fortalecimiento y Fomento a las Culturas Indígenas, Subsecretaría de Asuntos Indígenas, Chiapas.

Pozas, Ricardo

1959 Chamula: un Pueblo Indio de los Altos de Chiapas. 2 vols. *Memorias del Instituto Nacional Indigenista* No. 8, Mexico City.

Proskouriakoff, Tatiana

1961 Portraits of Women in Maya Art. In *Essays in Precolumbian Art and Archaeology*, edited by S.K. Lothrop et.al., pp. 81-99. Harvard University Press, Cambridge.

Rapp, Rayna

1987 Toward a Nuclear Freeze? The Gender Politics of Euro-American Kinship Analysis. In *Gender and Kinship: Essays Toward a Unified Analysis*, edited by Jane Collier and Silvia Yanagisako, pp. 119-131. Stanford University Press, Stanford.

Rodriguez, Josefina

1988 *La Mujer Azteca*. Universidad Nacional Autónoma de México, Mexico City.

Rosaldo, Michelle

1974 Woman, Culture and Society: a Theoretical Overview. In *Woman, Culture and Society*, edited by Michelle Rosaldo and Louise Lamphere, pp. 17-42. Stanford University Press, Stanford.

Rosen, Bernard

1982 *Industrial Connection: Achievement and the Family in Developing Societies*. Aldine, New York.

Rosenbaum, Brenda

1990 Maruch and I. Paper presented at the 1990 Annual Meeting of the American Anthropological Association, New Orleans.

1992 Mujer, Tejido e Identidad Etnica en Chamula: un Ensayo Histórico. In *La Indumentaria y el Tejido Mayas a Través del Tiempo*, edited by Linda Barrios and Dina Fernández, pp. 157-169. Museo Ixchel, Guatemala City.

Rosenbaum, Brenda and Christine Eber

In Press Trayendo el Margen al Centro: Mujer y Género en Mesoamérica. *Mesoamérica* 23 (1992).

Rus, Diane

1990 *La Crisis Económica y la Mujer Indígena: el Caso de Chamula, Chiapas*. Instituto de Asesoría Antropológica para la Región Maya, San Cristóbal de las Casas.

Rus, Jan

1969 *Pottery Making in Chamula*. Bachelor's thesis, Dept. of Anthropology, Harvard University.

1988 Changes in Employment Patterns Among Chamula Men 1977-1987. Paper presented at the Annual Conference of the Latin American Studies Association, New Orleans.

1989   The Caste War of 1869 from the Indian's Perspective: A Challenge for Ethnohistory. In *Memorias del Segundo Coloquio Internacional de Mayistas*, vol.2, pp. 1033-1047. Universidad Nacional Autónoma de México, Mexico City.

In Press Contained Revolutions: Indians and the Struggle for Control of Highland Chiapas, 1910-1925. *Mexican Studies/Estudios Mexicanos*.

ms   The 'Comunidad Revolucionaria Institucional:' Indian Resistance and Indian Policy in Highland Chiapas, 1936-1990. Manuscript in author's possession. Instituto de Asesoría Antropológica para la Región Maya, San Cristóbal de las Casas.

Rus, Jan and Diane Rus (editors)

1986   *Abtel Ta Pinka*. Taller Tzotzil, Instituto de Asesoría Antropológica para la Región Maya, San Cristóbal de las Casas.

Rus, Jan and Robert Wasserstrom

1980   Civil-Religious Hierarchies in Central Chiapas: A Critical Perspective. *American Ethnologist* 7:466-478.

Sacks, Karen

1979   *Sisters and Wives: The Past and Future of Sexual Equality*. Greenwood, Westport.

Sahagún, Bernardino de

1956   *Historia General de las Cosas de Nueva España*, edited by Angel María Garibay K. 4 vols. Editorial Porrúa, Mexico City.

Scott, James

1976   *The Moral Economy of the Peasant: Rebellion and Subsistence in Southeast Asia*. Yale University Press, New Haven.

Shapiro, Judith

1988   Gender Totemism. In *Dialectics and Gender*, edited by Richard Randolph, David Schneider and May Diaz, pp. 1-19. Westview Press, Boulder.

Shashahani, Soheila

1986   Mamasani Women: Changes in the Division of Labor among a Sedentarized Pastoral People of Iran. In *Women's Work*, edited by Eleanor Leacock, and Helen Safa, pp. 111-121. Bergin and Garvey, South Hadley, Massachusetts.

Shore, Bradd

1981   Sexuality and Gender in Samoa: Conceptions and Missed Conceptions in Sexual Meanings. In *Cultural Construction of Gender and Sexuality*, edited by Sherry Ortner and Harriet Whitehead, pp. 192-215. Cambridge View Press, New York.

Silverblatt, Irene

1987   *Moon, Sun and Witches: Gender Ideologies and Class in Inca and Colonial Peru*. Princeton University Press, Princeton.

1988   Women in States. *Annual Review of Anthropology* 17:427- 460.

Siskel, Susanne

1972   Schooling in Chamula. Manuscript on file. Harvard Chiapas Project, Harvard University, Cambridge.

1974   With the Spirit of a Jaguar. A study of Shamanism in Ichinton, Chamula. Bachelor thesis, Dept. of Anthropology, Harvard University.

Slocum, Sally

1975   Woman the Gatherer: Male Bias in Anthropology. In *Toward an Anthropology of Women*, edited by Rayna Reiter, pp. 36-50. Monthly Review Press, New York.

Stephen, Lynn

1991   *Zapotec Women*. University of Texas Press, Austin.

Stephen, Lynn and James Dow

1990   Introduction: Popular Religion in Mexico and Central America. In *Class, Politics and Popular Religion in Mexico and Central America*, edited by Lynn Stephen and James Dow, pp. 1-26. Society for Latin American Anthropology Publication Series Vol. 10. American Anthropological Association, Washington, D.C.

Stoll, David

1990   *Is Latin America Turning Protestant? The Politics of Evangelical Growth*. University of California Press, Berkeley

Strathern, Marilyn

1981   Self Interest and the Social Good: Some Implications of Hagen Gender Imagery. In *Sexual Meanings: The Cultural Construction of Gender and Sexuality*, edited by Sherry Ortner and Harriet Whitehead, pp. 166-191. Cambridge University Press, New York.

1988   *The Gender of the Gift*. University of California Press, Berkeley.

Taggart, James

1983   *Nahuat Myth and Social Structure*. University of Texas Press, Austin.

Tax, Susan

1966   Actividad de Desplazamiento en Zinacantán. In *Los Zinacantecos*, edited by Evon Z. Vogt, pp. 298-312. Instituto Nacional Indigenista, Mexico City.

Thompson, J. Eric S.

1966   *The Rise and Fall of Maya Civilization*. University of Oklahoma Press, Norman.

Tiano, Susan

1986   Women and Industrial Development in Latin America. *Latin American Research Review* 21(3):157-170.

Tozzer, Alfred

1907   *A Comparative Study of the Mayas and the Lacandones*. AMS Press, New York.

Vogt, Evon Z.

1969   *Zinacantán*. Harvard University Press, Cambridge.

1970   Notes on an Episode in a Marriage in Nab ta Peteh, Chamula. Written communication to Gary H. Gossen.

Wali, Alaka

1974   *Dependence and Dominance: The Status of Women in Zinacantán*. Bachelor thesis, Dept. of Anthropology, Harvard University.

Warren, Kay

In Press   Transforming Memories and Histories: Indian Identity Reexamined. In *Americas: Interpretive Essays,* edited by Al Stepan. Oxford University Press, Oxford (1992).

Warshauer, Maxine

1969   Marriage in Chamula. Manuscript on file. Harvard Chiapas Project, Harvard University, Cambridge.

Wasserstrom, Robert

1983a   *Class and Society in Central Chiapas.* University of California Press, Berkeley.

1983b   Spaniards and Indians in Colonial Chiapas 1528-1790. In *Spaniards and Indians in Southeastern Mesoamerica,* edited by Murdo MacLeod and Robert Wasserstrom, pp. 92-126. University of Nebraska Press, Lincoln.

Weedon, Chris

1987   *Feminist Practice and Poststructuralist Theory.* Basil Blackwell, Oxford.

Weiner, Annette B.

1976   *Women of Value, Men of Renown. New Perspectives in Trobriand Exchange.* University of Texas Press, Austin.

Williams, Raymond

1977   *Marxism and Literature.* Oxford University Press, New York.

Wolf, Eric

1959   *Sons of the Shaking Earth.* University of Chicago Press, Chicago.

Yanagisako, Sylvia and Jane Collier

1987   Toward a Unified Analysis of Gender and Kinship. In *Gender and Kinship. Essays Toward a Unified Analysis,* edited by Jane Collier and Sylvia Yanagisako, pp. 14-52. Stanford University Press, Stanford.

Young, Kate

1978   Modes of Appropriation and the Sexual Division of Labor: A Case Study from Oaxaca, Mexico. In *Feminism and Materialism: Women and Modes of Production,* edited by Annette Kuhn and AnnMarie Wolpe, pp. 125-154. Routledge and Kegan Paul, London.

Zaretsky, Eli

1976   *Capitalism, the Family and Personal Life.* Harper Colophon Books, New York.